note defective index
note spelling "Charngarnïer" for Changarnier. I know no warrant for it.

MONSIEUR THIERS

MONSIEUR THIERS

MONSIEUR THIERS

BY

JOHN M. S. ALLISON
PROFESSOR OF HISTORY, YALE UNIVERSITY

W · W · NORTON & COMPANY, INC.
NEW YORK

First Edition

PRINTED IN THE UNITED STATES OF AMERICA
FOR THE PUBLISHERS BY THE VAIL-BALLOU PRESS

TO M. L. M.

WHO GAVE ME LIFE AND MADE IT POSSIBLE
FOR ME TO LIVE IT ABUNDANTLY

PREFACE

THE author desires to acknowledge his indebtedness to the Director of the Bibliothèque Nationale, the Chef des Archives at the Ministère des Affaires Étrangères, the Director of the Archives Nationales, and the Curator of the Musée Arbaud at Aix-en-Provence for the privileges and courtesies extended to him during the studies in preparation for this book. He owes a special debt of gratitude to Monsieur Henri Malo, former Director of the Bibliothèque Thiers at Paris and now Curator of the Musée Condé at Chantilly, for his kindly interest and assistance, and to Professor S. B. Hemingway of Yale University for his helpful criticism. Acknowledgment should also be made to the Houghton Mifflin Company for their courtesy in permitting him to use, in the first part of this book, selections from an earlier effort entitled *Thiers and the French Monarchy* and published by them in 1926.

J. M. S. A.

New Haven, Connecticut,
April, 1931.

CONTENTS

CHAPTER I

THE ROAD TO PARIS

"I AM sprung from the bourgeoisie. I am a child of the Revolution."

This confession Thiers, when an old man, made to his friendly and indefatigable interviewer, William Nassau Senior.

No doubt when he uttered these words, he did so with a sense of pride, yet a pride that was not without certain qualifications. For he who became the intimate of Talleyrand, of Leopold of Belgium, and of Metternich, that most incorrigible of aristocrats, was very likely painfully aware of the fact that his origins were more revolutionary and more sordid than he wished later associates to know. In spite of his frequent protestations to the contrary, everything in the early experiences of Thiers contributed to make him part of New France rather than the Old Régime.

The place of his birth was Marseilles. That city had been one of the first of the great towns of the provinces to send delegates to a Radical Federation in Paris. At the time of Thiers' birth it was a hotbed of patriotism; for the Allies—one of whom, the British, had closed her seaport—left her ships rotting at the docks, and destroyed her former prosperity. The year was 1797, the second year of the Directory, when France was resting from the Terror, and when the victories of General Bonaparte were still hiding from Frenchmen the inherent weakness and corruption of the Directors themselves. And if time and place of his birth signified Revolution, the milieu into which Thiers was born was typically bourgeois. But it was bourgeois that was touched with a bit of eighteenth-century scandal that made it a little less monotonous. A lively and charming Mademoiselle Marie-Madeleine Amic, of good Middle Class stock, enamoured of a notorious Pierre Louis Thiers, adventurer and unworthy son of a much respected father: a scandal when Mademoiselle was discovered to be with child: a horror when Pierre was found to be already married: followed by an unexpected and happy dénouement when, after the birth of the child, the considerate hand of death intervened opportunely to remove the first wife from the scene. And then, the honour of the Amics restored by the hasty marriage of the lovers at a Civil Registry, and the small Adolphe sealed with the respectable but somewhat belated seal of legitimacy. When this had been accomplished, Pierre disappeared, and Marie-Madeleine and her offspring became charges of Grandpapa and Grandmama Amic. This much the records of Civil Registries and Contract Bureaux expose, although the scandalous memoirs, cartoons, and the political diatribes of Madame de Girardin and Balzac can add a great deal more illustrative material that is not without interest but, for the most part, devoid of truth. For his early years, one must turn to the statements of Monsieur Thiers, his family, and his friends.

The public life of Monsieur Thiers began, most properly, with baptism. This ceremony took place in the house of his aunt, Madame Victoire Pretty. Tante Victoire was *dévote,* and as the laws of the Revolution had closed the parish church she arranged for a secret administration of the sacrament in the cellar of her residence at 25 rue des Capucines. Such an inauguration of her nephew into the Christian mysteries partook of the primitive, and it was an appropriate beginning to which he often referred with a smile. Thiers' devotion to the Church left much to be desired.

The fortune of Madame Pretty had apparently not suffered so much from revolutionary panics as that of the other relatives, and so it was that lady who undertook to defray the expenses of his education when, six years later, he began the study of Latin and of his mother tongue at a day school in France. By this time, however, the family had come to find their young charge a good deal of a problem. Grandmama Amic complained that he was *difficile,* and Marie-Madeleine was alarmed for her son who was possessed of an energy far beyond his natural strength and a stubbornness that could not be conquered. It was obvious that a heavier hand was needed. And that soon came. In 1804, along with the rest of France, Louis Adolphe Thiers became the docile subject of Napoleon I and in the seventh year of the New Dispensation and the Empire he was received as a scholar at the Lycée de Marseilles. It was there that he met with sentiments and influences that left their indelible marks upon him.

In 1811 the Napoleonic régime was at its height. Like all other institutions the schools of France were completely under the Emperor's thumb, breeding grounds for the army and for patriotism, where the youth of the country were being trained to free the rotting seaports of the Mediterranean and to carry the eagle of Bonaparte across the wide expanse of Europe. For France, said the Emperor, had girded herself for peace; and peace, with Napoleon, could only mean conquest. It was not in vain that the Imperial Catechism had trained French children to repeat: "Christians owe to the Princes who govern them, and we, in particular, owe to Napoleon I, our Emperor, love, respect, obedience, fidelity, and the taxes levied for the support and defense of the Empire and of his throne." And so the schools, pursuant to this latest revised version of the duties of Christians, became in great part war schools. The great machine of the Imperial Monopole Universitaire, an educational dictatorship, prescribed a scientific, patriotic, and military training; History, Mathematics, Topography, and Geography held the center of the scholastic platform. Youngsters pored over great maps, and learned campaigns—the campaigns of France, of course. Young France imbibed a passionate and dangerous love of glory that it took years to forget. Such a system bred generals, martyrs, and fiery-tongued statesmen. Incidentally, at this particular Lycée at Marseilles, Napoleon's system made of one of its pupils an acute military historian and a patriot with an intense and perilous desire for the glory of a French Empire which at first fascinated him but which he learned in time to distrust.

These advantages, however, did not make themselves felt at the time, and no one could foresee what good would come to the young Thiers from his life at the school—he himself least of all, if one may judge by a reference that he made to it later on in his life: "The goverment took possession of me, as it did of all the youths with whom their parents could be induced to part, and it put me into a military school from which the seniors were drafted off every year; the few who had distinguished themselves to be made officers, the rest to be spent in the next campaign. The life was very hard, but its hardships, instead of killing me, as had been most probable, gave me, in a few years, an iron constitution."

Such an experience did not teach Thiers the gentleness of life, nor for that matter did it bring him success. On the contrary, his career at the school was adjudged a failure by his superiors and by his family. It had only served to accentuate his dislike of restraints and of discipline. Against these his nervous, feverish temperament was in a state of almost constant revolt. In despair, his sponsors set about to discover a more congenial occupation for him. The idea of commerce annoyed him; he believed himself to be above the ordinary pursuits of tradesmen. Finally it was decided to have him try the law. An indulgent professor from the Lycée gave him a high recommendation, and family influence procured for him at last a scholarship at the most distinguished law school in the south of France. In the autumn of 1815, while the fate of France was being settled over dinner tables at Vienna, Thiers, his mother, and Madame Amic left Marseilles for Aix-en-Provence. At Marseilles Thiers had met with Revolution and Napoleon; at Aix, he encountered the New France and its old traditions.

In spite of the fact that Aix was only some thirty kilometers from Marseilles, the young Thiers was really entering a new world and an atmosphere hitherto completely unknown to him. Marseilles was on the sea, while Aix was high in the hills. One was becoming, again, a stirring seaport, active, noisy, and dirty, while the other was a quiet, dreamy little town not given much to commerce or to great activity. The sea town had been a hotbed of Revolutionary interests and of up-to-date practices, but the small hilltop community had continued to live in the past, a past that extended far back into the romantic days of the Middle Ages. Furthermore, many Aixois failed completely to understand the Marseillais and what they represented. Then, as now, Aix was a seat of the old aristocracy of Provence. Elegant, conservative, proud, it pursued its old life, and most of the good citizens who walked along its quiet stately avenue with the plane-trees meeting above them, thought little of the Revolution and less of Revolutionists. These people, in 1815, breathed freely again, for the fall of Napoleon had been brought about at last, and the restoration of the Bourbons in the person of gouty Louis XVIII was a *fait accompli.* If there were radicals at Aix, most of its citizens chose to ignore their existence, and Paris was so far away that they knew little of republican sentiments that were now sleeping but were destined to awaken again.

But, the Aixois boasted not only of their conservatism; they prided themselves as well on the hospitality which was a tradition of ancient Provence. And the encounter with this last characteristic was a new experience for Thiers. Hitherto he had known only the harder side of life, the impatience and occasional neglect of his capricious mother, the prudish kindness of the Amics, and the harsh régime at the Lycée. But at Aix there came comrades, walks over the hills, long talks, and a few choice associations that endured for a very long lifetime. It was here, in an atmosphere conducive to peace of mind, that he began to develop that remarkable capacity for deep, almost passionate friendships that became so typical of the later Thiers. At this time, he met the quiet, faithful Mignet who was to remain by his side when all France seemed to have deserted him. He made for himself, as well, a place in the household of a few liberals in whose midst he learned much. These men, Monsieur d'Arlatan de Lauris and Docteur Arnaud, were older, more patient, and wiser than he; they quietly moulded his views, and later, when he went to Paris, they secured for him an entrée to liberals of their sort in the capital. For all these friends he developed a deep and lasting affection; but it was not a matter of personal liking alone. Even to the young Thiers, friendship partook of an intellectual quality, a give and take of ideas and experiences. To one he wrote: "Our mutual silence has lasted too long. The ties of blood and friendship unite us, but our friendship is too silent. We ought to know each other better. People love each other more, only when they are better acquainted. Frankness, gayety, good nature—that is what two friends need. With that, we shall have much to say to each other. . . . For my own part, I wish to set you a good example, and if I do not fill my pages with ideas, I shall, at least, give you words. I shall write you of cases, politics, moral philosophy, and gallantry. I shall be sincere about the faults of others. In short, I shall not spare you any of the follies that indicate the wisdom of our hemisphere."

To his intimates he was always gentle, amusing, and playful. His frankness and enthusiasms delighted them. But as time went on the general impression that he made upon his fellows at Aix was not so favourable. He was impetuous. He desired to cut a figure and so to obliterate, perhaps, the fact of his obscure and rather sordid origin. He envied the elegance and goodly manners of the well-born Aixois, and in many instances his envy turned into hatred. He became a bit of a poseur, and therefore the object of remarkable legends to many of which his behaviour gave an appearance of verisimilitude. In short, it was not long before many good Aixois, whose gentility annoyed him, became suspicious of him; and the fact that he was a very indifferent law student did not improve matters. It was noised about, and the report was true, that he talked against the restored Bourbons. He wrote a tragedy entitled *Tiberius Gracchus* in which he gave vent to the wildest political opinions, and he announced to his small world that he had in preparation a work on Kosciusko. To these pursuits he gave the time that he should have devoted to law books. Certain people credited the rumour that he had joined the Carbonari and taken an oath to kill the harmless old King. Thiers never learned the gentle art of holding his tongue. He found many hearers but, as time went on, fewer sympathizers and among the latter his professors were not to be numbered. He was known as a "partisan outré de la Revolution," the *enfant terrible* of the law school at Aix. Of this sentiment against him he soon became painfully aware.

In 1817 the recently founded Academy of Aix announced a prize for the best study of Vauvenargues, the author of the "Maximes." Thiers, to whom competitions of all sorts were far more attractive than law briefs, set to work with eagerness. He presented his essay at the appointed time. When, however, the academicians met to consider the matter of the award, his liberal sponsor, Monsieur d'Arlatan de Lauris, supported one particular essay so warmly that the venerable lords of letters became suspicious. They suspected, and justly, that this essay probably emanated from the notorious young law student in their midst, and, unwilling to countenance in any way the radical opinions with which Thiers was credited, they voted to postpone the competition until the following year. This decision, however, did not daunt the ambitious young protégé of Monsieur d'Arlatan. On the contrary, he composed immediately a second essay and in 1818 he submitted the two anonymously, the second having been sent to Paris and mailed to Aix from there. Again the wise men met and solemnly debated the merits of the two compositions. Finally, delighted at the opportunity to discountenance Monsieur Thiers, they awarded the prize to the unknown contestant from Paris and bestowed a simple *accessit* upon the essay which they believed to have been written by the radical law student in their midst. But when they opened the envelopes containing the real names of the authors, they discovered to their dismay that both essays had been written by the man whose opinions they had wished to censure.

The episode of the Vauvenargues essay marks a real turning point in the life of its author. While it displayed to his small public his real ability, what is more important, it revealed to himself the fact that there were other careers that were open to him. And this revelation came at a most opportune time, for the law had proven to be no more to his liking than the army had been.

Although he had been admitted to the bar in 1818, he was not happy in his profession. With Mignet, he had opened an office. Of the two, Mignet had been the more successful. He was patient, methodical, and plodding; Thiers was impetuous, hasty, and too daring. One supplied careful preparation and the other a rather fickle brilliance. Thiers amused his audience by his flights of oratory, his display of overdone sentimentality, and his spectacular attitudes. At one time, they were called upon to present the case of a man accused of incendiarism and murder. The two young barristers prepared elaborate cases. Apparently their prodigious efforts impressed the judges and jury, for Thiers had the prisoner acquitted of the first charge, while Mignet had him condemned for the second. The verdict was rendered and the young novices were given a tremendous ovation by their friends. But pride must have a fall. After the trial had been closed, it was discovered beyond a doubt that their client had actually been guilty of incendiarism and innocent of murder!

At the bar of Aix the eloquence and lucidity of Thiers' style were recognized; but he had handicaps and faults that frequently made him the butt of his older colleagues. He was small of stature and of unimposing appearance. His use of short, quick gestures betrayed his nervousness and lack of confidence, and this unfortunate impression was not mitigated by a high pitched falsetto voice that amused his hearers sometimes to the point of laughter. More and more he became convinced that if he was to succeed it would not be in the law courts of the provinces. Aix had done all that it could for him; it had helped him in revolution. Vauvenargues had taught him philosophy, and his lack of social success had shown him that his future lay with the New France and not with the Old. In Aix he was still known as the young man who was born almost a waif on the rue des Petits Pères at Marseilles. It was the recognition of this fact and the consciousness of his own defects that finally led him to burn his bridges at Aix and to seek his fortune at Paris whither Mignet had already gone. To that ever restless heart of France his friend had already summoned him. "Law is not your chosen calling; before you there lie the salons, literature, history, and art. Vauvenargues proved your strength and pointed you the way."

Such arguments aroused the desire that lay dormant in his heart. Aix could never offer him the brilliant future which he believed was reserved for him. Its society was old, conservative, and closed to such as he. He had learned at the feet of Monsieur d'Arlatan and Docteur Arnaud that the Old Régime, whose acquaintance he had made, was a machine that would not work. Bourbonism could not last, and already a new France was being born in Paris. The young Thiers must go out to meet it, for it would be years before it would come up into the hills of Provence. In Paris lay the hope of the future. In September, 1821, with true Gallic emotion, he wrote: "I leave tomorrow: I am overcome with tears. My two mothers break my heart with their grief. I am ill; my heart burns; I breathe with difficulty. I must leave or dry up on the tree. The future is awful, but the present is unendurable. It is ground that is withering; I must go, no matter what it costs."

These lines betray more than the ordinary sorrow of a son in parting from his family. As a matter of fact another tie bound him to Aix. There are other letters, not included in the "Lettres Politiques de Monsieur Thiers" at the *Bibliothèque Nationale:* they are epistles that escaped him and the careful elimination carried on by his heirs. These mention again and again "ma pauvre Émilie," a provençale, and the companion of his student days, whose parents now became alarmed at a departure that they were not mistaken in interpreting as a case of desertion. But the mind of Monsieur Thiers was made up. Cost what it would, Paris must be won. "As to myself, I am going to follow my destiny. Will it be good or bad? I know not. Whatever happens, I am resigned, for they call us philosophers and we must be worthy of the name."

Destiny and Philosophy then were the influences that took him to Paris, and not even Émilie would be allowed to stand in his path. With a magnificent emotion in which he thoroughly revelled, he took the diligence to New France. Paris soon dried his tears just as she had comforted many another youth of the early nineteenth century.

CHAPTER II

THE CONQUEST OF PARIS,

THE city towards which young Thiers was journeying in the autumn of 1821 presented a strange aspect; it was divided in social and political opinion. In 1814 the Émigrés of the Old Régime had returned to it, confident in the possibility of a complete and a real Restoration. They had invaded Paris as victors. Backed by the Allies and their armies, and aided by the adroit Talleyrand, who hoped in vain for a reward, they had placed Louis XVIII on the throne and surrounded him with what remained of the aristocracy and splendours of former times. In spite of his gout and other incapacities, the old King had stood the ordeal well and carried off his part of the play with a moderate dignity. Once again the vaults of Notre Dame had resounded to the *Domine salvum fac regem,* but even the restoration of Mother Church to her former position in the State had not been able to conceal the fact that this installation of a king was different. For the new King had given France a charter. He had not deigned to accept the one that a few of them had made out of whole cloth for him; and, while his charter proclaimed the sanctity of many of the precious Rights of Man, it also provided convenient straps for tightening these theoretical privileges if the King and his entourage so desired. The truth of the matter was that no one really knew what Louis XVIII meant by the Charter of 1814. Very likely that is exactly what he desired. For in spite of his infirmities this King was wise, in his ponderous fashion, and he was not going to allow anyone to lead him by the nose. It was, however, only very gradually that the various parties in France learned this lesson, but once the lesson was learned, it was unequivocable. Charles d'Artois, a younger brother, and his band of Ultra-Reactionaries tried to force him into an Old Régime system, and they failed. Some over-enthusiastic Republicans attempted a few but very noisy demonstrations, and they were quieted. In brief, Revenge and Republicanism were two words that were not to be found in Louis XVIII's vocabulary. When he chose to do so, he made a few graceful moves towards the Moderate Liberals in order to show the Ultras that they were not the Masters and to prove to the Holy Allies that he would not be entirely their creature. In this lies the importance of the early years of Louis XVIII's reign; he was too astute to become a real Reactionary or to believe that he could ruthlessly crush a liberalism that even Napoleon I had not been able to annihilate completely. By this very fact he allowed liberal sentiment to live—he gave it a breathing space; with the result that in 1821 the Émigrés had changed their minds. They no longer believed that a real Restoration could be accomplished during the present King's life. They became instead prisoners of hope. They shut themselves up in their old houses in the Faubourg Saint-Germain; and in the salons, under their crystal chandeliers, they nodded and wagged their old heads, and talked of the day when Monsieur Charles d'Artois, *le beau chevalier,* would succeed his fast aging brother on the throne of France.

But while, in the Faubourg, Ultras were biding their

time, in the Chaussée d'Antin other heads were planning for the future, and other plans were developing. For in France after the Revolution came gradually the Industrial Revolution; and a new class of aristocrats was coming into being. Doubtless it was not so respectable, not so *dévot,* and certainly, not so romantic. In 1821 the great bourgeois too had their salons with marble *cheminées* and red plush. They lived conveniently near the source of their power, the Bourse. Over them, Jacques Laffitte, Casimir Périer, and Baron Rothschild reigned. And all of them foregathered with their fellow money-makers and an occasional young writer or two, a Hugo or a de Vigny, who lent an air of refinement to the general atmosphere of stock-broking, loans, bonding, and iron-mongery. Bourgeois minds were often Voltairean. And so they talked of limited monarchy—monarchy limited by themselves, of course; and of a God who was not so Catholic, and less concerned with personal affairs; and they delighted in the songs of Béranger, sole surviving poet of the Revolution. But that is not to say that they were radicals or revolutionary; Béranger's songs amused them; the theories behind his verses they never tried to comprehend. Middle Class Liberalism was becoming successful because it was wealthy.

Republicanism had fewer and less spacious haunts; it was to be found almost entirely in student quarters and workingmen's sections. It had few leaders and practically no voice. But bourgeois opinion had its newspapers, the *Globe,* the *Constitutionnel,* and the *Courrier Français,* wherein occasionally appeared a moderate protest against the Ultras or a respectful prayer to the King to give his merchants and traders a voice in the government. Although they had all these advantages they cannot be said in 1821 to have been a party or to have developed a definite programme. Even the magnates among them were not yet recognized as real political leaders. Nevertheless this new society was beginning very gradually to revolve about its own particular sun and to pin its hopes and plans on the fate of one person.

From time to time when Louis XVIII's policy irritated them, or when Charles d'Artois and his Ultras behaved foolishly, the liberal Bourgeoisie turned its attention to one man who was not on the throne but who was perilously near it. Périer saw in him the possibilities of the King of the Middle Class; Laffitte beheld in him the Great Compromiser between Middle Class and Republican sentimentality; the man of the street, when he thought of him at all, recalled a pear-headed, democratic Duke who waddled along the Boulevards with his large green umbrella tucked securely under his arm, and who was glad to stop at any café and drink a *verre* with any man. What Louis Philippe, Duke of Orléans, saw in himself, during these early days of the Restoration, no one knows, and probably never will know.

Guided by instinct, or else by painful experience, this gentleman went everywhere and established himself nowhere. He avoided conspiracies, and appeared to have a positive horror of demonstrations. He played with Royal Château and with Chaussée d'Antin. He consulted the King about the education of his children, but in spite of his royal cousin's expressed disapproval he sent them to the public schools. He tried to consort with the Faubourg Saint-Germain, but Messieurs les Ultras had good memories and snubbed him. They had not forgotten that his father had voted for the death of Louis XVI in 1793. And so, like his parent of evil fame, Louis Philippe began to give himself more and more to the New France of the Liberal Bourgeoisie. He welcomed the return of the exiled liberal Manuel to Paris, and he lent money to Benjamin Constant who was writing dangerous pamphlets about a theory of Constitutional Government that he did not understand. Perhaps it was not without significance that Jacques Laffitte handled the Duke's finances. And one day Louis Philippe tried to joke with Monsieur Charles, Count of Artois; on the next, he hobnobbed with Talleyrand and poked fun at the Ultras who had snubbed the two of them. He opened the doors of his sumptuous Palais Royal to nobles, a few liberal priests, and a quantity of journalists, young writers, and men of business. Within his residence, the walls were hung with tapestries of the Revolution and the Empire. He made a fad of collecting revolutionary portraits and prints. These are the evidences of conspiracy, if there was conspiracy, in 1821. Faubourg Saint-Germain, Chaussée d'Antin, Quartier Latin, and Palais Royal had made of Paris a city of divided and, as yet, disorganized political and social opinion.

Into the outskirts of such a society, Thiers, newly come to Paris, made his début. Monsieur d'Arlatan and Docteur Arnaud had given him letters which he guarded carefully on the road, and presented upon his arrival to Manuel, almost the sole exponent of Liberalism in the Chamber. With Mignet, he took a room in a hotel in the passage Montesquieu. The house was small and mean. The street was dark and dirty. It was a gloomy and rather pathetic ménage, for the first months were not easy. Thiers was homesick for the Provence that he had deserted, and his purse was almost empty. Again, the memory of Émilie and the rumours of the intentions of her irate parent alarmed him. And for sustenance and divertissement, there was only hack writing; articles for the *Courrier* on politics of which he knew as yet very little, on art of which he knew less, on the theatre, or on anything, it mattered not what. For a short time relief came when Thiers served as secretary to an Ultra-minded Duke at Lieusaint, but soon incompatibility of temperament and ideals ended this relationship. The month of December, 1821, found him again in Paris in search of permanent employment. With the turn of the year, however, came a change of fortune. Manuel, himself a resident of Aix, offered a helping hand to his young compatriot.

The event which had brought Thiers more closely in touch with the leader of the Liberals among the Deputies was the conclusion of his Provençal romance. Bon papa Bonnefoux, exasperated at the vague assurances of the recalcitrant Adolphe, came to Paris and demanded satisfaction for his daughter's broken heart. Monsieur Thiers was somewhat embarrassed, for his circle of acquaintances was still small; but Manuel gallantly proposed to stand as his second. There ensued a meeting at dawn in the Bois at which Bonnefoux père shot and missed while his opponent did not fire. Like the thin smoke from her father's pistol, Émilie vanished from her lover's life, and shortly afterwards Manuel found for Thiers steady employment. An introduction to Monsieur Étienne, editor of the *Constitutionnel,* gained for him a position on that paper. Soon neither Manuel nor Étienne regretted this act of charity.

The *Constitutionnel,* while the advocate of Middle Class Liberalism, was old and stuffy, mild in its sentiments, and timid in its attacks. But soon the paper changed its character. The recklessness of youth and the fire of Provence put new life and real daring into the hitherto prosaic phrases. Thiers redressed its old and banal arguments and gave them a new form and a real point. There was even a sting to certain articles. Nothing that could be criticised was allowed to pass uncensured, for the young Thiers had never heard of a land where angels feared to tread. He wrote on Constitutional Government, although he did not comprehend it; he reviewed the Salon of 1822, in spite of the fact that he had barely made the acquaintance of Art Galleries. He forced his way into *ateliers* and watched Gérard as he painted the lovely Duchesse de Broglie. Even the sanctuaries of the learned did not frighten him.

Boldly he climbed the steps of the temple and penetrated into its innermost mysteries. Every Friday he met at table with Lebrun, Paul-Louis Courier, Victor Cousin, and Béranger. In preparation for these intellectual feasts, he would memorize whole passages of learned works and recite them before his scholarly acquaintances at great length, to their admiration and consternation. His feats of memory were prodigious. Nor did old Docteur Véron and his *Comédie Française* escape him. He became a familiar figure in the *coulisses,* and, to display his acquaintance with the dramatic Muse as well as to fill his purse, he published, with an elaborate Preface of his own, *bien entendu,* the "Memoirs of Mistress Bellamy of Covent Garden." This was the début of Monsieur Thiers in Paris.

The letters from Aix to Manuel paved the way for Thiers' introduction into one section of Parisian society, but it was a fortuitous circumstance that finally put him definitely into the limelight and brought him under the influence and patronage of the great. Up to the year 1822 his vocation had been uncertain. The law, commerce, art criticism, dramatic criticism, and political essays had all been tried. In 1822, however, he was brought to a decision, and he ended by committing himself to politics and to journalism.

It was in that year that Louis XVIII was confronted with the last really difficult problem that was to concern him before the matter of a holy death began to occupy his mind. Once again in Europe Revolution had raised its head against the Metternich system of Reaction. Uprisings had occurred in Naples, Piedmont, and Spain. It was in the latter country that the movement had made the greatest headway, and had finally driven the absolutist Ferdinand from the throne. In 1822 the unfortunate King appealed to Metternich; and at Verona, in spite of England's protest, the Allies had committed to Louis XVIII the task of re-enthroning Ferdinand. The old King of the

French, eager to prove to his sceptical subjects that the Bourbons as well as the Bonapartes could bring glory to the flag of France, assumed the task. To his surprise and dismay, the enterprise did not meet with the approval that he had expected. The Ultras, of course, demanded a policy *à outrance,* but the Liberals of the LaFayette and Manuel groups had declared, in public and in the Chamber, and with equal heat, that a war to suppress freedom ought to fail and would fail. Discussion of the question became quite general throughout the country. This situation provided an excellent opportunity for an enterprising publisher and an able writer. The editors of the *Constitutionnel* themselves undertook to bring out a series of articles on the Spanish question and they set about to send an observer to the Pyrenees. They had the good sense to select the young writer whose articles had revived somewhat the popularity of their paper.

In October, 1822, after a brief visit at Aix-en-Provence, Monsieur Thiers set out on his first adventure. From its very beginning the enterprise seems to have been regarded with suspicion by the government at Paris. The order went out to the local Prefects to follow carefully the movements of "ce jeune avocat qui n'exerce pas sa profession." Evidently Messieurs les Préfets were diligent, for a whole carton of correspondence exists in the archives of the Secret Police. With infinite care Monsieur le Préfet d'Aix reports at length on the past history of Monsieur Thiers and transmits a list of persons upon whom he called while he was at Aix. His passage through Ariège to the Hautes-Pyrénées is minutely described to the officials in Paris. But then there comes a gap in the correspondence. Evidently agile Monsieur Thiers had given them the slip. Quite certainly he did for he tells us himself that he escaped across the Pyrenees and interviewed the leaders of the Spanish Revolutionists themselves. But such facts did not appear in the columns of the *Constitutionnel* nor in the book that he finally published under the innocent title: "Les Pyrénées et le Midi de la France pendant les mois de Novembre et Décembre, 1822." Statements of government officials, however, and of Monsieur himself, lead one to believe that to observe was not his only duty during his tour of inspection of the Pyrenees. There is very good reason to credit the story that he actually carried messages from French Liberals in Paris to their Spanish brethren across the frontier. It was not then without reason that he wrote home to a friend: "There will be nothing of what really impressed me, for the book is not written for those who quarrel over war and peace."

What secrets he left out of his book were compensated for by the jibes that he took occasion to make against French officialdom. No one who has ever suffered with passport officials can fail to appreciate the following extract from a description of his own experiences with a similar official:

THIERS: "I declare that I desire to circulate freely and that I desire a passport."

COMMISSAIRE: "For what destination?"

THIERS: "For foreign parts."

COMMISSAIRE: "For foreign parts? And at such a time as this! Where are you going?"

THIERS: "To Switzerland."

COMMISSAIRE: "What business calls you there?"

THIERS: "None."

COMMISSAIRE: "None! And do you imagine that without reasonable motives Monsieur le Préfet will allow you to leave?"

THIERS: "If I choose to travel without reasonable motives must Monsieur le Préfet find them for me? Anyhow is not the fact that I wish to see the country sufficient?"

COMMISSAIRE: "That is enough: the authorities will see what they can do for you. Come back in three days."

THIERS: "In three days! And what if I am in a hurry, all my arrangements made?"

COMMISSAIRE: "In three days."

THIERS: "But, please, has anyone complained to Monsieur le

Commissaire about me? Is there any reason to suspect me?"

COMMISSAIRE: "None whatever."

THIERS: "Monsieur le Commissaire is therefore pleased with me? For here good citizens must be those with whom he is not acquainted."

COMMISSAIRE: "In three days."

The "Voyage aux Pyrénées" was not merely a rather lengthy and in places a rather delightful travelogue. For the scholar who cares to search for them, there are plenty of good reasons for regarding the book as one of the most clever, veiled, and yet pointed attacks on the system of the Restoration in France. This aspect of the work was not lost to many of its readers, and opened to its author the doors of the leaders of the Middle Class Liberals so that he became a frequenter of the salons of Laffitte, Dosne, and Périer. Owing, in part, to an argument arising out of the book, the young Thiers won the interest of the man who became the most faithful and most valuable political mentor. The most important result of his trip to the Pyrenees was the fact that Monsieur le Duc de Talleyrand expressed a desire to meet him.

When for their own convenience Bourbons and their adherents chose to regard Monsieur de Talleyrand as old, retired, and no longer redoubtable, they were deceiving themselves grossly. On the contrary the very fact that Monsieur Talleyrand had been retired made him all the more dangerous. He became the nestor of the disaffected. In Paris, or at Rochecotte, the château of his interesting niece, Madame de Dino, this old man of the French Revolution was being flattered and much sought after by the newer society of the Industrial Revolution. It was shortly after his return from the Midi, at the house of Laffitte, that Talleyrand requested that the young Thiers be presented to him. Almost immediately, a strong friendship developed between the old man and the young writer. It became very shortly a sort of tripartite arrangement in which the vivacious Madame de Dino shared, and at which, perhaps, sometimes not without reason, good society raised its eyebrows. For Madame was not always discreet in her expressions of admiration for the young protégé of her uncle, and the young protégé himself had already established a modest reputation for conquests among the wealthy bourgeoises. In view of this fact, is it likely that he would have allowed a benevolently inclined Duchess to pass by unnoticed?

In any case, Thiers soon became a frequent visitor at Rochecotte. In his own words: "Talleyrand adopted me from the very first." Quite probably, too, Monsieur Thiers adopted Monsieur de T. The young man found in the experienced old statesman a counselor, sympathetic, loyal, and inspiring, who did not confine his good offices to counsel alone. There were more material advantages: good dinners, a splendid riding horse in the use of which he made valiant struggles, and a new coterie of friends. Furthermore, Talleyrand's friendship gave him the chance to become, for the time, part owner of the *Constitutionnel.* At the Duke's plea, Jacques Laffitte and Baron Cotta bought his "actions" for him. And this arrangement was an advantage to Monsieur de Talleyrand as well as to Thiers, for from 1823 on Thiers often voiced the opinions of his mentor at Rochecotte in his articles. "He never asked me to do anything, but he had a certain way of looking at me and of addressing me that I soon came to understand. Whenever he had something to say to the public, he always mentioned it before me." In the same breath, however, Monsieur Thiers was careful to recall that at that time Talleyrand did not conspire with him. "He was not foreseeing anything; he was only waiting. But when the event came he accepted it and no one had a better eye than he for seizing the advantage."

The "Pyrénées" put Monsieur Thiers to school in the practices and ideas of Talleyrand. It also placed him in the very milieu where conspiracy would begin when the Bourbons had had time enough to exasperate the Middle Class Liberals to the point of rebellion.

The success of his book, the friendship of Talleyrand, and his new relation to the *Constitutionnel* made living somewhat less of a problem for Thiers, and the fortunate year brought about a complete change of custom and habit. His life became less monotonous. There were demands upon his time. There were the conventions of society to be observed. He must frequent the salons of bourgeois hostesses and establish himself there. In the circle of Middle Class society, he became a familiar figure, a short little man, with eyes singularly bright, so bright that they seemed to illuminate the large glasses which covered them; his mouth twisted into that dry little smile that became so familiar to France, and that was so dreaded in later years by his enemies; talking with an unparalleled vivacity and *esprit,* on all subjects from finance and astronomy to religion. There was more assurance, more confidence, than had appeared in the eager and nervous barrister of Aix. Paris had changed him, but the transformation was not only in manner; there was also an alteration in his appearance. He was meticulously neat in his dress, and he had lost most of the outward characteristics of a provincial. To succeed he must do as young Parisians of his age were wont to do, and in following their lead he frequently ran into debt. Like them he must indulge in some form of recreation. Alas! when he attempted to master the equestrian art he selected the recreation that was probably least suited to him. This was an effort for which he was manifestly unfitted because of his small stature and his quick, nervous temperament. But Thiers was not to be dissuaded. He frequented the *Manège* of Carrega, a former officer of the Empire, noted and admired by the young blades of Paris for his skill as a horseman. Under that veteran's direction he experienced hours of torture and discomfort. To one of his friends, he declared that he wished to become a second Alexander. Monsieur Thiers was not content with being a mere editor. He would become a sportsman, if necessary, and then, perhaps, a man of letters!

CHAPTER III

HISTORIAN AND JOURNALIST

On August 16, 1824, the long expected death of Louis XVIII occurred. A week later he was carried to the tomb with all the pomp that Royalist France could muster. *Requiescat in pace,* chanted the priests. There were tears in many eyes, but in the eyes of the Ultras, there shone the hope of another resurrection. At last, a few of their number thought, they might reap the harvest of revenge.

Charles d'Artois, who, as Charles X, succeeded his brother, had been taught very little by the French Revolution. He was himself the epitome of Conservatism. He was Ultra in politics, in religion, and in clothes. It is related that, on the famous night of August 4, 1789, when, for the sake of peace, so many nobles had sacrificed their inherited feudal rights, Charles had declined to renounce his privileges. In August, 1824, his mind had not changed so very much; he was determined to regain what had been taken away thirty-five years ago, and to restore to his nobles and clergy as much of their former position as possible. Very likely the new King and his entourage were convinced, in 1824, that the Old Régime could be restored, and it is possible that, in this opinion, they were not entirely mistaken.

There was, in fact, a large section of the provinces where the feudal spirit still survived. In many small rural communities Monsieur le Comte and Madame la Comtesse had become again the center of social life, and the lord of the local château was regarded once more as the father of the little village of souls that clustered around the walls that enclosed his mansion. He was their protector and the arbitrator of their disputes. Most of France was still made up of such communities. The Industrial Revolution was, as yet, in its infancy, and while discontent and a certain liberal tendency could be found in the larger commercial areas, these were not yet numerous enough to be effective. Furthermore, liberal spirit in the provinces lacked, as yet, co-ordination and intelligent leadership.

In fact, what Charles and his Ultras chose to regard as Liberalism was at this time in a very weakened condition. If there really was a Liberal party it was divided and dispersed. LaFayette, the great living symbol of democracy, claimed alike by Extremist and by Moderate Left, was out of the Chamber, and had gone to America to find consolation for his defeat in the honours that the young Republic desired to offer him. Manuel, a veteran of some twelve years' standing and first patron of Thiers, had been expelled from the Chamber by reason of his violent opposition to French intervention in Spain. Only General Foy, of Napoleonic fame and still loyal to the principles of the Revolution, remained in the Legislature. To his name should be added that of Casimir Périer, wealthy banker and man of iron. The General was feared because of his former association with the Empire, and the capitalist was suspected because of his association with the Bourgeoisie. With such men as leaders, Republicans would have nothing to do. And so, the old opposition, lacking intelligent leadership, was incapable of serious effort.

Charles X was correct, then, in adjudging that the Liberal movement was practically dead, but he was grievously mistaken in regard to another matter. He failed completely to realize that, right at his elbow, was a new and different opponent; new, in that it was not dependent on the rabble, the Quartier Latin, or the École Polytechnique; different, in that the methods it employed were contrary to those of the Republicans. These new Liberals did not use lodges, secret societies, street corner speeches, demonstrations, and riots, and they made no appeal to the mob. In fact, they abhorred it. As yet, no one of them, except Périer, was in the Chamber. But, they were increasing in number, as the economic condition of France improved, and they were spreading their sentiments through progressively minded professors at the University and liberal writers on the *Constitutionnel* for whose "seditious" articles some wealthy bourgeois sympathizer would pay the fine. Very gradually, under the influence of these men, Middle Class Liberalism was formulating its programme. Oddly enough, it was not first propounded from the tribune of the Chamber, but through the popular literature of the day. Among these productions was the first ambitious historical work of Monsieur Thiers that covered the rather immoderate number of ten tomes.

The first volume of the *History of the French Revolution* made its appearance at a very appropriate time. The full Restoration so desired by Charles d'Artois and his coterie seemed to be on the point of accomplishment. Nobility was declaring its rights and proclaiming its virtues, when the *History* recalled its flagrant vices and abuses. Reactionary Monarchy was vaunting its recent victories in Spain for the cause of Holy Alliance when Thiers, in his book, reminded his readers that liberated France had, at one time, defeated Holy Alliance. A few rash Republicans thought on riot, and the *History* described the Terror and warned France of the danger of the multitude. It was revolutionary propaganda that this book contained, but it was propaganda for the best of the Revolution. It was sympathetic to an aspect, but, in contrast to previous works on the subject, it was not opposed to Revolution nor was it favourable to its excesses. Its author, Monsieur Thiers, was preaching a sermon on Moderate Liberalism; he was trying to formulate for his own generation their political credo. Odd as it seems, the stern and puritanical Professor Guizot from his platform at the Sorbonne and the fiery and emancipated young hack writer from Provence were aiming at the same thing. Clio was again being prostituted for political edification.

And, as a matter of fact, this is not another's interpretation of Thiers' intentions. On the contrary, it is his very own. "I have been preaching now for three years a doctrine that the Left lacks common sense, that they are as foolish as the Émigrés." Truly, this was a theory that was bound to satisfy Messieurs les Bourgeois who, for reasons of purse and business, desired neither revolution nor a too sudden transformation back into the Old Régime. It was Thiers, in his *History,* who, through the narrative of the Revolution, taught these men the advantages of government *à l'anglais.* In this one respect, at least, the *History of the French Revolution* is nothing more or less than a ten-volume pamphlet against the Ultras and their extreme opponents of the Left.

In another aspect, however, it is an almost unique work. It is an echo of the discussion and reminiscences that took place in the bourgeois salons where Bonapartist, Republican, and Constitutional Monarchist foregathered, and where, sometimes, they were bored almost to distraction by the questioning of that insatiable little ferret with the huge *lunettes* who had such a passion for facts. And what a galaxy of heroes there was to be consulted! Talleyrand, Jourdain, Baron Louis. Boswell-like he plied them with questions, and, from the living wreckage of the Revolution, he gleaned his material. As time went on, he came to regard his work more seriously; he wished to become a real savant. Perhaps already the tempting glory of academic laurels began to hover before his eyes. He haunted the rendezvous of artillery officers and, through them, obtained admission to army manœuvres. It appears, even, that this change of attitude was not without its effect. The later volumes show the results of care and greater investigation. Sometimes, however, he wearied his prey with his persistence. One day he encountered the brilliant Madame Gay who had lived in the society of the Directory.

THIERS: "What I regret not to have seen are the brilliant receptions during the Directory, the joy of meeting again, the need of social intercourse, the Greek *toilettes*. Tell me all about it."

And the obliging lady began to talk of the soirées, of Madame Tallien, and of Madame de Beauharnais. On and on he led her, farther and farther back, until the poor lady cried:

"And are you not going to ask me how they dressed and amused themselves at the marriage of Marie Antoinette?"

This question silenced, for once, her relentless interviewer. He had made the unpardonable mistake of asking a lady about things that had happened before she was born.

The *History* took Paris by storm. From the date of its completion its author was recognized as a writer of merit. This success led him to make a momentous decision: an historian he would be, and the *History of the French Revolution* would have a sequel. On April 2, 1826, he signed with Alexandre Schubart, Publisher, a contract for the *History of the Consulate and the Empire*. This work was to be in four or five volumes. When finally it appeared it took the form of twenty tomes! Far different were the terms of this second contract; Monsieur Thiers was to receive three thousand five hundred francs per volume issued for the first edition of two thousand copies, and, in the interval of its composition, Monsieur Schubart was to advance sums of money that were to be arranged *à l'amiable.* Evidently, the young Thiers had not studied Revolutionary finances in vain.

Meanwhile, Charles X had had himself crowned at Rheims, his brow anointed with oil from the *sainte ampoule,* and the sword of Charlemagne girt to his side. Did all this paraphernalia of the Middle Ages symbolize the return of the monarchy of the Ancien Régime? That was the question that bourgeois France asked itself. Reaction was in the air, but, for a time, Liberals in France had to wait its appearance, and when it appeared it was not of the sort they had anticipated.

Ever so gradually, the war drew on. The new King was acting cautiously. And this was thanks almost entirely to the wise President of the council, Monsieur de Villèle, a moderate reactionary with a modern head, who, unlike his master, was perfectly aware of the fact that Charles X must rule two countries—Old France and New. Villèle was determined that, since reaction must come, its advent should be as painless as possible. He had decided to anæsthetize the patient and then perform the difficult operation.

Prosperity-talk was the first anodyne administered, and prosperity-measures. Then, in 1825, came the proposal to indemnify the Émigrés. Bourgeois clutched their money-bags in alarm. Indemnification was followed by the Law of Sacrilege to protect Holy Church, and the unauthorized return of the Jesuit Order. Bourgeois became even more annoyed and, over the open graves of Manuel and General Foy, two Liberals, they challenged the Government. Funeral orations became again, in France, defiances of Royalty. The *Constitutionnel* and other liberal papers, too, voiced their discontent, and the National Guard failed to cheer their King at a review. Then it was that Monarchy, insulted, retorted with a Vandal Press Bill that brought more rigorous censorship, and the establishment of a careful surveillance on the part of the Secret Police. As for the rash guardsmen, they were compelled to doff their uniforms and pack them away for a more auspicious occasion.

In short, near the end of the year 1827, Charles's Government was becoming uneasy about its programme. It must discover the extent and nature of this new but determined opposition, and so it took to dogging the footsteps of any of those who had been in any way associated with the new Liberals. Even young Monsieur Thiers came, again, under its surveillance, and when, his *History* completed, he set out on a visit to his mother at Aix-en-Provence, it appears that his every move was followed.

In the Archives Nationales, Section F 7, there is a *dossier* of considerable proportions that relates to this comparatively innocent journey. Monsieur le Ministre de l'Intérieur requests Monsieur le Préfet du Departement des Bouches-du-Rhône to watch this young writer and extraordinary historian and to report on his activities. Evidently, Monsieur le Préfet observed instructions to the letter for when, on January 8, Monsieur Thiers was already en route to Paris, the faithful servant of the government replied:

"Monseigneur, Sire Louis Adolphe Thiers, formerly a lawyer at the bar of Aix, and one of the editors of the *Constitutionnel,* to whom Your Excellency called my attention, did not limit his stay to Aix. He went on to Marseilles where he remained three days, during which time he was visited, on several occasions, by Monsieur Borélly, Vice-President of the Civil Tribunal, and by

Monsieur Thomas, lawyer, one of the Constitutionalist candidates at the last election, and by several other persons connected with the legal profession in the city.

"These *relations* are, indeed, ground for conjecture, and there is nothing to indicate that Sire Thiers came to Marseilles for private affairs. (It is likely) that the purpose of this visit was to communicate with these gentlemen who are known for their extreme liberal opinions, to inform himself of the general spirit and sentiment among the inhabitants of the city."

Upon his return to Paris, Monsieur Thiers found much to interest him. Because of his lukewarm attitude to the case of the liberty-loving Greeks, Villèle had fallen, and the King had finally been forced to select the more liberal Martignac. Monsieur Thiers informed his friends of the Midi that, at the height of the crisis, Villèle had even asked Laffitte, a leader of the bourgeois, to join with him. As to the new Ministry, in spite of Martignac's own good intentions and sincerity, it cannot last. It has no colour; it is grey; everyone of worth is refusing the positions offered by the President of the Council. Many, even, do not expect the Ministry to survive until the opening of the Chambers.

There was much truth in these reflections that he transmitted to his friends. The Martignac Ministry found favour with no one. Charles X hated it, the Ultras despised it, and the Liberals were not of a mind to support the mild reforms that were proposed by its well-meaning head. Already the words—relentless opposition—appeared to have gone forth. Martignac's Council lasted longer than Thiers expected, for the bourgeois party moved slowly, and, at first, aimed simply at preventing the Cabinet from accomplishing anything. To many, the real crisis appeared to be still in the far distance. To Thiers, this meant that his opportunity was not yet come. And so, *en attendant*, he felt the need of an absorbing occupation.

He had tried his hand at many trades, as historian,

reviewer, dramatic critic, and art critic. To his own mind, the most satisfactory had been history. Once again, therefore, he returned to Clio's arms. It was the day of monumental history. Perhaps Romanticism had had its part in this new rage. At any rate, the *History of the French Revolution* now seemed small in scope and content to its ambitious young author. Monsieur Thiers desired to outdo them all by writing a narrative of the world. But this work, he wrote a friend, would really go beyond the bounds of pure history; it would be something greater, more potent, something of which, he confessed, he had often dreamed. "My next book will be at one and the same time a poem and a philosophy."

Hardly had this decision been reached than fortune smiled again on him. The door of opportunity was opened to him, when, through the favour of Hyde de Neuville, Minister of Marine, he was invited to be one of a small company that was to travel on the ship *Favorite* around the world. Here, indeed, was a splendid preparation for his proposed historical manuscripts. Preparations were made; bags were packed. And then, a few days before the departure, the hand of Charles the King at the Château designated Polignac, the Ultra, as the successor to the unfortunate Martignac. The *tour du monde* was abandoned immediately. The crisis had come! Into politics Monsieur Thiers would go. "War and politics," he wrote, "are the true portrayers of a man's real character, for all his soul is in the one or the other. Look at the works of the most famous poets, savants, and authors. Even their finest productions will never reveal to you what was the real temper of their minds. There is only one thing that is equal to the art of war, and that is the art of governing."

With these words, he took leave of his Muse and abandoned the profession of historian and critic for seven years.

The most immediate result of the appointment of Polignac was a change in the character of the Opposition. Until August, 1829, there had not been any generally organized action against Charles X. Such action as had occurred had been sporadic and individual. Thiers, as a member of the staff of the *Constitutionnel,* had visited and consulted Borélly and Thomas, the leaders of the Opposition at Marseilles, but he had done so as one of a group in Paris and not as the emissary of a large, organized political machine.

After the nomination of Polignac, however, groups of malcontents began to coalesce, but, even then, real party machinery did not develop. Such organization as took place was entirely sectional, and was brought about under the guidance of regional leaders who appear to have acted quite independently of each other. In some places, even, the clubs were revived, but these should not be confused with the earlier Carbonari sections in France; their purpose was not so radical, nor were their methods so elemental. While they were opposed to the Government, they did not desire to use bloodshed to overthrow it; instead, they proposed to embarrass it by legal means. The "League of Breton Resistance," for example, refused to pay taxes not sanctioned by the law. The Society known as "Help Thyself and Heaven will Help Thee" sought to obstruct legislation that was incompatible with the Charter. All these groups, whether Moderate or Radical, did much to disseminate the spirit of opposition throughout France, but little to unify it, and practically nothing to educate it and make it intelligent.

Frenchmen confessed that they were discontented with the existing government, but they seemed to be unable to suggest a satisfactory substitute. Many, except the workmen and the *exaltés,* shuddered at the word Republic, for the years 1789–1795 were still too vivid a recollection in their minds. Even the workmen, for that matter, distrusted Republicans. In other words, while Charles and his Government appeared to be doomed, it is not at all unlikely that they might have survived longer had not a new force arisen to educate the several opinions, and to provide information and afford a sort of leadership to an ignorant and incohesive Opposition.

The first development in this direction had been made by the Republicans when they had inaugurated a new paper, *La Jeune France,* in June, 1829. But this paper was too radical to gain much support from the bourgeoisie; the banker and industrialist saw in its propaganda a menace to their own security. For the needs of these more cautious gentlemen, a moderate and less extreme system must be proposed, and its safer theories disseminated. It was to this end that the *National* was founded during the latter part of the same year.

This latest addition to Paris journalism was an outgrowth of certain elements from the *Constitutionnel* and the *Globe*. These two sheets had been advanced for the early years of the Restoration, but, by November, 1829, they had fallen far behind the aims and desires of some of their subscribers and, more especially, of certain younger editors who had served on their boards. Most of their stockholders, however, were conservative bourgeois who were afraid of jeopardizing their business interests by countenancing all that these rash young writers desired. It appears that Thiers, supported by Étienne and Évariste Desmoulins, actually attempted to make over the platform of the *Constitutionnel,* but he was allowed to go only so far. When, therefore, he became convinced that it would be impossible to transform the political programme of the paper, he retired from its staff to join with Mignet and Armand Carrel in a new journalistic enterprise. The *National* was founded and soon became the organ of the advanced wing of the bourgeois Opposition.

It stands to reason that Thiers would not have taken such a step without the advice of other men, older than himself and more experienced. For the three to have founded the *National* alone would have been out of the question; no one of them possessed a sufficient income, and, as yet, the position of none was assured in Paris. Of the three, Thiers was the best known and was regarded as a young man of promise; Mignet was recognized as a competent historian, a little more dispassionate than most of his fellows; and Carrel had recently published a study of the Counter-Revolution in England that had brought him a certain notoriety. But no one of them was strong enough, at that time, to have stood alone. There must, therefore, have been encouragement from a powerful source that led the trio to attempt a new venture in Paris journalism, but it is difficult to discover exactly where the support and assistance originated.

Undoubtedly, Prince Talleyrand was concerned in this enterprise from the very beginning, for, by 1829, he had become a sort of pivot for that section of the Opposition with which Thiers had become identified. During the short-lived Ministry of Martignac, the Prince had carried on a brief flirtation with the Restoration Monarchy, but, with the coming of Polignac, this remarkable navigator of the political seas shifted the air and steered his ship straight into the harbour of Orléanism, where Sébastiani, Broglie, Villemain, and Molé had already established themselves. Nevertheless Talleyrand, and even his garrulous niece, Madame de Dino, were careful to leave no trace of their relations to the *National* in the papers and letters that they bequeathed to posterity. Jacques Laffitte, that friend of Louis Philippe d'Orléans and protector of Thiers, and the mysterious Baron Cotta of Cottendorf, gave financial assistance to the plan. But who was the first sponsor? Some would like to throw on old Talleyrand the onus of the entire venture. They present a story that is attractive. They take us to Rochecotte, the château of the Duchesse de Dino. There, in the country, far from prying eyes, came Baron Louis, former associate of Talleyrand in Bonaparte's Government. With the Baron were two young men, Thiers and Mignet. And these three, in the presence of the old Prince and his niece who, like her uncle, never missed a trick in the political game, arranged the plan for the *National* that was to prepare France to depose one King and enthrone another. This is the tale told by Monsieur de Gérainville: undoubtedly it was whispered in the corners of Paris salons during the spring of 1830 when the *National* became the most discussed paper in France. It may be true in every detail; in its essence, it most certainly contains the truth. Talleyrand aided them with his advice, and Baron Louis very likely gave them a more material blessing. As Chateaubriand remarked: "The Prince de Talleyrand did not contribute a sou; he only soiled the spirit of the paper by contributing to the common fund his share of treason and corruption." Monsieur Colmache, Talleyrand's secretary, remarks that after the last of November, 1829, the young Monsieur Thiers was an assiduous visitor wherever Talleyrand happened to be located, and that he held long and serious consultations with the Prince.

Advised and supported by these various powers, the three editors established their headquarters in the Place des Italiens, rue Neuve-Saint-Martin, No. 10. Within a very short time after its appearance, the *National* became the recognized authority to define and explain the aims of a large and growing section of the Left. In this way, an Opposition that was not united in any sense received unofficial guidance and direction from the journal whose words they read with delight and whose suggestions they frequently followed. The writings of its young editors inspired many readers who had become weary of the dull, old-fashioned platitudes of the *Globe*, the *Constitutionnel*, and the *Courrier Français*. In fact, it was not long before the example of the *National* reacted upon its older and more timid contemporaries: in time, the *Tribune*, the *Temps*, and the *Globe* came to follow the pace set by the younger paper. This was the début of the *National:* what, now, was its real purpose?

Over this question there has been much discussion. In later years, Armand Carrel became a radical Republican, and this has led some to infer that, from the very day of its inception, the *National* was a Republican sheet. As a matter of fact, Carrel's case of Republicanism was very mild until the July Days. To disclose the true and original colour of the paper, one must turn to the man who first acted as its editor-in-chief, and to his friend, Mignet. Neither one of these two was Republican in 1830, and that is why Thiers broke with Carrel later in that year. Furthermore, neither the editor-in-chief nor Mignet ever advocated violence against the existing Government until the July Days. A few of his most hostile critics assert that Monsieur Thiers desired to see France return to Jacobin principles. But, in that case, his bourgeois supporters would never have aided him and it would have been entirely contrary to everything that he had written. In 1830, he was still loyal to the opinions that he had expressed in the *History of the French Revolution*. While he advocated revolution, the methods that he and his friends advised were legal. *Legitimacy*, as represented by Charles X and Polignac, was their only enemy, and it must be reformed or else done away with entirely. But, in their opinion, public sentiment must first be created, and the first step in such a direction was to teach Frenchmen history and politics. Instruction, then, was one of the primary aims of the *National*. In this respect the paper was merely the continuation of the *History of the French Revolution*.

To a certain extent, the early policy of Polignac assisted the paper at the outset. It gave the young editors a breathing space and an opportunity to establish themselves in the mind of Paris. Contrary to popular expectation, the Minister did not attempt to immediately inaugurate a drastic reaction. Due, in part, to the timidity of certain of his colleagues, Polignac at first did nothing. He gave the *National* a chance to teach before it set about to attack the actual policies proposed by the hated Ministry.

The first issue appeared on January 3, 1830, and contained a declaration of the paper's wishes for France. The leading article was written by Thiers. He had expended much effort and worry about it. He even went so far as to submit it to Chateaubriand, whose approval he sought in vain. "If, in this first article, which is a subject of great anxiety to me, I have managed to express opinions of which you approve, then I am reassured and certain of finding myself in the right way." Needless to say, he did not secure the *imprimatur* that he desired. There is, however, nothing radical or Republican in the first instruction that the editor-in-chief of the *National* addressed to the French public:

"A king hereditary, inviolable, depositary of the Government, obliged to confide the exercise of the same to responsible ministers who declare for him peace and war, draw up the laws, and administer the public funds. . . . A king so placed in a region superior to petty ambitions, above public hate, where, when all is well, he enjoys the affection of his people, and is only reproved by their silence when all is wrong. Beneath this king, a peerage which is independent of the ministers by the fact of its hereditary character, and which its lights make dependent upon public opinion; a peerage richly endowed in a country of divided estates, filled with the most illustrious names, conservative both in its traditions and in its political maxims, and opposing a resistance to yield to the general impetuosity of human minds. Beside this peerage, an elective assembly composed of all the men distinguished in industry, arms, science, and art, sent up to represent the country and to proclaim the nation's mind, not to nominate ministers, but to have them nominated by its votes; not administering of itself, but by means of those who have its confidence. Such an ensemble constitutes the most stable and free, the most balanced and vigorous (government). It is such (a government) that we should and do desire for France."

This is Thiers' ideal "representative monarchy." It is nothing more or less than the English system that he had praised in the pages of the *History*.

Lessons like this one were continued in the subsequent articles that appeared in the *National*, and they were immediately taken up and attacked by the Government papers. The center of the controversy became Thiers' conception of kingship and it was during this newspaper discussion that he finally uttered that political mot of his that has been attached to his name ever since— "The King reigns and does not govern." In the *History* the first suggestion of the phrase appears in the words, "The nation wills, and the King fulfils." Later, in the *National*, the same theory is clothed in different terms: "Again, in a word, he (the King) reigns, and the country rules itself. The King does not administer, he does not govern, he reigns. Thus the King reigns, the ministers govern, the Chambers judge." And, finally, in a later number of the *National* it receives its final form: "The King reigns and does not govern."

To instruct the public in a new type of monarchy was the first purpose of this group of editors. Their second aim was to expose the character of the existing government. At first this was done only by implication, but as the days wore on and the *National* began to prosper, it became very daring. On January 5, thanks to Martignac's more liberal Press Law that was still in force, Monsieur Thiers launched his first strong attack when he reminded his readers of the absolute incompatibility of Chamber and Ministry, and pointed out to them that Polignac had only two alternatives, either to "retire ingloriously" or to dissolve the Chamber and change the electoral law by means of a coup d'état. From January 5 the *National* threw discretion to the winds and set out to propose a radical remedy. Thiers himself, although he expressed to his friends a "regret for the quiet of my studies to which I hope to return after a little while," had definitely decided to fight the matter out through the columns of the *National*. Now that he and his supporters believed that a coup d'état was being considered, he even went so far as to suggest, in veiled terms, a possible substitution not only for Ministry but for King. The phrases that he used are veiled but there is also another thing about them—they are highly coloured and idealized. To him, as to many others, the idea of the deadly parallel between England in 1688 and France in 1830 became predominant. The House of Orange had been substituted for the House of Stuart. Why, likewise, should not Orléans be substituted for Bourbon? A bloodless revolution! The idea seized upon his imagination, and Monsieur Thiers became a *doctrinaire*. But what a romantic and imaginative *doctrinaire* he was when he wrote this description of Louis Philippe, the head of the House of Orléans, whom, incidentally, he had never met! "France, as a matter of fact, is, indeed, disillusioned in regard to persons; France loves genius, and she has seen what that cost her. Simple virtues, modest and solid, that a good education can always assure in the inheritor of a throne, that a limited power cannot spoil, that is what France needs."

And, all the while, Louis Philippe lived in his Palais Royal, this paragon of bourgeois simplicity, surrounded by his paintings and tapestries of the Revolution, and his children fresh from the public schools of France. A Catholic, but not too Catholic, a Voltairean but not too sceptical, the follower of the Golden Mean in all things.

Meanwhile, Polignac began to act. There were processes

against the *National* but wealthy bourgeois paid the fines, and the fines were small. It was a sign, however, that Polignac was beginning to be active. The time had come when he and his King must meet the Chamber. To prepare the way for popular favour, a gigantic enterprise of conquest in Algiers was inaugurated. France followed it enthusiastically, but when the Chamber opened, Charles X spoiled it all. There was a phrase in his Speech from the Throne that sounded like a threat: "If guilty inclinations raise against my government obstacles that I cannot and shall not foresee, I will find the force by which to surmount them."

Consequently, an angry Chamber entered upon a long debate over its Reply to the Throne. Finally, an Address was accepted by a vote of 221 to 81. It had been written by Étienne, the friend of Thiers, and by Guizot. The Address was virtually a demand for the retirement of Polignac. Charles curtly refused to heed the request and called for elections that brought him almost the same stubborn opposition.

The crisis prophesied by Thiers in his article of January 5 had indeed come. What was the Government to do? Should it retire or break the law? On July 20, the chief editor of the *National* wrote these words for the morning issue of his paper:

"Sinister rumours are abroad in Paris today. In spite of the general incredulity which people have shown until now, we are all struck with the thought that a *coup d'état* will be attempted before the end of the month."

CHAPTER IV

EXIT CHARLES X

ON July 21 the *National* had signalled the coup d'état, and on the evening of July 25 that prophecy was fulfilled when Charles signed, at St. Cloud, the four famous ordinances. As he laid down his pen, the King is said to have remarked: "There, Messieurs, are strong measures, and a great deal of courage will be required to enforce them. I count on you, and you may count on me. We have a common cause. Between us, it is a question of life or death." The next morning the ordinances appeared in the official paper, and the plan of the Government for maintaining its control of France was exposed to the world. The first ordinance suspended the liberty of the Press; the second dissolved the Chamber. The third changed the electoral system to the exclusion of the bourgeoisie and the advantage of the great landlords, while the fourth law called for an election according to the new system.

These decrees caused surprise in Paris. The Liberal Press had long since warned the public of the possibility of such action on the part of the Government. Indignation ran high, and it should be remembered to the credit of some of the most loyal supporters of the Monarchy that they were not all unanimous in approving this latest move of Charles's Government. Marshal Marmont, to whom was given the command of the troops in Paris, is said to have remarked to Arago: "Well, the fools have gone beyond their limits. You have nothing to worry about, you who are a citizen and a Frenchman, but how much should I be pitied; I, who in my quality of soldier may perhaps be forced to give up my life in the defence of acts that I abominate and of persons who for some time have seemed to be trying to fill me with disgust." Probably Marmont was not alone in this sentiment. And yet, in spite of the disgust of Loyalist and Liberal, Charles and his partisans seemed to feel that there was a basis of legality for their actions and that this basis would bring many to their support. The ground for this contention lay in Article 14 of the Charter of 1814. According to this clause, the King was empowered to make "the necessary regulations and ordinances for the execution of the laws and for the safety of the State." But it was certainly a very exaggerated interpretation of this provision that would permit a king to make regulations transforming the character of the Monarchy. It was impossible to contend, as Charles virtually did, that Article 14 nullified all the other fundamental laws of the Charter.

Obviously, the ordinances affected principally three groups in Paris, the deputies, the disfranchised voters, and the Press. Of these, the Press was the first to take any action, while, at the outset, deputy and voter appeared to be struck dumb. The journalists were placed under very peculiar disabilities by the second law. For the publication of a periodical or newspaper a preliminary authorization was to be required, and this must be renewed every three months. Furthermore, the Government reserved the right to revoke its authorization at any time. This amounted to the temporary suspension of all publications from the evening of the twenty-fifth, and no paper could be issued until an application had been made and passed upon. Great was the need, therefore, of the Press, and it was quite natural that they should be the first to act. It is indeed with reason that the revolution that ensued has been called a "Newspaper Revolution"; at least two of the four July Days belong to the journalists and kindred trades.

Shortly after the appearance of the new laws in the *Moniteur* of July 26, a group of journalists representing the *Constitutionnel,* the *Temps,* and the *Débats* called at the law offices of Charles Dupin to consult about the legality of the disabilities that the Ministry had placed upon them. A little later, Dupin was joined by several other lawyers, Merillon, Barthe, and Odilon Barrot. With these men Dupin went into consultation, and during their conference other members of the Press foregathered in the outer office. It was before quite an audience, therefore, that Dupin finally announced his decision: "The law alone is in force. The ordinances of July 25 are not able to abrogate it or to abolish it; these ordinances must not be enforced. If I were a journalist, I should resist by all means of fact and of law; and I add that, in my opinion, any paper that submits or requests the authorization imposed does not deserve to have a single subscriber in France." These were bold words. Dupin was willing to urge them on, but he would not allow the journalists to take any action in his office, and so they adjourned to the bureau of the *National,* rue Neuve-Saint-Martin, No. 10, to deliberate.

It was in the offices of Thiers' paper that the first organized protest of the Revolution was made. The Paris journals had latterly become leaders of public opinion and now, in the July Days, they reached the height of their power and might almost be said to have directed the first day of the Revolution. Out of courtesy to the paper whose guests they were, it was agreed that Thiers should preside at the meeting. But the fact that he acted as chairman does not seem to have prevented him from speaking frequently, and at length, from the floor! Various measures of retaliation were proposed, but none appears to have met with the support of the chairman until Monsieur Jean Pillet proposed that a collective protest be published. Again Thiers left the chair, this time not to combat but to approve. "Names are necessary; we must risk our heads," he declared. The proposal was finally adopted. In the meantime, during the discussion, some of the more timid journalists left the room. After their departure, a committee was appointed to draft a formal Protest. Thiers, Chatelain, Cauchois-Lemaire, and de Rémusat were selected for the task of composing the Protest, and it was the first named who drafted the statement of the Paris journalists that was to appear in the morning.

The document as printed in the *National* was brief, concise, and to the point, written in its author's best and most lucid style. Obedience to the Government, the Protest declared, is no longer a duty. For that body by its recent acts has violated the law and need no longer be obeyed. Article 8 of the Charter declares that the Press must conform to the law; it does not mention the ordinances. Article 35 states that the electoral colleges shall be determined according to the law; it does not specify that they shall be determined by the ordinances. Heretofore the Government has recognized these laws; now it has violated them. "Today the Government has lost the legal character by which it commands obedience. As far as our own rights are concerned, we will resist to the utmost. As for France, let her decide how far she ought to carry resistance against tyranny." Appended to this statement were the signatures of representatives of the *National, Globe, Temps, Figaro, Constitutionnel,* and *Courrier Français.* With such words the Press of Paris would address its readers on the morrow, and the concluding phrase, "As for France, let her decide how far she ought to carry resistance against tyranny," would be the tocsin of a new revolution. But today Paris was quiet and silent. Charles X might return from a day's hunting and hear from Polignac that the city had not stirred. He might have one more night of freedom from anxiety.

Beginning with the morning of the 27th, however, ripples were visible upon the surface of comparatively serene Paris. The *National* and other papers appeared with Thiers' Protest printed in bold type. Extra editions were soon exhausted. From early morning the boulevards and streets were thronged with groups of workmen with nothing to do, gazing into the barred shop-windows, reading extra copies of the *Temps* and the *National* that were distributed gratis, and prey to the whim of any passing moment. A drunken labourer or the sight of an elegant aristocrat might have led at any moment to a repetition of July 14, 1789. But fortunately July, 1830, could offer no Camille Desmoulins, and the aristocrats were all gathered at St. Cloud. For the present, these idle groups were enjoying an unaccustomed leisure, and the atmosphere was one of holiday, but soon that would become irksome and gradually the serious question of food for the family would present itself. For many of these labourers were destined to a longer holiday than they desired; they had been shut out of their shops. When they had gone to the scenes of their labour that morning, they had discovered placards posted on the doors, announcing the fact that the factories had been closed for an indefinite period. Apparently, during the preceding night, industrialist as well as journalist had been at work. The first of the shops to adopt such a measure had been those closely allied to the journalists, the printers. At the suggestion of Monsieur Barthe, who had been one of the legal lights at Dupin's office on the 26th, a meeting of the printers had been called at the Café de la Rotonde. There it had been agreed to close the shops and to throw the printers on to the streets. Other industries followed their example, and by midday of the 27th labouring Paris was idle. But as yet its state of mind was not dangerous.

The first occurrence to arouse the mob to anything more than a passive interest in the novelty of the whole situation was the arrival of Government officers at the headquarters of the *Temps*. Their purpose was to dismantle the presses. From the *Temps* bureau the mob followed the *agents* to the *National*, where the officers performed their duties, while Thiers watched serenely from behind his enormous glasses. There can be no doubt but that he was enjoying the situation hugely. No sooner had the *agents* taken their departure than some machinist in the crowd set to work to assist the editor in reconstructing the presses. When the latter were again in order, Thiers prepared the issue for the 28th. This was to be printed on a single sheet. The issue of the 27th had sounded the tocsin, and the succeeding edition repeated the call in words more bold and, too, more impertinent: "We still can talk to France today. Yesterday, the Charter was torn into shreds, and those who found in it their guarantees lost them; yesterday, everyone was made free to act according to his power, and now no one should expect security save through using force."

The morrow's issue prepared, Thiers and Mignet hurried from the scene of their labours and left Paris for parts unknown. In fact, there was good reason why the two young Liberals should flee the capital. They had been advised by Royer-Collard to leave at once, for warrants had been issued for their arrest as signatories to the Protest of July 26 which the Government regarded as seditious. In company with another of their colleagues, they took refuge near Montmorency at the house of Madame de Courchamp. There they remained until the authority of the restored Bourbons had been driven from Paris.

With the disappearance of the two writers the first Day of the Journalists ends.

In the meantime, the Paris mob had concentrated at two main points, around the Palais Royal, whose lord was absent, and in the vicinity of the home of Casimir Périer, where those Constitutionalist Deputies who had had the courage to remain were assembled. Marmont, appointed on the eve military Commander of the city by Polignac, sent two small detachments to disperse the mob. At the Palais Royal an officer, losing his temper, fired upon the crowd, and a riot ensued. Barricades appeared in the rue St. Honoré, and Marmont sent to St. Cloud for reinforcements. The crowds did not interfere very much with the movements of the troops; they contented themselves with watching the soldiery, frequently even fraternizing with them. Towards evening the uniform of the suppressed National Guard appeared on the streets. This was not without its significance. It boded ill for the morrow.

July 28 is properly called the "People's Day." The mob once turned out on the streets, the Deputies who remained seem to have made a feeble and not too sincere attempt at conciliation with the existing Government. Failing in this, they waited and allowed the people to drive the Ministry from power and the Royalist troops from Paris, before themselves taking up any constructive programme. As early as five o'clock in the morning, groups of armed men had appeared in the vicinity of the Porte Saint Martin and the Porte Saint Denis. Soon other parts of Paris presented the same aspect. During the night several arsenals had been raided, and arms and munitions secured. Actual fighting first set in, of course, in the crowded quarter of the Bastille and the Hôtel de Ville. By noon, the tricolour floated from the towers of Notre Dame. Marmont, now thoroughly alarmed, concentrated his forces at the Louvre in preparation for an attack. At the same time he sent a message to Charles, apprising him of the situation and counselling an attempt at conciliation. From St. Cloud the King sent his reply; it was a curt refusal. By evening, the fighting extended to the Boulevards.

Meantime, what of the Deputies of France, those repositories and guarantors of law and order? Many had fled to their homes in the provinces, and the remnant that had remained in Paris was of the Constitutional party. On the evening of the 27th, some of them had met at the house of Casimir Périer, but the general confusion and the howling mob outside prevented their accomplishing anything. Again, on the morrow, these worthies convened at the house of Audrey de Puyraveau. To them came Laffitte and LaFayette. The presence of the banker and the general, both of whom were popular and whose Liberal opinions were recognized, gave a sense of assurance to the meeting. Some action must now be taken. Should an appeal be made to the King, or should a Provisional Government be established? Undoubtedly, the latter was the desire of the extremists. Probably LaFayette favoured this as much as he can be said to have favoured any definite policy at this time of his life. But the combined efforts of Périer, Sébastiani, and Laffitte won the day. A committee of five was appointed to visit Marmont and to present a protest through him to the King, against the Ministry that had issued and was seeking to enforce the ordinances. Gérard, de Lobau, Périer, Mauguin, and Laffitte set out for the Tuileries on their mission. Arriving there, they met with Arago, who joined his instances to theirs and besought Marmont to forward their Protest. To this Marmont consented, but, as he had foretold, the attempt failed. Both Charles and Polignac refused to communicate with this group of Deputies. Upon the return of the delegates to Puyraveau's house, the meeting decided to publish the Protest. The same thing occurred among the Peers, who had assembled at the hôtel of Pasquier. In the meantime LaFayette had been dispatched to the Hôtel de Ville, where the Republicans were already in possession. During the night fighting continued in the streets, and when July 29 dawned, Paris was free from her detested King. The Royalist troops had evacuated their stronghold at the Louvre and were retreating in the direction of St. Cloud. The tricolour now floated above the Tuileries; Paris was in the hands of its citizens.

Monarchy had gone from the capital, but what was in its place? That was the serious question that everyone was asking himself on the morning of the 29th. As yet, nothing had been substituted, but unless the Deputies acted a Republic was a possibility, even a likelihood. LaFayette held the Hôtel de Ville, and once there, he came under the influence of the Republican group. Bastide, Cavaignac, Thomas, and Joubert reigned at the Tuileries, and at the Café Lointier, the rendezvous of a very active group of Republicans, a proclamation calling for the election of a *Constituante* was in the process of composition. Consequently, when the Deputies reconvened at the house of Laffitte on that morning, one thing was uppermost in their minds—the necessity of establishing their control over the movement that they had allowed to break out and that they had done nothing to restrain. Obviously, if their predominance was to be established, they must set up a Provisional Government and make sure of the recognition of LaFayette and his party at the Hôtel de Ville before the latter had joined with the other Republican groups. Otherwise, the Constitutionalist Deputies would be outnumbered. Accordingly, de Rémusat was sent on an embassy to the Hôtel de Ville. He returned with a characteristically vague answer from the old General, but at any rate it was favourable enough to encourage the

Deputies to act. Thereupon they set to work and appointed a Provisional Government that was announced by the following Proclamation:

"The Deputies present in Paris have met to remedy the great dangers that are menacing the security of persons and property.

"A Commission was named to safeguard all interests in the absence of a regular organized Government. Messieurs Audrey de Puyraveau, Comte Gérard, Comte de Lobau, Mauguin, Odier, Casimir Périer, de Schönen compose this Commission.

"The National Guard is in control of Paris at all points."

It was well that these gentlemen spoke of the dangers menacing persons and property in the past tense. Wisdom dictated the statement that the National Guard was in control at all points; such was not the case, but it might be if LaFayette were made commander, for Republicans adored the old hero. The appointment of LaFayette might prevent the possibility of a union between the Hôtel de Ville Republicans and the desperadoes of the Tuileries.

When Dupin had drafted this Proclamation, it was spread over Paris. The Deputies were dealing desperately in futures, but only by dealing in futures could the possibility of any sort of Monarchy survive. In this way a banker and an industrialist became the temporary and uncertain masters of the July Revolution, and it is well to remember that the banker had managed the business affairs of the House of Orléans for twelve years.

A Provisional Government established and the means for restoring order in Paris set in operation, the next problem was the future of France. What should follow the temporary arrangement? One might expect that the answer would come from this same group of Deputies. As a matter of fact, this was the case, but it does not appear that the first to mention publicly the plan was one of its number. The journalists of Paris appear again on the scene.

With the success of the People's Day the two young gentlemen who had taken refuge near Montmorency returned. Upon their arrival, they found much to interest them, and they set out to explore the new Paris that had come into being during their very brief absence. According to Thiers, this very simple promenade became a very momentous occasion. They walked along the streets, past the Tuileries, stopping often to speak to friends or even to exchange greetings with strangers, for the spirit of "Fraternité" was again in the air. They declared that they were impressed by the frequency with which they heard the word "Republic" pronounced. LaFayette was asserting it in loud tones, and one Monsieur de Laborde was forming a legion of Young Republicans. In the course of their walk the two young friends turned into the rue de Richelieu, where, in those days, there were many fashionable shops. Thiers remarked that the shopkeepers who had been furnishers to the King, or to the Duc or Duchesse de Berry, and who had proclaimed the fact in large gold letters, were now hastily removing the same from their shop-windows. As they went on, however, they noticed two shops whose windows were decorated with the coat-of-arms of the Duc d'Orléans, and this was allowed to remain. Thiers was struck by this fact. "I said to Mignet, 'Do you think that they are considering the Duke of Orléans?' With that I went to Laffitte."

It is indeed hard to believe that it had not occurred to these two that Louis Philippe might receive the crown of France. Otherwise, why the articles in the *National*? Why the school of 1688? So much innocence could hardly go hand in hand with so much perspicacity as these two had shown. But here again there is an element of truth in Thiers' statement that should not be forgotten. It is evidence of the fact that there was no real, organized conspiracy for Orléans until July. Time and time again, in later life, Thiers affirmed this fact, and many others supported him. The Duke sought the throne, but he did not conspire in the earlier days, and his candidacy does not appear to have been discussed openly even among his friends until the People's Day had driven the authority of the Bourbons from Paris. Then it was that the candidacy of Orléans, a matter that had undoubtedly been in the minds of many, became recognized as a desirable fact. The first men to mention it were, then, the originators of the July Monarchy, and these men were Laffitte, Talleyrand, Sébastiani, Thiers, and, to a lesser degree, Périer.

The name of Louis Philippe was first pronounced in public at the meeting at Laffitte's house on July 29. To this meeting came Thiers, newly returned to Paris. He tells us that as he entered the house he was still impressed by the evidences of Republican spirit that he had beheld during his walk, but that once he found himself within the walls of Laffitte's mansion, where were gathered Deputies, bankers, and generals, he found a sentiment quite the opposite. All were opposed to any form of Republican rule. "You've got it," he cried, as he entered the room, "(the Republic) is spreading everywhere. You will not escape it. Only the Duke of Orléans can possibly get you out of this." In his opinion all concurred. But there was a difficulty, for none of them seemed to have the slightest idea what Louis Philippe would do or say to a proposal from them. They needed him to lead them, but would he come? Then it was that Thiers made a stroke for his beloved "representative monarchy." "What matter?" he said, "*compromise him without consulting him.*"

As was to be so frequently the case in later times, the daring of the little man swept the informal gathering. The older and more experienced of them accepted the proposition of one who was but a few years ago a complete stranger to them, and active conspiracy began. Most of the gathering retired to reconvene on the 30th, when they were to bring their friends with them. Only the arch-conspirators remained to draft the Proclamation with which Paris was to be placarded during the night. They had just completed their work when someone knocked at Laffitte's door. The Old Régime in the persons of Marmont and a few Carlist peers had called to present the draft of a revocation of the ordinances to which Charles had at last consented! But the Deputies had gone home; the decision had been taken; and the presses of the *National* were being oiled to print for Parisians the momentous decree that had been declared by a small group of men not all of whom were Deputies. In the dim light Laffitte read to his latest visitors the draft of the Orléanist Proclamation, and the emissaries of the Bourbon Monarchy retired defeated. Thiers stayed by the presses until the Proclamations were through. Laffitte dreamed of statesmanship, and, off in his corner of Paris, Talleyrand saw again a stage on which he could play a part.

On the following morning, Parisians awoke to find themselves Orléanists. Every billboard bore the poster relating the marvellous virtues of the great man who had lived so quietly and so modestly in their midst. Could the Duke have read it, it is doubtful whether even he would have recognized himself. The wording of the declaration was cleverly done, and even without his own assertion to that effect, one could be sure that it was the work of Thiers. But it is difficult to find in the portrait the real Louis Philippe of the pear-shaped head—"la poire couronné" they called him—of the slow, heavy gait, the great wide-brimmed hat, and the inevitable green umbrella tucked under his left arm that his right hand might be free to greet bourgeois, labourer, and aristocrat as he sauntered down the rue de Rivoli. The glowing words of the youthful enthusiast who did not yet know him, and who had previously refused to meet him, created a new and altogether ideal Duke. Perhaps it was just as well that Thiers did not know him, otherwise he would have been compelled to forget as much about the unprepossessing appearance of Louis Philippe as he, the historian, had had to forget about history when he had formed the thrilling words of the Proclamation:

"Charles X can never return to Paris; he has shed the blood of the people.

"The Republic would expose us to dangerous divisions; it would involve us in hostilities with Europe.

"The Duke of Orléans is a Prince devoted to the cause of the Revolution.

"The Duke of Orléans has never fought against us.

"The Duke of Orléans was at Jemmapes.

"The Duke of Orléans is a Citizen-King.

"The Duke of Orléans has carried the tricolour under the enemies' fire; the Duke of Orléans alone can carry it again. We will have no other flag.

"The Duke of Orléans does not commit himself. He awaits the expression of our wishes. Let us proclaim those wishes, and he will accept the Charter as we have always understood it, and as we have always desired it. It is from the French people that he will hold his crown."

These sentences were well calculated to attract the public eye. The catchwords, Revolution, Jemmapes, Tricolour, and Citizen-King made fainter the already dim recollection of the disgraceful Égalité, Louis Philippe's father. Meanwhile, the subject of this panegyric was in hiding in the Parc de Riancey. Had he gone thither, like the prophets of old, to meditate on his mission, to protect his property, or because he feared the warrants of Charles X for his arrest?

Paris generally seemed to accept tacitly the sentiments placarded through the efforts of Laffitte and his lieutenant. But there were still difficulties and hindrances in the path of the new Orléanist party. LaFayette was an uncertain quantity, and no definite statement of attitude had emanated from the Duke or from any member of his household. The sooner the adherence of Louis Philippe could be obtained, the more likely it was that LaFayette would hand over the Hôtel de Ville to him. This, therefore, was the principal concern of the Deputies who foregathered at Laffitte's on the morning of the 30th. As he joined them, Béranger remarked: "The only subject of conversation this morning is your prince. His name is on every tongue." But would the Duke come to Paris? Of this Laffitte felt quite sure, but Sébastiani and a number of others at the meeting expressed considerable doubt about it. Time, however, was passing, and every minute lost by the Orléanists was a minute gained by Republicanism. Finally, Thiers and others urged that someone be sent to ascertain the sentiments of Louis Philippe. According to Thiers' statement, this was a difficult thing to manage, because there was no one at the meeting who was intimately acquainted with the Duke. Then it was that one of the group suggested that Thiers be selected to ascertain the sentiments of his Grace, and to discover if he would accept the Lieutenant-Generalcy of the Realm of France. To this proposal the young gentleman objected, protesting the fact that he was not even acquainted with their candidate. The reply to this settled the matter: "We will give you letters, and by means of these, you will present yourself in our name." So it was that adventure again fell to the lot of the young journalist from Provence, and he became the delegate of bourgeois Paris in search of a king.

At first glance, the selection of Thiers may seem to have been an odd one. It is quite certain that he had never been presented to the Duke, and that once, on Étienne's advice, he had declined that honour. Laffitte, however, may have urged his nomination as the Commissioner of the Deputies on the ground that an invitation offered to Louis Philippe by one of the leading journalists of Paris might appear to be more of a direct request from the Parisians themselves. There is also another reason that may have occurred to Laffitte. His protégé was not only the friend of the Constitutionalist group; through his more radical colleagues on the *National,* he was also the friend of many Republicans, and the fact that Thiers, instead of a prominent member of the high bourgeoisie, had been selected might make Carrel and his associates more willing to accept the Monarchy.

With Monsieur Scheffer, who gave drawing lessons to the young princesses, Thiers set about the preparations for the journey to Neuilly, whither Louis Philippe's family had retired. Two horses from the stables of the Prince de Muskowa, son-in-law of Laffitte, were saddled for them. How grateful must Thiers have been for his recent lessons at Carrega's riding academy! The pair set out, accompanied by an officer of the National Guard. This officer carried passes from General Fagal to the military outposts, and the principal of the trio had in his possession a paper bearing Sébastiani's signature and a note from Laffitte that contained these words: "I beg Monsieur le Duc d'Orléans to receive Monsieur Thiers with all confidence and to hear all that he is charged by me to say to you."

Due to the fact that the passports had not been viséd, the two envoys and their escort experienced some difficulty, and were swept by the fire of the sentries several times, but they managed to reach Neuilly before the morning was spent. Upon their arrival, however, Thiers had a great disappointment. He was informed that Louis Philippe had left in the direction of St. Cloud, where he possessed some property about which he was anxious. Finally, he succeeded in gaining admittance to the Duchess Marie Amélie. This lady could not have been so ignorant and as unconcerned as she appeared to Thiers to be, for she had already interviewed at least one other delegation from Paris. Dupin and Persil had seen her before the arrival of Laffitte's envoy, and it is not unlikely that Gérard and Talleyrand had communicated with the family early on the morning of the 30th. The Duchess began by protesting to her latest interviewer that the Duke was absent. Of this he did not appear to be convinced, and told her that the moment was decisive, and that no time could be lost. He broached the question of the Lieutenant-General. This time the answer of Marie Amélie convinced him that Louis Philippe was really away. Having persuaded him of this, however, she made haste to assure him that she would gladly listen to whatever he had to say, and repeat it to the Duke upon his return. She then sent for Madame Adelaide, Louis Philippe's sister. This action on the part of the Duchess of Orléans indicates clearly her attitude to affairs in France. When, earlier in the day, Dupin had visited her and urged upon her rather violent reasons for pressing her husband to act, she had burst into tears and declared that she wished to remain a stranger to politics. It is not unlikely that, in the case of this second interview, she wished to shift the burden. After her sister-in-law, Madame Adelaide, had entered, the future Queen of France sank completely into the background as far as Thiers' account of the interview is concerned. Madame Adelaide's was a far more masculine and active nature, and it was to her that Thiers addressed most of his remarks. To her mind, the principal obstacle to her brother's acceptance of the position of Lieutenant-General was the fear that such an act would be regarded by the foreign Powers as a "révolution du palais." She feared the consequent anger of European courts. At this, Thiers called forth all of his young and audacious eloquence. It was Paris that called, it was not the Orléanists who sought. He conjured up his beloved "representative monarchy," and finally even hauled William of Orange into the drawing-room of the ducal house at Neuilly. Here was the supreme effort. If he could succeed in this mission, his own future was made. He extolled the virtues of public conscience and its glorious infallibility. Never would a family have had so divine and so certain a sanction to mount a throne. "All the world will know that you have not of yourselves sought the crown, for surely today it is so dangerous a possession that no one would seek it of his own accord."

The eloquence of the Midi conquered, and finally Madame Adelaide, apparently overcome by the visions that the young magician had conjured up, turned to him, and said: "If you think that the adherence of our family will be of advantage to the Revolution—a woman is nothing in a family, one can compromise them—I myself am ready to go to Paris. There I will share the destiny of the Parisians. I make but one condition, namely, that Monsieur Laffitte or General Sébastiani come themselves to fetch me." Thiers appears to have been satisfied with this declaration from one member of the ducal household. One can easily imagine the studied grace with which the little bourgeois delivered himself of these words: "Today, Madame, you have placed the crown in your own house." Deserted son of the rue des Petits Pères, Marseilles, journalist, historian, and King-maker! He then asked her to write to the Duke at once, and added thereto a little advice as to the arguments she should advance for his acceptance. One can see him so easily. He bows, begins to back out—ah! just one word more! And then, a word or two on government along the lines of "representative monarchy." Then, the final bow, the door closes behind him—and a shrewd smile comes over the face of the little man, for Madame Adelaide has betrayed to him a fact that he later puts into these words: "Louis Philippe n'a pas conspiré; il a aspiré."

No sooner had that strangely smiling little bourgeois mounted his great horse and galloped off to Paris, than out from the palace at Neuilly sped the Comte de Montesquieu with the message for Louis Philippe, who was in hiding at Riancey.

Meanwhile, Thiers, Scheffer, and the officer were hastening back to Paris to report to Laffitte and Sébastiani the result of the mission. They must have made good time, for, in spite of pickets, outposts, and sentries, they arrived at Laffitte's door a little before one o'clock. During the absence of the trio, the Deputies had established themselves at the Palais Bourbon, and thither Thiers hurried to make his report to his superiors. Like him, they interpreted Madame Adelaide's remarks as compromising the entire Orléans family. To give to the matter the appearance of certainty, they spread the rumour that one member of the Duke's family was expected momentarily, and that soon all of them would be in Paris. This done, they could refuse the last overtures of Charles in which the King had even consented to a Ministry that would include Marmont, Gérard, and Casimir Périer.

At this point, the second adventure of Adolphe Thiers concluded with his retirement to the *bureau* of the *National,* where he dictated to Monsieur Martin, his secretary, the account of the greatest day that he had yet experienced.

Parts of Paris were now eagerly awaiting the arrival of their hero, the Duke. What would these Parisians have thought if they had known that he who would declare in his first proclamation, "I have not hesitated to come and partake of your dangers," had, once he was on the road to the city, actually turned back his carriage, and started off in the opposite direction! At last, however, the Duke arrived, and was received at the Palais Royal by Laffitte, Sébastiani, and those others most interested in his return. He was welcomed cordially by these men, but one section of Paris held aloof; LaFayette and his Republicans did not venture forth to greet him. And so it was decided by Louis Philippe himself that he would go to them. It was a perilous undertaking, and his supporters were uneasy. The march to the Hôtel de Ville had its dangers, but for once in his life, a Duke of Orléans showed that he was capable of facing a trying situation. He rode through lines of silent and sullen men. On he went to the Hôtel. There he dismounted, and climbed the steps to LaFayette's *bureau.* That march gave Louis Philippe the crown of France. Then occurred the famous scene—the old General and the future King, wrapped in the folds of the tricolour, on the balcony before the square full of Republicans. Of this scene, that arch-cynic, Metternich, remarked: "A kiss is a slight effort to make to stifle a Republic; so you think that such a power can be expected of kisses in the future?" To some Republicans it must have seemed to be the kiss of a Judas.

The return from the Hôtel de Ville was as triumphant as the previous march had been melancholy, and when Louis Philippe finally reached the Palais Royal he felt far more secure than when he had set out. At once he set himself to his task. There were supporters to be gratified, friends to be made, and innumerable delegations to receive. During the first days there were very few trappings of royalty where royalty lived. No lackey in gorgeous liveries opened the doors. Common soldiers and volunteers in the uniform of the revived National Guard, or in no uniform at all, crowded the anterooms and lounged on the stairways, while the Lieutenant-General held council seated upon a tabouret. The Council room was open to all.

It must have been in the midst of some such scenes that Thiers met for the first time the man in whose cause he had been so active. The occasion for one of their first encounters was an odd one. In fact, no one but Thiers could have thought of such a thing. He had found that not all of his friends, even some of his colleagues in the *National*, were behind the move of Laffitte. With Mignet and a few others who had joined him so heartily in his advocacy of the "representative monarchy," the little editor found sympathy for what had been done. Little did they realize at the time how undesirous Louis Philippe would be to have such sponsors. They were blinded; but not so Carrel, Cavaignac, Guinard, and Bauvilliers, who were ardent Republicans and who found themselves unable to reconcile their views to an acceptance of the Orléans régime. It was to these that Thiers now turned his attention. Having been presented to the Duke, he asked him to receive some of his discontented acquaintances, and to discuss their political difficulties with them. On the very same evening the interview took place. Perhaps the originator of this remarkable meeting may have been cherishing a hope that by such a presentation he might win this group of malcontents to the Orléanist cause, or at least effect an attitude of neutrality on their part. If this was the case, he must have been grievously disappointed, for his Republican friends were not convinced by their talk with the new royalty. When, at the conclusion of the conference, several of them expressed to Thiers their disgust with Louis Philippe, he, amused at their discomfiture, held his sides as he laughed and said, "J'ai fait là, ma foi, une belle ambassade."

CHAPTER V

MONSIEUR THIERS' POLITICAL DÉBUT

THE visit of Louis Philippe to the Republicans at the Hôtel de Ville determined the enthronement of the House of Orléans. With it the possibility of a Republican Government disappeared, and the Deputies who had been gathered together by Casimir Périer profited by a revolution in which they had not participated actively. On the first day of August they met to elect Pasquier their chairman and to inaugurate a new order. But, modest indeed was the New Régime: they were mindful of the bourgeois interest that they represented, and they were careful not to give too revolutionary a character to their proceedings. Casimir Périer, the strongest man among them, had declared that there had not been a revolution; what had occurred, he said, was only a change in the head of the State. These words set a limit, if such a limit was needed, to the intentions of the Deputies. They first accepted a Cabinet of Moderate Republicans, men of the Empire, and representatives of the vested interests. Then, on August 6, they assumed the task of government-making.

The Monarchy was shorn of its sacred character by the assertion that Louis Philippe held his crown from the French people, and, at the same time, several of the royal attributes, including the right of the King to promulgate laws in time of danger, were abolished. A limited suffrage was established to elect a Chamber of Deputies: for a time, the Senate remained hereditary. Unwisely, it was merely assumed that Ministerial responsibility would be observed. And then, in the hope of calming the Republicans, Freedom of Religion and the Press was declared. Within a few days, their work of "liberalizing" France was ended, and the Deputies resumed their accustomed calm. Louis Philippe assumed the crown, hailed by the misguided as the restorer of liberty and freedom, but denounced by the Radicals as a King who had come to power by means of "an aborted revolution." All of France, however, was not misled by what had happened in Paris.

After a short time, Legitimists and Republicans who had been paralysed, at first, by the rapidity with which the crisis had come and gone, regained their breath and assembled their forces with the resolve to become implacable foes of the July Monarchy. The Legitimists adopted a policy of obstruction. To impede the government in all possible ways by participating in an almost continuous overthrow of Ministries through alliance, if necessary, with men of the other extreme, became the favourite gesture of that party. To cast disparagement and doubt upon the sincere efforts which Laffitte and Périer were attempting in order to restore prosperity and confidence; to spread discouragement; in other words, to sacrifice the present for the past, was the permanent aim of these malcontents. Berryer, a bourgeois and a splendid orator, was their representative in the Chamber. His only weakness was that in him passion predominated more often than reason. In themselves, these Carlists or Legitimists were not dangerous, for their numbers were not great, but when considered with the Left, they presented a redoubtable phalanx.

These other gentlemen, strange bedfellows for the Legitimists, were of a totally different character. Representatives of Paris rather than of the provinces, they adhered to the old Jacobin traditions and methods. The more intelligent of them had accepted, temporarily, the July Monarchy. They hoped to stamp it with as Republican a character as possible, and, at first, they believed that the July Monarchy might serve as a convenient plank to a French Republic. Furthermore, they decided to keep this hope constantly in the minds of the Government and its subjects by means of frequent demonstrations in favour of a revision of the Charter and a modification of the suffrage. This was the creed and programme of the leaders of the Hôtel de Ville faction, LaFayette, Manuel, Danou, and Auguste and Victorin Fabre.

For this plan, the Republicans did not lack supporters. In fact, as the August Days wore on, it looked as if, in Paris, something more than Republicanism would come even before the leaders themselves expected it. Sections of the capital were still fertile fields for Radical doctrine and effort.

The workers of Paris, the very ones who had been put on to the street and who had driven out Marshal Marmont and his troops, stood in need. Industry was at a standstill; idle and poorly paid labourers were at the beck and call of independent agitators who called themselves Republicans but who were preaching the Socialist precepts of Saint-Simon and Fourier. Workers provided an audience that was re-enforced by members of the École Polytechnique and students from the University. Idlers, labourers, and students were herded into clubs and lodges with strange names and rites. The rivalries between these units were great and prevented them from becoming a serious menace. The same cannot be said, however, of one organization that, in time, nearly drove the others to the wall.

This club was known as the *Friends of the People.* In its midst were to be found the ablest of the young Radicals, Cavaignac, Marrast who, after the resignation of Thiers, was in complete control of the *National,* Raspail, Flocon, and Blanqui. Its members were sworn to strive for the establishment of a real Republic in France and Liberty in Europe.

In contrast to the other Radical organizations, the *Friends of the People* was practical. Its directors established their headquarters on the rue de Montmartre, convenient to the sections where the labourers and small shopkeepers lived. Here secret meetings and an open forum were held. They set up a bureau of propaganda and established affiliations with liberal societies in Belgium and Poland. They had a paper, the *Tribune,* in which to air their views. Twice during August and September they marched against the Chamber to demand that the Deputies resign their mandates and twice they caused embarrassment and, eventually, disgrace to LaFayette, Commander of the National Guard, who could not be brought to charge them. They gained considerably in numbers by asserting that they were the protectors of the working people. For their new protégés they demanded political rights, amelioration of living conditions, and even, at one time, the abolition of machinery which, they averred, was the root of all economic evil. Under the guidance of their young leaders, demonstrations and labour riots became an almost daily occurrence. It was, in fact, due to them that industry was at a standstill.

In the midst of this discord stood Louis Philippe supported by his capitalists and by the members of Young France who, like Thiers, had belonged to the *National* School. Laffitte who headed the King's Council was a good business man, a sentimental liberal, and a weak leader in time of danger. He could not be brought to take any decisive action against these disturbances. His more conservative and forceful colleagues, Périer, Broglie, Guizot, and Dupin could do nothing with him, and his popularity with the masses they regarded as dangerous. After several attempts to find the successful middle-road combination, the King finally discarded his liberal allures, and called Périer to settle France and to solve the question of France in Europe.

The enthroning of the Orléanist family had encountered even fewer sympathizers in Europe than it had found in the more liberal sections of Paris. The star of Prince Metternich was still in the ascendant. That faithful watch-dog of the Old Régime had found the Charter of 1814 too liberal, and, in 1830, he declared that its revised version was positively subversive. The July Days in Paris had inspired a revolution in Belgium against the King of Holland, and risings in Poland and Italy. Neither Monsieur Metternich of Austria nor Monsieur Nesselrode of Russia desired Charters of 1830 in and near their domains. Accordingly, these two worthies decided to attempt a revival of the Holy Alliance and to throw a sanitary cordon around France. Consequently they met at Carlsbad. For a brief moment, the situation augured ill for France. It was the King of the French and not his timid Minister who found the solution. Louis Philippe was clever enough to perceive the fundamental insincerities of an Austro-Russian alliance. His own perspicacity and the astonishing rapidity of the Belgian revolt delivered him. To England he sent, in haste, wise Talleyrand who had befriended that country at Vienna in 1815. Within a short space of time, the French and British Governments came to a secret agreement not to tolerate interference in Belgium. In this way Louis Philippe gained two friends in Europe, a fact which enabled him to keep at bay the frightened old gentlemen at Carlsbad. When, later, his daughter was married to Leopold of Saxe-Coburg, chosen ruler of the Belgians, the position of the July Monarchy was more secure.

It remained now to mollify the fears and hostility of the older Courts of Europe. But the Liberals in Paris prevented the King from realizing this design. They rioted again and demanded a more drastic participation of France in Belgium and the dispatch of military aid to the Poles and Italians. At this news Metternich wagged his head and said that the peaceful protestations of France could not be trusted. Metternich must be converted or, at least, placated. Laffitte had shown clearly that he was as incapable of mollifying Europe as he was of silencing Paris. The Conservative Chamber as well as the King was eager to be rid of him. On March 10, 1831, Casimir Périer became President of the King's Council.

Périer's Cabinet was a notable one, and it was strong—it was called the "Resistance Ministry." Some of the ablest men in France were appointed to it. Under their guidance, the July Monarchy had a chance to catch its breath, and France was brought to the prosperity that Laffitte had promised but had not been able to realize. As a parliamentarian, Périer was far superior to his predecessor, and he exerted a very real control over the Chamber. His success was due in part to the fact that he was just as conservative as the majority of the Deputies, and, in part, to a very wise practice, followed by the President, of keeping outside of the Ministry those who, by reason of their situation or talents, could be of use to him in the Chamber.

Périer was above corruption and he served France only to be of benefit to her. He scorned the customary methods that Ministers used to defend their policies. He refused to employ the ordinary practice of buying up the papers to support him. He declared: "I have the *Moniteur* to register my actions: the *Tribune* of the Chambers to explain them; and the future to judge them." It was under the ægis of such a man that the young Thiers began the serious part of his political schooling. It is significant that what Thiers learned under this wise leader, he never abandoned. From March, 1831, the character of the Périer régime was indelibly impressed on his mind, and he changed somewhat the views that he had held when he was on the editorial staff of the *National*. The first year of the Bourgeois Monarchy had made of Monsieur Marrast a Republican while his former colleague, Monsieur Thiers, was becoming a Conservative.

Immediately following the July Days, Thiers had served as an Under-Secretary of Finances under Baron Louis. In August, he had stood for election from Aix-en-Provence which he chose to regard as his native city, and September, 1830, had found him defending the budget proposed by Laffitte's first Cabinet. His maiden speech had not convinced his hearers: then, as now, the French Chamber was merciless to its orators, and Monsieur Thiers must needs endure jibes, criticisms, and insults. As time went on, he wrote of his discouragement for himself and for Laffitte whose *laissez-aller* policy annoyed him. More and more he came to see the necessity for strong government, far more powerful than he had allowed for in his articles in the *National*. Upon the fall of Laffitte, he retired for a time to Aix to visit his mother and to study. The fruit of these meditations was a brochure which appeared in April, 1831, and bore the title "La Monarchie de Juillet."

Its enemies had raised the argument that the House of Orléans had not the sanction of popular sovereignty to rule France. Monsieur Thiers rushed to their defence and, in this pamphlet, once and for all discarded popular sovereignty when he acknowledged that this sanction had not been given to Louis Philippe and then asserted that the consent of popular sovereignty would not have been wise in this instance and was not necessary. "Popular sovereignty calls into the government the intervention of the masses, and these have never appeared except to upset the government and to make it anarchical, violent, and blood-thirsty. On the other hand, the sovereignty of the majority calls in a factor true, natural, and legitimate, for then the nation, consulted not *en masse,* for that is impossible, but consulted consecutively in the persons of electors, deputies, and peers who represent the élite of the nation, expresses a wish that is the real public law. There is the true principle by which the country governs itself according to stable and regular laws."

Monsieur Thiers never lost this ideal of a government by the élite. Born of mean and low estate, he yearned always towards an aristocracy of intelligence. In 1831, the Périer Ministry seemed to him to be the embodiment of his doctrine. Almost immediately upon his coming into office, France felt the strong hand of Casimir Périer. The Radical agitators, among whom were Cavaignac, Blanqui, and Trélat, were brought before the courts on charges of inciting riot and disturbance. Even the editors of papers of the Extreme Left, the *Tribune* and the *Amis du Peuple,* had their interviews with the magistrates. Legitimists, too, had their turn, and when the Duchesse de Berry aided by the Duc de Cases, the Duc de Saint-Priest, and Marshal Bourmont, connived with their fellows in France to stir up a rising in the West, Périer dispatched an army into the Vendée. All of these plans met with the support of the majority in the Chamber. Périer had made good his promise that, under him, law and order would prevail in France.

In all these moves that he had made, he had been eagerly seconded in the parliament by three men whose services had become almost invaluable to him. These men were Guizot, Dupin, and Thiers, whom the two Oppositions maliciously called the Triumvirs. Guizot assured the President of the adherence of the Constitutional

Monarchists, or Doctrinaires, of the Right: Dupin, still loyal, rallied from the Left all those who could be gathered from the ranks of the old Opposition that had existed during the Restoration. Thiers, on the other hand, confirmed the timid and unstable, and controlled those who, like himself, still delighted to regard themselves as independent. These three henchmen of the President represented the finest oratory in the Chamber. In the face of such a force, the Opposition had little to offer. LaFayette was too old and was somewhat discredited by his behaviour during the Paris riots, and Odilon Barrot was only trying out his flights of oratorical passion. Of them all, Ministerial and Opposition, the most interesting orator in the Chamber was the youngest of the Triumvirs.

Practice had begun to have its effect upon Monsieur Thiers, and he had regained his confidence. His method was novel for the orators of the 'thirties. He possessed none of the passion of a Berryer, and none of his glowing phrases and persuasive eloquence. This new orator was not of the silver-tongued variety. He was clear, logical, and his method of presentation was almost didactic. He taught his audience its lesson. There was a hint of the schoolmaster in his art, and also an echo of the historian. Frequently he prefaced his arguments with a résumé of the events that smacked of the *History of the French Revolution.* At this time, he had just begun the study of Napoleon and there were frequent references to the period of the Consulate and the Empire. Périer, his chief, had described his foreign policy as one of "non-intervention," and when the Left demanded, in reply, that France renounce this attitude and send an army to assist the Poles, Monsieur Thiers replied to them by a dramatic narration of Napoleon's difficulties in Poland. This is not to say, however, that his discourses were dull and arid. They were relieved by witty sallies directed at his opponents. These extemporaneous quips delighted his hearers, and his apt and short retorts frequently turned the laugh against his interrupters.

Périer, aided by his Triumvirs, was rapidly approaching the point of victory when, suddenly, the cholera swept Paris. On May 16, the President of the Council fell, a victim to the disease. Great was the alarm of Guizot and Thiers and the Conservatives whom they represented: great was the delight of Legitimist and Republican some of whom actually proposed an illumination of Paris "to celebrate the deliverance of France from an unscrupulous dictator." Even Louis Philippe, always too fond of half-way measures, commented: "Casimir Périer is dead: is this an advantage or a misfortune? Time will show." For Thiers, the passing of Périer meant the conclusion of his political apprenticeship. The situation created by Périer's death opened the way to a Ministerial *fauteuil*.

When the news of the President's death reached Talleyrand, that ever faithful friend of the Government of the day left his post at London and hastened to Paris to advise the King. On May 25, a conference was held at the residence of the Ambassador. At this consultation it was proposed to form a Cabinet of which Talleyrand, Sébastiani, and the Triumvirs would be the shining lights. But the Left protested so strongly against such a combination which would guarantee a continuation of Périer's policy of repression, that Louis Philippe desisted, and finally appointed a Ministry of which he was virtually the head. A period of disturbance followed during which the King, to control the Radicals, had to declare Paris in a state of siege, and was forced to arrest Berryer, Legitimist leader, whom he held accountable for the sudden arrival of the Duchesse de Berry in the Vendée.

During this interval, Thiers had been away from Paris. Whether intentional or not, his absence had been wise. Twice the faithful Mignet had summoned him from the provinces where he had retired to study. Dupin desired his presence and so did the King's party. Here was opportunity beckoning him. But Monsieur Thiers was coy and wary and, at first, he did not come. Meanwhile, the King's situation became more difficult: Louis Philippe now wanted Périer's system continued but he did not desire to take the blame for it himself. In September, 1832, Thiers returned. The King summoned him and greeted him as a long-lost friend. He recalled his service to his House in July, 1830, and exclaimed: "With what pleasure I see you again! You are my man, the one whom I prefer to take over affairs. . . . We are destined to lose each other often and to find each other again. Twenty times you shall be my Minister. I think that I have a long future ahead of me. Circumstances may force me to separate from you, but I shall come back to you again."

These words were words of prophecy: they were far more true than either of them realized at the time. But they were also a gage of friendship and a promise. Consequently when, in October, 1832, Louis Philippe finally called for Marshal Soult to relieve his royal master of the ministerial functions that he had assumed, Monsieur Thiers was not surprised when he was invited to tuck the portfolio of the Ministry of the Interior under his arm.

Contrary to the expectations of his critics, his first reactions to this sign of royal confidence and favour were not of a cheerful nature. He was already a veteran of the Chamber and he bore the scars of hard, vigorous combat. His persistence in calling himself a parliamentary free lance had cost him a great deal and, in many quarters, people had not complete confidence in his sincerity. He was accused of being an opportunist and a self-seeker. At this time, Monsieur Thiers was a much discussed person and all of the interest was not centered on his public life. He was subject to certain family embarrassments in the persons of a profligate father and a collection of natural brothers and sisters, and these circumstances made him the butt of Charivarii, of the *Pilorii*, and even of the music-halls. The iconography of Thiers in caricature is enormous for the 'thirties. Even Daumier did not spare him, and Thiers is said to have feared that cartoonist as he feared the plague. To all this criticism he was keenly sensible and, on the morrow of his appointment to the Ministry of the Interior, he wrote to his friend General Bugeaud: "Support me, I beg you. Give me courage for I have need that people of heart support a young man calumniated and beaten by the winds of envy and mistrust. Write me—I shall be grateful for that. I am weighed down under the awful impression of the newspapers, and I write you with too much feeling, perhaps. . . ."

In all probability, it was not alone abuse and criticism that oppressed him: it was also the fact that, at last, he had come to the test. He had made the conquest of the Chamber and, in doing it, he had supported eloquently and successfully his late chief's policy of repression and order. And now, in October, 1832, the Government expected him to continue Périer's internal policy and to act as the chief policeman of the realm.

His first acts showed that he was, at all events, prepared to make good the words that he had uttered from the tribune of the Chamber. He sent out to the departmental police strict orders in regard to the treatment of public meetings and demonstrations. Rioters of the Left he put into prison. But, after all, the problem of the Radicals was not his greatest difficulty, for he could treat them with a ruthless hand. There was, however, another matter that required more tact and discretion.

Maria Carolina, Duchesse de Berry and widow of the heir of the exiled Charles X, had secretly come to France and was making sudden appearances among the Vendéans, ever loyal to the Bourbon cause. But the Minister of the Interior could not give the same treatment to the Duchess that he had afforded to a Flocon or a Blanqui, for there were certain courts in Europe that were interested in her cause. Austria was undoubtedly sympathetic to the Legitimist party in France, Prussia was related to the Duchess by ties of sentiment and kinship, and the Tsar hated the Orléanist family and would have been delighted at its overthrow. Drastic measures against this royal lady might have involved Louis Philippe in serious difficulties with the counter-revolutionary courts of Europe. Furthermore, there could be no doubt but that her cause was gaining in the provinces. In certain parishes prayers were offered publicly for the Duchess, and the movement in her favour had spread even to Aix and Marseilles.

One thing was certain; the uprising in the Vendée could never be quelled until the fair lady was safely and decently lodged in the care of the Government. But she could not be captured as a common criminal, and her appearances and disappearances were most disconcerting.

By a fortuitous circumstance, Monsieur Thiers learned the name of one of her agents on the very day that he accepted the portfolio of the Interior. This man was named Deutz, son of a Jewish rabbi, later a convert to Rome and a creature of the Jesuits who had accredited him to Maria Carolina. As he gazed over the Dossier of Deutz, Monsieur le Ministre became convinced that Deutz was more concerned with personal gain than with the success of the cause of his patroness. Not long afterwards, Monsieur Thiers received an anonymous letter in which the writer proposed a rendezvous in the vicinity of the Champs Élysées. There, for a consideration, he would divulge the hiding place of the lady who was causing the Government so much trouble. The invitation was accepted in spite of the opposition of the Secret Police who declared that the affair was not without danger to the Minister. Monsieur Thiers relates that he concealed two revolvers on his small person and stationed his secret agents in the vicinity. Then—he went alone to meet his correspondent. As he had surmised, he proved to be Deutz, who, in his turn, was most compliant. He was bundled into a train for Nantes and lo! on November 6, the capture was made and the prisoner carried off to Blaye where she was comfortably lodged under the watchful eye of General Bugeaud.

France was flooded with Legitimist pamphlets reviling her captor. For the moment, it seemed as if Monsieur Thiers had only succeeded in increasing the popularity of his victim. La Vendée was reported as aflame. Fortune, however, again played into the hands of the Minister when it was discovered that Maria Carolina was with child, having contracted a secret marriage with a person below her station. The Legitimists, in honour, retired from the scene discomfited. The successful conclusion of the affair, however, did not result in an increase of popularity for the Minister who had managed it. Republicans reviled him for his leniency while the Right was denouncing him as a cruel monster. To quiet this criticism which reflected on the Ministry, he was transferred to the post of Minister of Public Works. He had, however, silenced for the first time since the July Days the Opposition of the Right.

In his capacity of Minister of Public Works, Thiers had a freer hand. He presided over the first Congress of the prominent agriculturalists, industrialists, and merchants whose meeting marked the economic revival of France. His own interest, however, was not in tariffs, factories, and railroads, but in something that was more akin to his character of a romantic patriot. This man was not of the sort who behold in dollars and in cents the glory of their country: perhaps, even, he thought too little about such things. To him the glory of France lay in her dignity, her beauty, and her military strength. He believed that his principal duty as Minister of Public Works lay along these lines. Napoleon again came to his mind. The Emperor had undertaken to give Paris magnificent buildings, stately vistas, and wide, open spaces; Monsieur Thiers would do likewise. With this in mind, he nearly threw the Chamber into a state of apoplexy when he suddenly demanded of them the sum of one million francs for public buildings. By dint of argument he won his point, and under his enthusiastic direction the Arc de Triomphe, the Madeleine, the Quai d'Orsay, the Panthéon, and the Basilica of St. Denis were restored and completed. He also planned out the work for the completion of the Place de la Concorde. He added to the buildings of the École des Beaux Arts and, because of his friendship with the artists of the time, he became particularly interested in its development. He gave a ready ear to their suggestions. For a time, he was regarded as their patron, but when their little Mæcenas offered liberal subsidies to such men as Ingres, Delacroix, and Vernet, in an effort to induce them to go to Italy and make copies of great Italian masters for French art schools, they turned from him. Fortunately, all of his enterprises at this time were not so disastrously æsthetic.

The study of History had taught him the value of armament to a nation, and at the same time that he was hobnobbing with painters, he was consorting with military engineers. Great maps and plans littered the long tables of his office. Perched on a high stool over these he pored for hours at a time, for his study of Napoleon had taught him the game of war. The result of this venture into military fields was his wise proposal for the fortification of Paris by the construction of a ring of forts around the city.

In spite of the fact that he succeeded in forcing through the Chamber most of the measures that he desired, the

Minister tells us that, at this time, he was not satisfied. He was not content alone with a reputation of an *homme d'état*. Throughout his long life, this little bourgeois was always asserting that the affairs of the world meant nothing to him and that what really satisfied him were matters of the intellect and of taste. Even during his busiest moments his mind was obsessed by grandiose designs for historical and literary efforts. Their variety was appalling; he would write a History of the World, a History of Florence, or, perhaps, a detailed study of Chinese art. He was even the victim of an ambition to be recognized as a scholar and an art collector. Amusing and pathetic are some of his efforts. An unfinished History of Florence for which he collected copious notes, and the vulgar reproductions of Italian masterpieces along with pathetic bits of Chinoiserie at the Place Saint Georges, are evidences that he has left of the ideal to which he never attained.

Probably the nearest point to satisfaction of this craving was reached in 1834 when, upon the death of one of its members, Monsieur Thiers, in the customary fashion, proposed his own name as candidate for election to the Academy. His enemies were amused at his audacity, but others who knew that his chances were good, were not surprised when it was announced that he had received seventeen of the twenty-five votes. On December 14, he was received among the Immortals. Facing him were Talleyrand and Royer-Collard. Above him, in one of the boxes, Madame la Duchesse de Dino smiled down on him, and Madame de Lieven, *la belle russe,* was also there to witness the triumph of her latest admirer.

His learned and fashionable audience was somewhat shocked when the young débutant delivered an address that partook more of the nature of a political argument than of a scholarly effort. Some of them smiled when he characterized himself as "a disciple of letters, temporarily separated from their service." He took this occasion to proclaim that although he was a patriot, he was anti-revolutionary in literature, philosophy, and politics. While, as was proper, he eulogized Andrieux whose seat he was taking, he threw into his discourse a glowing tribute to Talleyrand, his old mentor, who had recommended him to the attention of Louis Philippe. At this moment of triumph, the young pupil did not forget the debt that he owed to his first master.

When Thiers uttered these words, he and the Soult Cabinet to which he belonged had just passed through a crisis. Once the Legitimist intrigue had been averted, the problem of the Extreme Left became acute.

Aided by Cavaignac and Trélat, the *Society of the Rights of Man* had been founded and had begun its propaganda. The *Tribune* assisted in spreading the doctrines of this organization, and the example set by the Paris chapter and its newspapers was followed by the provincial sections. Young Italy and Mazzini were at work in the country: a *Congrega Centrale* was established in Paris, and the Italian patriot was in active correspondence with Armand Carrel of the *National* and with the *Tribune*. From liberal centers in Italy and in Geneva, French radicals were receiving encouragement. Saint-Simonism was spreading, Considérant was preaching his labour doctrines at Tours, and others of his agents were located in many of the industrial centres of France. Labour unions known as *Mutuallistes* had sprung up at Grenoble, Dijon, Metz, and Strasbourg. The year 1834 bade fair to be a troublesome year, and because of this danger, the young man who had been the lieutenant of Périer was returned to the Department of the Interior on March 25. It was just before the crisis was reached.

The reinstatement of Thiers was regarded by the Radical leaders as a declaration of war on the part of the Ministry. His attitude to their former activities was well known: in his speeches he had not refrained from expressing a frank disapproval of their methods. Nor was he afraid to meet them. As he himself remarked, even the victor of the Pyramids had faced revolts in his own country. In April, his own strength and courage were severely tested when, in that month, the famous revolt of Lyons broke out.

Its origin was not political but the movement soon assumed a political character. The higher bourgeoisie had profited by the economic progress that had been made since 1831, but the labouring classes, although steadily increasing in numbers, had gained nothing. The city of Lyons was the largest industrial centre in France, and it was natural that the labour situation should first become acute in that region. There had already been a serious riot anent the question of tariffs, and for a time the workers had been masters of the city. This revolt had been quelled by reinforcements sent from Paris. Since the earlier trouble, however, the Republicans had been at work among the labourers. They had talked to them of universal suffrage which, they asserted, was the panacea for all their sorrows, and had turned the discontent of the Lyonnais into political channels. When, therefore, on April 9, the Government opened proceedings against several leaders who had been instrumental in bringing about a general strike, their fellows seized the opportunity to commence a second revolt. The example of Lyons was followed by the radicals at Vienne, Perpignan, St. Étienne, Clermont, and Marseilles. By April 13, the Government troops had abandoned the city. The situation became even more alarming when the Faubourgs Saint Antoine and Saint Jacques in Paris joined the movement.

On April 11, Thiers had obtained from the Chamber a bill that forbade the formation of all associations except for commercial purposes without a previous authorization from the Government. But by April 13 law alone was not sufficient; force was necessary. That evening Thiers and Bugeaud laid out their plan of campaign. A barricade was erected to shut off the disaffected Faubourgs from the rest of Paris. It was an undertaking that was fraught with danger. At the time, Thiers was wearing the costume of a Minister, and this made him an easy target for the rioters who fired upon him. They missed their mark, but struck down his secretary who had stood by his side. It was not until the next day that quiet was restored in Paris. During the crisis Thiers had directed the operations himself, for Bugeaud had been dispatched to Lyons where his policy of the sword and no quarter was soon successful.

His courage and quick action won for the young Minister the warm support of the Conservatives in both Chambers. The April Days obliterated what doubts they may have had of his integrity. Once again, the bourgeoisie had triumphed and the Republicans, like the Legitimists, were crushed and silent for a time.

It was a victory for the Monarchy but it was a victory that cost a heavy price. The Government had shed blood that was spent in the name of Liberty. Monsieur Thiers, too, had definitely set himself along the path of Conservatism, and the hopes that Liberals in France and Europe had set in the July Revolution vanished. There was left a bitterness, too, among some of those in the Chambers who were not radicals but who felt that a compromise with Labour would have been a better and more successful method. Among those who broke from the Government was Dupin, once a triumvir with Thiers. As a result of this schism, parliamentary rivalries followed and Louis Philippe must needs reconstitute his Ministry. But there were other and more dangerous consequences. Louis Philippe's action had identified him with Capital. This action Labour could never forgive and then, as now, irritated Labour would not always follow the counsels of those who are capable of leading them. Conspiracies against the King's life began. Of these Monsieur Thiers had knowledge. On July 28, a review was held in commemoration of the Three Glorious Days of 1830. Thiers warned the King not to attend it, but his advice was not heeded. It all happened as Thiers predicted and Fieschi made his attempt on the King. Louis Philippe, his sons, and Thiers escaped unhurt, but Marshal Mortier dropped at Thiers' side.

Fieschi's attempt filled France with horror, and the Conservative Ministry of Broglie found itself strengthened by it. Now, the Chamber was willing to institute a policy of Périer *à outrance:* all radical Opposition must be crushed. Aided by the general sentiment in France, Broglie, supported by Thiers, put through the September Laws. These were the most reactionary legislation that France had known since the eve of the July Revolution. Special courts were allowed to try summarily all those who attacked the security of the State. The accused might be judged even when absent. The liberty of the Press was curbed by the heavy fines for seditious articles.

The transformation of the July Monarchy was almost completed. Ill and worn out from his cares, Thiers demanded a leave. He was oppressed and discouraged; in serving his King he had lost some friends and made a host of enemies among the Left, and, in 1835, he wanted his reward. As a matter of fact, it was not far off. Old Talleyrand had watched him and had nodded his head in approval and the King believed that he owed to his Minister of the Interior the power that he now had. Soon Thiers would replace Broglie as President of the Council.

"I remain what I have been, the faithful friend of the July Revolution. *But I am convinced of this great truth, that to save a Revolution, you must prevent it from going too far.*"

Adolphe Thiers, Discours, 22 February, 1836.

CHAPTER VI

THIERS AND HIS RELATIONS

THIERS and his relations afford an interesting reflection of the confused condition of French society during the second decade of the nineteenth century. A bourgeois he was, and a bourgeois whose people had suffered and not profited by the Revolution. He was born into material poverty. But this was not all; Thiers as well was born into a moral poverty. In fact, he may be said to have had all the disadvantages of sonship and none of its real advantages. Certainly, he knew none of its joys.

His father, Pierre Louis Marie Thiers, was an adventurer, the son of a prominent archivist of Marseilles who had markedly royalist sympathies. Pierre Louis did not share his father's opinions and soon was swept up by the well-known Republican sentiment of his native city. Before the Revolution he had sought adventure in the Antilles. Upon its outbreak he fished in the troubled waters, seeking here and there a fortune, winning it and as quickly losing it. The affair with Mademoiselle Amic was merely one of a series of amorous adventures, and when he had finally endowed the result of this episode, Louis Adolphe, with legitimacy, he went again on his way in quest of adventure and diversions. He was in Spain,

Italy, and Switzerland, in the company of another like himself, a man from Toulouse who called himself the "Chevalier de Foinville." With this disreputable character, Pierre Louis dealt profitably in foodstuffs for the armies and spent the intervals between business transactions in travel, associating with all the low castes of the Levant, and, once in a while, venturing north where usually there was an affair with a dancer or a singer. One hears little else of him until Adolphe Thiers has arrived at a place in public life where he might be of use to his extravagant parent.

It was in 1825 that the mysterious father seems to have crossed his son's path for the first time. The son, already prominent among the Liberal bourgeoisie and enjoying, by that time, a certain fame as a journalist and writer, is made the object of a request for money. The episode is soon closed. The young Thiers, himself known as a gallant and a *bon vivant,* assumes towards his parent the tone of a grandfather and writes him a long letter reproving him for his excesses. How deplorable, he exclaims, that a son of twenty-eight must expostulate with a father of sixty for his follies! How dare that father write of privations that he has endured when he deserted his unhappy wife! But the son will be merciful. "When Monsieur Thiers (elder) has proven that he can do nothing for himself, that it is to maintain life in his body that he begs, and not to give himself over to further excesses, then his true sons will agree as to what they should do. Monsieur Adolphe Thiers will aid his father not from sentiment, however, for he recognizes only the love and duty that he bears to his mother."

All this in the third person singular. Cold formality, and cold formality seems to have kept the profligate parent silent for seven years. But, after the July Revolution, the opportunity was too tempting; Thiers junior had become a minister and a promising future appeared to be in store for him. Like a pack of hounds, Pierre Louis and his other natural progeny pursued their prey. At Marseilles a radical paper, *le Peuple Souverain,* opened a subscription for the avowed purpose of rescuing the relatives of Monsieur Thiers from "famine and prostitution," while the father rushed to Paris to make new demands in person.

The visit to the capital was successful. Pierre Louis gave a promise of silence and a consent to his son's marriage in return for forty thousand francs and the assurance of a pension of six hundred francs for his natural daughter, Madame Brunet. For two years trouble between father and son continued until, finally, in desperation, the future President of the Council placed his father under the personal surveillance of Monsieur Floret, subprefect of Carpentras, with the distinct understanding that Pierre Louis must remain discreet and out of the public eye. To this arrangement the father reluctantly agreed. He observed his promise until one morning when he read in the paper the announcement of his own death, inserted, it is unkindly rumoured, by someone at the instigation of his son. Only in 1843 was this burden removed, when Pierre Louis at last expired at the home of his daughter, Madame Brunet, whom Adolphe Thiers had presented with a tobacco shop.

Mention has been made of Pierre Louis Thiers' other natural children. Of these, only four seem to have caused Adolphe Thiers much concern. Madame Brunet was satisfied with her modest *boutique* and was never the source of other importunities. A second half-sister, Madame Rippert, was quieted with a pension. There remained two brothers, Louis and Germain. Both of these were the cause of considerable embarrassment to the statesman during his early career. Of the two, Louis was the more serious problem. Placed by Thiers in the supply service at Colmar, Louis was charged with theft. He was finally rescued and sent to the East by Thiers. Germain, on the other hand, though not so bad a character, was still a reason for embarrassment. Previous to 1832 he was concerned in a tobacco industry at Montargis. In 1832, when the Périer Ministry came in and Thiers was appointed Minister of the Interior, Germain established himself in Paris and scandalized his brother by opening a shop in Paris that bore the sign: "Thiers, peintre en bâtiment, et frère de Monsieur le Ministre de l'Intérieur." In 1835, Germain was sent to Calcutta.

When one turns to Madame Thiers, the mother, the problem is more difficult for here there is a real mystery. There is also, however, a hint of tragedy. Marie-Madeleine Amic was born of respectable bourgeois stock, but poor. Disappointed in her hopes for a happy married existence, and deserted by the man whom she loved, she and her parents devoted themselves to the education of Louis Adolphe, her son. In spite of their poverty they procured for him the best schooling available, and in his early days Thiers seems to have been devoted to his mother and to his maternal grandmother. "Mes deux mères," he calls them in a letter to his friend Rouchon whose acquaintance he made at Aix.

Madame Thiers lived at Aix with her son while he was studying at the law school. Then came the separation, a separation that he seems to have regretted deeply. After the death of his grandmother in 1824, Madame Thiers visited him in Paris, but the visit was spoiled by her son's apparent reluctance to have her with him and by the police inspections and questionings to which the Government of the restored Bourbons subjected her. In 1833, the relations between mother and son appear to have become strained. At this time Thiers wrote to Rouchon about his approaching marriage. He besought Rouchon to ask Madame Thiers for the formal consent demanded by the law. He seemed to foresee difficulties; his mother did not approve of a bride whose family ignored her own existence. Nevertheless she gave her consent. But from then on, relations were not cordial, and when, in 1836, Madame Thiers, the mother, came to Paris to live, she received a small pension from her son, and stayed in a house near the magnificent hôtel of the Place Saint Georges whose doors, she avers, were always closed to her. Finally, she moved to the Batignolles when her son, now so engrossed in his new relations, visited her only occasionally. In fact, after 1833, Thiers' real family became his wife's parents, Monsieur and Madame Dosne.

Among the group of wealthy bourgeois prominent in Paris during the early 'twenties was Alexis Dosne. Monsieur Dosne, who was a banker and industrialist of Lille, married, in 1811, a Parisian named Euridice Matheron. Mademoiselle Matheron was the daughter of a cloth merchant. She had spent her childhood in the Faubourg Montmartre, but she aspired to the Faubourg Saint-Germain, and there her marriage to Alexis Dosne, a very prosaic man of affairs, finally placed her. Madame Dosne soon set up a salon. Her habitués were drawn from those who belonged to the *Juste Milieu* or had decided leanings towards the moderate Middle-Class Liberalism represented by Louis Philippe, Duke of Orléans. She was ambitious, brilliant, and domineering, and it was not long before her hôtel at the Place Saint Georges became a rendezvous for the rising generation of journalists, writers, and men of affairs.

About the year 1822, young Thiers, who, since his arrival at Paris, had modified his revolutionary enthusiasms and donned the colours of Talleyrand's school, was presented at the house. It was Madame Dosne who took possession of Thiers, and he shortly became one of her most ardent devotees. The lady herself was not a bad judge of character and she soon expressed the belief that this latest addition to her court would make a name for himself. Consequently, she became his patroness. Madame Dosne was an able manager; Balzac calls her "une espèce de Père Joseph en jupons." Thiers and the ambitious hostess of the Place Saint Georges were of the sort to be congenial. He with his past of the rue des Petits Pères, Marseilles, and she with her memories of the Faubourg Montmartre; both of them with the Faubourg Saint-Germain before their eyes! It was not long before they joined forces, and formed an alliance to which Paris and even certain journalists made uncomplimentary allusions. Suddenly, in 1833, the *haute monde* of the Middle Class learned that Madame Dosne was preparing to add to her rôle of a confidante that of a mother-in-law: the young Thiers was betrothed to Élise Dosne.

Thiers as a lover is a disappointment. There is very little romance; there is too much reason. To Rouchon, loyal friend at Aix, he writes of his prospects and commits to him the delicate task of obtaining the consent of Madame Thiers: "I write you at a very important time of my life. I am to marry a young person, lovely, amiable, raised for me with infinite care. She is not even too young for a man of thirty-five years who has a healthy body but a mind worn and fatigued by the immense cares of government. I shall not be able to give her all that a young girl expects, but she is devoted to me; she has been brought up by her mother who has taught her that it is her duty to live for me alone. She is attached to me; she has placed all her pride in me. I think that I can make her happy. What is not less precious to me is her family, in whom I find repose, confidence, consolation, and all that I need more than anyone and more than ever. Her fortune will be great some day, especially for me, who have nothing, and I am proud of that for I have made nothing out of my position."

On November 5, 1833, the marriage was celebrated with great pomp. The contract was signed by five pages of distinguished witnesses, including such men as the President of the Council, the Duc de Dalmatie, Guizot, Broglie, d'Argout, Gérard, Sébastiani, and the faithful Mignet. Not content with this showing, a mandamus was issued to permit the record to be transported to the Tuileries for the signatures of Louis Philippe and of Marie Amélie, the Queen. The Faubourg Montmartre had arrived at last at the portals of the Faubourg Saint-Germain. A brilliant future was assured Madame Dosne. As for her son-in-law, his repose was secured, for Thiers brought his wife in furniture and effects ten thousand francs and a house valued at sixty thousand but mortgaged for more, plus a house at Aix, while Élise Dosne brought a trousseau and furniture at ten thousand francs and three hundred thousand francs dowry. In this way, Thiers found a new interior in which he was happy in spite of the scorn of his more aristocratic friends. Talleyrand's niece, the Duchesse de Dino, complained: "Since his marriage, Thiers lives in a sort of solidarity with the smallest people in the world, ill-famed, pretentious, *parvenu par le coup et non pas arrivés.*"

In his wife Thiers found all the satisfaction that he sought. She was lovely, and her beauty was frequently commented upon. In later days, she graced his salon well and performed ably and gently her social duties. But during the early years of her marriage she seems to have been overwhelmed by her indefatigable and restless husband. Unlike her mother, politics do not seem to have interested her and, for a time, she remained a good deal in the background. This may be accounted for by her extreme youth, for at her marriage she was only sixteen, or by a rather indifferent health that frequently caused both her husband and Madame Dosne considerable alarm.

In marrying Mademoiselle Dosne, Thiers allied himself to an important influence in his life. To a certain extent, Madame Dosne was worthy of the title that Balzac gave her. She watched over Thiers, she protected him and she advised him. It was not an infrequent occurrence to have a midnight conference with his colleagues interrupted by "Madame-Mère" who appeared in dressing gown and curl-papers to expose her opinion. Even her letters are replete with warnings and suggestions. She read the French and English newspapers assiduously, and she seems to have been possessed of a remarkable political sagacity. She gloried in the fame of her son-in-law and daughter. "I read yesterday an account of your reception in Berlin. The article gave me great pleasure, first because it gave me news of you, and then because I saw that people appreciate you both. My *amour-propre* was flattered when I read that 'Monsieur Thiers and his lovely wife arrived at twelve o'clock.' "

The Salon Thiers-Dosne became a great political center and served its purpose in shaping the fortunes of the young statesman who stood, in 1835, on the threshold of his first political experiment. Here the newly arrived bourgeoisie and the followers of true Orléanism met. It was the period of great salons but, in its way, that of the Place Saint Georges was unique. Madame de Flahaut was merely a rallying point for the aristocracy; that charming Russian, the Princess de Lieven, reigned but did not govern; but Thiers and, at times, Madame Dosne through him exercised a very real power.

In fact, contrary to the usual custom, the hôtel at the Place Saint Georges was the scene of almost continuous receptions. Thiers and his family received nearly every evening, and never went out except when they had a loge at the Théâtre des Italiens. At these functions, Madame Dosne usually presided. Even so hostile a critic as the Duchesse de Dino comments on her striking appearance and her masterly air. With her received Madame Thiers and Mademoiselle Félicie Dosne. In these days, we are told, Madame Thiers appeared to carry the weight of the whole company on her shoulders. Her father, the prosaic Monsieur Dosne, made his appearance very infrequently. During the early part of the evening even the young statesman was not visible, at least not visible to the uninquiring eye. But if one sought him, he might be found asleep in a *fauteuil* in an obscure part of the salon. For Thiers had formed in his youth a habit that he continued to observe in his later years, the practice of a siesta after dinner. There, in a retired corner, the distinguished young hero rested while his guests passed softly by his peaceful form and respected his slumber. Then, suddenly awakening, he would jump up, stretch himself, come out from behind the screen that protected him, and, "as if the rest had rejuvenated his thoughts, become the most brilliant conversationalist in the world." He was always courteous and obsequious, and always accompanied the ladies to their carriages when they made their departures. He was known as a charming and agreeable host, and he never distinguished between the really worthy and the ignominious and plutocratic bourgeois who thronged his salon.

Thiers at home was always a success, but, during the early years of his prominence, Thiers in the rôle of a young man of society, outside the Place Saint Georges, was not always so successful. He had continued to acquaint himself with the usual accomplishments and diversions of the young Parisian of his day. In all of these, however, he was not adept. He did not relinquish his avowed or assumed fondness for horses after his first entry into public life. It pleased him to demonstrate his equestrian ability at the promenades to which the King invited him. These usually took place at Compiègne, at St. Cloud, or at Fontainebleau. He disliked to ride in the open landaus with the older and more important guests. He preferred to ride on his horse beside them in the company of the young Princes. Mounted on a horse called "Vendôme" that he, with his Southern accent, persisted in pronouncing "Vandomme," he loved to ride ahead of the cortège at triple gallop, vie with the Prince de Joinville, his particular favourite, and display his prowess. Sometimes, by chance, he passed a peasant girl. If she smiled up at the little Minister as he galloped by, he would rein in abruptly, drop a handful of coins into her hand, and then off he would go at a terrific pace, jumping fallen trees and ditches and playing the gallant for all that he was worth.

Sometimes, however, his performances were not so impressive. His love of the spectacular and his naïveté occasionally called forth the laughter and even the ridicule of his audience. The younger son of King Louis Philippe, Joinville, who seems to have had a real affection for the little Minister, recalls an incident that occurred on the occasion of the restoration of Napoleon's statue to the column on the Place Vendôme. To this ceremony, Thiers, as Minister of the Interior, had devoted much attention. It was the time of the revival of interest in the Napoleonic Legend when Thiers himself was an effective but unconscious advance agent of Bonapartism.

"The troops, the National Guard were under arms; and the military bands with drums and a magnificent drum-major at their head were massed at the foot of the column. We approached, *en grand cortège,* via the rue de Castiglione. In front of us was the column surmounted by the statue that was covered with a veil which, at a given signal, was to fall. Upon our arrival at the scene, Monsieur Thiers, *en grand uniforme,* wearing a hat with waving plumes and mounted on 'Vandomme', spurred his horse, left the cortège *au grand galop* and passed before my father, crying shrilly in his high falsetto, 'I bear the King's orders.' He accompanied these words with a wave of his plumed hat that unkind tongues declared he had copied from the pose of General Rapp in Gérard's painting, 'The Battle of Austerlitz', at the Louvre. At his gesture, the drums began to beat, the band struck up, and the veil fell from the statue. But Monsieur Thiers was no longer master of 'Vandomme', who, wild with enthusiasm, charged head down, upset the drums and the magnificent drum-major, and tore off with the little Minister hanging on to him like a monkey at the Hippodrome."

Sometimes, Monsieur Thiers' love for the theatrical nearly occasioned his downfall. This was true in society, but never in the Tribune whose principal occupant he so soon became.

that Monsieur Thiers did not carry out his intentions of travel. The explanation is obvious when one finds that a fortnight after his dinner party he was summoned to the Tuileries and begged by a much distraught Monarch to see if he could form a Cabinet that would be sure of a majority. Monsieur Thiers accepted the invitation with alacrity.

To all of the men in his first Council, the new President was decidedly superior. Many of them were older but few had had as much experience. No one of them was so able or so agile before the Chamber. Thiers himself acknowledged that his Cabinet was not a party Cabinet; like its leader, it could claim no permanent party affiliations and, under his guidance, it followed the dangerous and exciting practice of finding a majority when it needed one. Prince Metternich described exactly this policy of Thiers' when, in August, 1836, he wrote to Count Apponyi: "Monsieur Thiers is in every way a very dangerous man. . . . The cart that he drives is always veering from Right to Left, and he will have many severe lessons before he learns to keep it steady." The wise old statesman added: "He understands how to manipulate parties in France. But it is different in the case of Europe. Strange combination of revolutionary doctrines, journalistic audacities, and governmental despotism, this Minister represents his country to his country; but he is not fit to represent it before Europe."

Metternich shuddered, England feared that her hitherto docile ally would become an *enfant terrible,* and France, ever philosophical, sat back to watch.

On February 22, when Thiers made his first appearance before the Chamber, everything was in his favour. The *Viscomte de Launay* remarked in *La Presse:* "Paris is going to become more and more difficult to live in, for, aside from the great dynastic divisions that separate society, we shall now have all the factions to which disappointed personal ambitions have given rise: faction Molé, faction Guizot, faction Broglie, and finally, faction Thiers. And every one of them as hostile and bitter as are the Legitimists and Orléanists."

This situation was reflected in the Chamber, and it delighted the new President of the Council who wrote to a friend: "The Chamber cannot recede and does not wish to advance any more. It is obliged to stop right on my ground." He knew that, out of these divisions, he could create a majority when he needed it. And it was by such a dangerous game that Thiers, who had followed carefully similar movements in England, put through the Chamber bills adjusting tariffs to meet the needs of each industry and trade, and authorizing a few suburban lines to tie the outlying districts with trade centres in the provinces. In June, 1836, after considerable effort, he even found a majority to support his new and modern method for the colonization of Algiers. Most of these measures that concerned the internal affairs of France alone had been put through by the support of the Left with which he had been coquetting. Oddly enough, when it came to foreign policy, Monsieur Thiers' cart veered, at first, more to the Conservative side.

Even beyond the borders of France, it was common knowledge that the new President was desirous of inaugurating a foreign policy of reconciliation. England even suspected that he wished France to break away from her apron strings. But this suspicion was not entirely correct. He desired to maintain the friendship already established between the two countries but he did not wish the English Alliance to prevent the possibility of a rapprochement with the more conservative courts of Europe.

Consequently, from the beginning of his administration, Monsieur Thiers walked circumspectly and tried to manifest a very moderate enthusiasm in regard to liberal developments in Europe. When Cracow became the center for a movement to revive the spirit of Polish independence, the President was only mildly sympathetic, and his language in regard to Geneva, "that city that breeds Young Italy, Young Germany, Young Europe, even, Young France," was very firm. For such an attitude he was severely criticized by his temporary allies of the Left, but he did not heed them. Instead, he bided his time, for these declarations were simply the reflection of his desire to bring about a change in the relations of his country with Vienna, Berlin, and St. Petersburg. The Teutonic stodginess of the Court of St. James did not appeal to him: he longed for the brilliance of Vienna and the glittering jewels of the Court of Russia. *There* was dignity, and there he desired to see his France again. To this end, at first, all other lines of his foreign policy converged. He must create, for his King, a good impression: he must show to Prince Metternich that even Monsieur Thiers himself was not too revolutionary, and then he could aspire to an intimate alliance with the aristocratic governments of Europe.

The medium by which these new relationships were to be created was daring, to say the least. Thiers desired to see the grandson of regicide Philippe Égalité married to a Hapsburg! He would seek the hand of an Austrian Archduchess for the heir to the French throne. He would break forever the "matrimonial blockade" that Metternich and Nesselrode had set up against the House of Orléans. Such a change, he wrote to his ambassador at Vienna, would give the monarchy more éclat at home and would consolidate its position in Europe.

The stage had already been set for this bit of comedy; the object of the affections of the Duc d'Orléans had already been selected for him by his royal Mother. Marie Amélie, Queen of France, had chosen Maria Theresa, a daughter of Archduke Charles of Austria. Poor Broglie, when President, had tried to sound out Metternich but before the rebuff of that Prince he had retired discomfited. It was in the early spring of 1836 that the hopes of the Orléanist House revived when Monsieur Thiers, in buoyant spirits at his elevation, declared that he was not afraid to resume negotiations. Shortly afterwards, he announced that the young Duke and his brother were about to make a *grand tour* of Europe.

Instructions went out to the embassies at Vienna, Berlin, and St. Petersburg, to prepare the way for this peaceful invasion of a new reigning family. Sometimes these official advices were extraordinary: "Do not say much about marriage. France is not begging for a marriage alliance, but the French Government is thinking of marrying off its Princes. Voilà tout." "But," adds Monsieur Thiers, "it is at Vienna that there are Princesses galore: I can enumerate three at least. *My Young Princes* will be seen and will see; there is the truth. You know as much about it as I do. If the *voyage* should have no other results than to show that our Princes are well received at the palaces of Legitimate Princes, and to bring together the reigning families and their subjects, the advantages would be considerable." And then having paved the way, there were so many little homilies to deliver to the Princes themselves. To Orléans, he said: "Where you do not seek a wife, you must, at least, establish friendship for yourself and for your country. Your task will not be an easy one." But for this effort the young Duke was far better suited than was Monsieur Thiers. The charm of Orléans was great: he was attractive, intelligent, and gracious.

In May the Duke and his brother set out upon their journey. The first stop was at Berlin where the princely pair met with an immediate success. "Your King has been pleased to show in a fashion that can be understood by the whole world the union that exists between himself and the Continental Powers," the Prussian King remarked to Bresson, French Ambassador at Berlin: "I responded immediately. This is only the beginning, the future will show us the results. I have performed my part, and it has been as easy as it was agreeable, thanks to your Princes who, I repeat, have won the hearts of all of us." When this success was announced by the delighted King and the President of his Council, a paper of the Left commented: "Monsieur Thiers is now the very humble servant of the *grands seigneurs* of Hungary, Prussia, and Russia, who are graciously pleased to forgive him for being, after all, only a humble plebeian like ourselves."

Berlin, however, was not the crucial point: Vienna was to be the test. Almost from the day of their arrival in Austria, the popularity of the Princes was assured. Only in Metternich did they encounter any coldness and, from Paris, Monsieur Thiers was determined to break down that statesman's reserve. Poor Monsieur de Sainte-Aulaire, the French Ambassador, was bombarded with instructions from his home government and was kept running to the Chancellery with fresh messages. The Ambassador despaired of success but, on June 10, Metternich actually informed him that he had transmitted the expressed wishes of the Duc d'Orléans to the Imperial Family. Negotiations for a marriage began in earnest. Then, suddenly, came the collapse of the whole scheme when, at Paris, Louis Alibaud made an almost successful attempt on the life of the King. The investigation that Thiers immediately began established the fact that, although the Alibaud attempt was the act of an individual, the moral complicity of the Press of the Left was undeniable.

This news raised again the ghost of Revolution before the eyes of Metternich, and it was a far more serious check to the fortunes of the French Ministry than any attack of Liberal Press or Deputies' opposition. The President must retreat before the scorn of Metternich, and Thiers' retreats were never dignified. There were threats and then a desperate attempt to save himself by pursuing with relentless vigour and rashness a new policy, totally at variance with the one that had failed. There were frantic letters to Sainte-Aulaire: warn Austria of the danger that she will run if she refuses to stand by the King to whom she has just proffered the hand of friendship. But such threats were of no avail. Metternich wrote to Apponyi: "The events of the year 1830 separated our two governments completely, and this separation was not one of theory but of absolute fact." When Thiers heard of this comment, he remarked: "There those Austrians are, just as I have always known them: It is with exactly such a spirit as theirs that, for half a century, people who walk backwards spoil everything."

Although it was through no fault of the President that the marriage policy had failed and that Metternich had slammed the door again in the face of France, these events might have caused the overthrow of his Ministry had not its leader had another interest to which he could now turn the attention of his country. If a foothold in European politics could not be gained through a union with Austria, France could force an entrance by asserting her concern and her devoirs in Spain. Thiers has been credited with having said: "Monsieur de Metternich need not worry. If I am too much Holy Alliance in Switzerland, I shall make up for the fault as far as Spain is concerned."

Thiers, however, did not take up the Spanish question simply to save himself and in the hope of avenging himself. From the very beginning of his Ministry, he had been much concerned about the fate of Constitutionalism in Spain. It is true, nevertheless, that, after the failure of the marriage proposal, his advocacy of intervention on behalf of the Spanish Queen became stronger.

Some time before he became President of the Council he had exposed to Louis Philippe his belief that a time might come when France, in order to serve the cause of Liberty in the Iberian Peninsula, might have to send an expeditionary force to the assistance of the two Queens. With this suggestion the King had disagreed, and turned, for comfort, to Soult and Gérard, old-school army officers of the Empire, who opined that only disaster could come to French armies in Spain and who warned the King that the country that had begun the undoing of Napoleon might easily do the same to Louis Philippe. To Thiers, who, from his studies, believed that he knew the real causes of Napoleon's failure, such talk was only so much superstition. Of the truth of this he could persuade the sons of Louis Philippe, but he could not change the belief of that monarch himself. Even as late as the Spring of 1836, the King openly declared that he would not countenance French intervention in Spain. By June of that year, however, the Constitutionalist supporters of the Queen became more insistent in their demands for French assistance. A treaty with Spain and Portugal by which England and France had guaranteed a joint support was the basis for their request, and a very sympathetic French ambassador at Madrid was, undoubtedly, the instigator. At first, however, Monsieur Thiers as head of the Government had temporized. He was convinced that the maintenance of a Liberal government in Spain was closely related to the permanence of the Constitutional Monarchy in France, and he envisaged the possibility of an eventual intervention in the Peninsula. But, he wrote the enthusiastic ambassador, he must first win the Right Wing of the Chamber to this opinion, and then the Chamber must win over the King. In the meantime he allowed a Foreign Legion to gather on the Pyrenees border, and promised that it would be increased. So far matters had progressed when, on June 25, Louis Alibaud made his attempt on the life of the King. This event resulted in the first break between Louis Philippe and the President of his Council. The disclosures that followed the attack convinced the King that, after all, Thiers had not brought him the security and peace that he had thought, while the subsequent behaviour of Metternich showed the French Monarch that his Minister had not won for him the esteem and confidence of Austria. Once again the King, never in favour of a too active foreign policy, drew back to the old plan of abstention. Monsieur Thiers, on the other hand, after the rebuff from Metternich, was more than ever anxious to show himself a Liberal and to aid a cause, like that of Spain, with which Metternich had no sympathy. Furthermore, the cause of Constitutionalism in Spain had, by now, become desperate. The King was resolved to abstain; Monsieur Thiers was equally determined to intervene. The question was posed: does the King reign *and* govern?

By the first of July, Louis Philippe had come to distrust his Minister. He secretly requested Montalivet, who was a member of the Cabinet and who was more devoted to the King than to the President, to watch Thiers and to report his actions. And the information that came to the King was not entirely satisfactory. It appeared that Thiers was not informing his royal master of all of the arrangements that he was making. In spite of royal admonitions to the contrary, recruiting for the Foreign Legion and Bugeaud, displeasing to the King, was announced by Thiers as Commander of the Army of the Pyrenees before Louis Philippe had even assented to his nomination. The King openly accused his Minister of publishing orders to which he was not party and of pushing France into a war of which he did not approve. The feeling of mutual distrust became acute and when, on August 24, General Lebeau, Commander of the Foreign Legion, announced that, in agreement with Thiers, a French army would cross the Pyrenees and enter Spain, the astonished Monarch who had never consented to the plan, published an official denial in the *Moniteur*. On August 29, Louis Philippe was glad to accept the resignation of the President and of six of his colleagues.

To his friends, the retirement of Thiers came as a disagreeable surprise. He had had no quarrel with the Chamber of Deputies, for that body was on its summer vacation. By the Deputies his action was interpreted as a personal disagreement with the King to whose elevation he had contributed six years ago. His greatest friends, the Talleyrands, were much perplexed, and the sentiments that they expressed may very well have been held by his other supporters: "You break with the King—is it because of that hideous Spain? . . . We are sad, anxious, and concerned about you. To resign from power is not always regrettable, but to see you leave the King and the Ministry for a cause that will not excite the slightest sympathy in France!"

But, in the opinion of the retiring President, there was a reason that was far more subtle than that of his sympathy for the Spanish cause: "I wrote in the *National*, 'the King reigns and does not govern.' I acted on it. I never allowed Louis Philippe to interfere with me when I was his Minister and, therefore, my time of office was short and interrupted."

Shortly after August 29, Louis Philippe remarked to the Prussian Ambassador: "I had to take Monsieur Thiers for six months in order to show France exactly what he is worth. It requires infinite patience and persistence for me to steer my ship."

Undoubtedly the King of the French was glad to be rid of the fiery young independent who had almost involved him in a war. But the feeling was mutual. The ex-President was equally happy to be free from his King, and for a time there was a coldness between the Tuileries and the Place Saint Georges. However, it was not a sentiment that changed, in any way, Thiers' belief in Monarchy or even in Orléanism. He was still loyal, but he was suffering, for the moment, from a surfeit of things political. He still believed that the existing Monarchy could be brought to its proper power but he was not anxious to perform the operation at present. He wanted to rest, but once rested, he would return. He protested that, in the future, he would not aspire to a ministerial *fauteuil* and in this assertion he was, very likely, sincere. It is even possible that at this time he came to realize that his greatest effectiveness had been as a deputy and not as the head of the King's Council. One of his critics who hated and yet admired him wrote of him at this time: "Monsieur Thiers is never so powerful as when he is on the ground; the ministerial pedestal does not become him. On the contrary, when fighting from the floor he gains force: his brilliant *esprit,* his happy phrases, give him at once the prestige that he has lost as a Minister." Such thoughts may very well have been in his mind when he retired temporarily from the scene, and took his family to Italy where he dabbled in Florentine History and was piloted about Rome by Ingres.

Meanwhile a new Ministry was rapidly undoing the work of Monsieur Thiers. His overthrow, it will be recalled, had not been accomplished by the Chamber, for that body had adjourned on July 12. In other words, the change had occurred over a matter of royal prerogative in which Louis Philippe had won out. Consequently, that monarch was now determined to retain the power that he had just gained. It was with this object in mind that the choice of the King finally fell on Count Molé who was docile and obedient, and, true to the desires of his royal master, the new President's Cabinet was composed of moderate men such as Duchâtel, Rémusat, Guizot, and the ever-faithful Montalivet. Its policy was announced as one of conciliation abroad and at home. The Army of the Pyrenees was disbanded, an amnesty was granted to political offenders, and under Molé's personal direction, wise measures were undertaken to construct bridges, canals, highways, and railroads. These last laws were designed to meet the demands of industrialist and capitalist who were beginning, by now, to lay the foundations for a real economic change in France. For a time it seemed as if a real peace had come. Molé was a wise and tactful administrator, he was a sincere and earnest peacemaker, but he did not realize that the expansion of industrial activity brought with it problems that affected labour as well as capital, nor did he know how to fight a parliamentary war and, under the surface, a storm was brewing. Born of petty jealousies that prevented a patriotic approval of the Count's wise measures, a tremendous opposition to the King and his President was arising. Its source was in the Chamber of Deputies but few of its leaders took serious cognizance of the Social Question that Molé's internal policy involved. Instead, they concentrated their attention upon purely political matters.

Molé did not represent any large faction in this body. On the other hand, Guizot, Broglie, and Thiers controlled large numbers of votes. Guizot and his followers resented the fact that the former Professor of History had not received the recognition that was his due, and, from personal pique, Guizot retired to oppose the Government from a Deputy's chair. This was the first factor in an opposition that finally wrought great harm to the Monarchy.

The second factor was Monsieur Thiers. His only occasional presence in Paris had not removed him from the minds of his colleagues in the Chamber, and the Deputies were being constantly reminded of the very important fact that they had not dismissed him and that they had not assented to the appointment of his successor. In other words, Monsieur Thiers soon was acclaimed by his cohorts as the victim of a King who had overstepped his powers and violated the sacred principle of a parliamentary and responsible Ministry. Faction Guizot and Faction Thiers were shortly joined by two other groups. Barrot, of the Left, with his Republicans, had stretched his imagination and was soon denouncing the Louis Philippe-Molé régime as a repetition of Charles X and Polignac, while Berryer with his Legitimists naturally joined in a coalition that seemed to be working to discredit the King as well as his Minister.

It was a time of the reign of personal animosities when Thiers and even Guizot did more permanent harm to the Monarchy that they professed to revere than to the name of Count Molé. Their relentless harangues (in one month Thiers delivered eighteen discourses!) revived the hopes of the Radicals and the charges of supine and timid foreign policy that they levelled against Molé more often stigmatized the King in the eyes of his people. This "guerre acharnée" was not confined alone to the Chambers. Monsieur Thiers, who was by March, 1839, astride the movement, carried the quarrel into the farthest corners of the provinces by the use that he made of the Press. Thanks to his contacts and friendships, he became virtual dictator to the *Journal des Débats, Constitutionnel, Siècle, Messager,* and *Courrier Français*. Balzac, not without a touch of malice, describes a typical *matinée chez Thiers* during this campaign: "Every morning Messieurs Cardonne, Guiraldi, Boilay, Veron, Walewski, Léon Faucher, Chambolle came to the rue Saint Georges, to the hôtel of Monsieur Thiers, to receive their orders, and to be informed what kind of articles to write. Monsieur Thiers was aided by two of his assistants,

Messieurs Martin and Sainty; the task of the latter was very difficult, being to translate into good French whatever Monsieur Thiers wrote. There, with Madame Dosne presiding, the cakes that were to be swallowed by the public were buttered."

By February, Molé was crumbling under the combined attacks of the Coalition and, finally, in a desperate effort to save this Cabinet, the King called for new elections. These resulted overwhelmingly against the Government, and on March 8, Molé resigned. The Chamber was in an uproar, the Radical Clubs were reviving in Paris, and the King, in despair, called for Thiers and his coalitionists to give him a Cabinet and a programme.

On March 19, a great dinner was given at the Place Saint Georges. There the leaders of the Coalition met for the purpose of drawing up an ideal programme for the future Ministry. Some of the clauses in this document are significant. They are the first indications of the birth of a Reform Movement in France.

"The New Ministry, representing the opinions of the Left Center, will not proclaim itself the continuation of the Ministry that has just resigned.

"The Laws of September will be maintained.

"No proposition for electoral reform will be made for the present; that question will be left for the future.

"No armed intervention during the present condition of affairs in Spain, but in the event of serious incidents, the Cabinet reserves a complete liberty of action."

This last clause led Louis Philippe to refuse their proposals. The King turned from them to form a Cabinet under Marshal Soult and the Coalition resumed its attack which was finally successful when, in February, 1840, the Cabinet resigned.

Out of this parliamentary war of the Coalition came three important results. The first was the rousing of spirit, hostile to the King and critical of his every act, that confirmed and strengthened the position of those leaders who were opposed to the idea of a monarchy in France. The Republicans took heart, and the Radicals whose temper had become more ambitious and hopeful, due to the teachings of Utopian Socialists, the followers of Saint-Simon and the experimentalists who accepted the theories of Fourier for the reorganization of industry, found among the labourers an increasingly sympathetic hearing. The second result was the beginning of a move to save the monarchy by the adoption of a definite programme of Moderate Reform—the first step towards which was made when the Coalition attempted to draw up a platform. And the third outcome was the acceptance by Thiers of the King's commission to form a Cabinet.

Again in 1840, as in 1836, Thiers was swept into power on the wave of a strong nationalistic sentiment that demanded a change in foreign policy. If Molé's practice of abstention had annoyed Frenchmen, that of Soult had exasperated them. In 1839, public opinion in France had become aroused over a quarrel between the Sultan of Turkey and his vassal, Mehemet-Ali, Pasha of Egypt.

It is not unlikely that the crisis might have been avoided but for the mutual rivalries of two great powers in the Near East. For some time England, the ally of France, had been watching anxiously the increase of Russian power in the Balkans and in Turkey. Ever since an agreement that had been made in 1833, the Tsar and the Sultan had been bound in a defensive alliance by which Russia enjoyed an almost exclusive influence in Constantinople. But England, too, had made gains in an easterly direction; her influence in the Ionian Islands was supreme, and in Greece her power was preponderant. These advantages had whetted the appetite of commercial England and now, under Palmerston's encouragement, British merchants were casting covetous eyes on

Trebizond and even on Constantinople itself. It was the quarrel between the Sultan and Mehemet-Ali that gave England an opportunity to try to offset the rival power of Russia.

The Pasha of Egypt desired to extend his rule into Syria. So successful had been his efforts in that direction that the Porte had finally decided to make peace by offering to invest him with the hereditary power in that country. Such an arrangement would have raised the Pasha to a position practically independent of the Sultan. Here was the opportunity for England; an offer to help the Sultan and to mediate for him might cause the balance of Turkish favour to swing from Russia to England. The first move was naturally for England to consult her ally, France. If that country agreed to the proposal, the British Government would feel free to act. In the meantime, however, the Tsar scented the danger to his own influence and instituted measures to effect a speedy accommodation between the Porte and Cairo. But this effort of Russia was checked when Soult declared that the question of Egypt was not an exclusively Russian affair, and that France and the other great European powers had a right to participate in such an arrangement.

So far, England and France had acted in agreement, but at this point discord developed between the two countries. Palmerston's plan was to win the gratitude of the Sultan by snubbing the Pasha, and, to this scheme, France refused her consent. Mehemet-Ali had allowed Frenchmen many commercial privileges and his romantic and rather spectacular career had aroused their admiration. Incidentally, his popularity had been increased by the influence of Thiers who regarded him as a second Napoleon and who saw in his cause the opportunity of France to assert herself in European affairs. When, therefore, Soult, in accordance with the wishes of his royal master to preserve peace at all costs, showed signs of giving way to Palmerston, the Coalition denounced his policy and, on another pretext, accomplished his retirement. This situation paved the way for the return of Monsieur Thiers.

Upon his assumption of the office of President, Thiers was resolved to be cautious and not to let loose the dogs of war for fear that they should turn and rend him again. He had persuaded the King that it would be possible to prevent the crushing of the Pasha by the united efforts of England and Russia, without resorting to other than diplomatic action. He had pointed out the glory that it would be to outwit Palmerston and thus to win for France a sphere of influence in the Near East by befriending the Pasha and not harming the Sultan. For his plan to succeed, he said, only secrecy and quick action were necessary.

Accordingly, special agents were dispatched to the Porte and to Cairo to negotiate a direct arrangement, by France, between the Sultan and Mehemet-Ali. The scheme was almost a fact when Palmerston heard of it. To the English Minister this covert move of the French Cabinet appeared to be directed towards the exclusion of Austrian, Russian, and British influence. Enraged at what he called "la politique égoïste" of France under its present administrators, Palmerston instructed Ponsonby, his agent at Constantinople, to send to Syria emissaries who should stir up a revolt against Mehemet-Ali. At the same time, ignoring Thiers and Guizot, French Ambassador at London, he called a secret conference of Russian, Prussian, and Austrian delegates. On July 15, he delivered his blow at France, when the four powers signed the Pact of London that called upon the Pasha to evacuate Syria within ten days and that threatened him with deposition if he ignored their demand. To give force to this ultimatum, an English fleet was dispatched to the Syrian coast.

The news of this action dumbfounded Thiers and angered him. His enemies ridiculed him in the Press and in the Chamber. But there was a more personal aspect to the affair: Thiers interpreted Palmerston's move as an attempt to bring about an estrangement between Louis Philippe and his Council. The world was aware that the French King would support his Minister only so long as there was no likelihood of hostilities, and it was believed that, once the phantom of Mars walked upon the scene, Louis Philippe would dismiss Thiers and take to cover. Palmerston's shrewd calculations were correct.

From the date of the publication of the ultimatum, the position of Thiers became increasingly difficult. It was no longer possible to divert the attention of the French public from the unfortunate turn that events had taken, and Palmerston's action only fed in France the desire for national prestige that had been fostered during the period of the Coalition. When many rash patriots rallied to the side of Thiers, he began again to lose the confidence of the King. In desperation, he veered to the side of caution when he attempted to obtain through Prussia a modification of the terms of the Pact. When this effort met with no success, he advised the Pasha to consider sacrificing Syria. But now, Mehemet-Ali was as stubborn as Palmerston. Thiers had reached an impasse: pacific measures had failed him and his only resort was to bluff. And so, he rushed to the King and asked for authority to call out the classes of 1836 and 1839, and to demand war credits. The fleet should be increased and preparations undertaken for a further fortification of Paris. He assured the agitated monarch that these measures were only threats to Palmerston and that he did not contemplate actual hostilities. To these requests, Louis Philippe, so peace-loving, gave a reluctant consent. But the King was becoming uneasy; the threats of Thiers had been taken by the Press. In alarm, he wrote to his Minister: "Please moderate the tone of the papers." In reply

Monsieur announced that he was no longer in the mood to preach moderation. At this, the King came to his own conclusions. "Let me tell you," he remarked to Sainte-Aulaire, "I shall not allow myself to be carried too far by my little Minister. At least, he wants war, and I do not want it: and when he will not allow me any other resource, I shall break with him rather than break with Europe."

By September it looked indeed as if the Minister's policy might lead to war. If, however, Thiers was serious, Palmerston was equally so and he soon gave evidence of it. On September 11, Beyrout was bombarded and the Sultan proclaimed the deposition of Mehemet-Ali. After this action, public opinion in France was not so completely behind the President of the Council. The crisis had lasted too long, and people were beginning to weary of it. Conservatives were asking themselves if Thiers had not gone too far, and many were coming to believe that the argument had descended to a personal quarrel between Thiers and Palmerston in which the Frenchman had been duped by the Englishman. When this defection began, Louis Philippe took heart while Monsieur le Ministre complained to Madame Dosne that he found the King more difficult and less amiable. As a last concession to the Cabinet, the King consented to send Thiers' memorandum protesting against the acts of the English Government and he convoked the Chamber for October 28. In the meanwhile he negotiated in secret himself. Through Leopold of Belgium, he received assurances that an accommodation with the powers could be reached, and he had a secret conference with Guizot at Eu. The result was that on the eve of the opening of Parliament, Louis Philippe refused to incorporate Thiers' bellicose phrases in his address. The Cabinet of March 1 resigned, and Guizot hastened from London to Paris to assist in the formation of a new Ministry.

The actual events of the two Ministries of Adolphe Thiers are not of such great importance. But there is behind them a theory of considerable significance. A Ministry avowedly parliamentary yielded to royal prerogative. Again, as in 1836, Thiers was not thrown out of office by the Chamber, and this fact has its point in the history of his political evolution.

The Period of the Restoration had converted him from Jacobinism to Orléanism, but he was only an Orléanist because he believed in "representative monarchy." The years that followed the July Revolution had led him to somewhat modify this theory. Périer and the behaviour of the Radicals had led him to proclaim the idea of representative monarchy controlled by the élite of the nation. Twice he had tried to teach France this lesson but those who could vote did not heed him, and the most unsatisfactory pupil of all had been Louis Philippe. From 1840, therefore, there was another stage in his political development. Now he beheld his ideal monarchy endangered by the King and by the statesmen whom he chose as his Ministers, and from that time he devoted himself to an effort to save his idea of monarchy and to drive all its enemies from power. He formed, therefore, what he called the Dynastic Opposition, and found himself in the anomalous position of a Monarchist who, on theory, opposed the monarch.

To many of his contemporaries, even to some of his friends, Thiers' two ventures as President of the Council appeared to be failures. They declared that he had done nothing to France except to arouse her ambitions and then to disappoint them. On the surface, this verdict appears to be true: France, under him, had not become a united nation, party enmities were stronger than ever, and, under him, France had bluffed and failed both in Spain and in Egypt. But there were many other results of his administration that remained to benefit France. Underneath all of the tumult and fanfare of the diplomatic wars that he carried on, there was a steady progress. He was busily laying the foundation of a greater France. To win the Centre parties, he urged the increase of railroads, the building of the great port of St. Nazaire, and the development of the French merchant marine to North and South America. But these efforts, laudable in themselves and significant in their results, did not spring from any really profound conception of the importance of the new industrial era upon which France, slower than some of her rivals, was beginning to embark. Thiers remained a stranger to the idea of a new economic order except in so far as it concerned the Middle Class—"that élite of the nation" of which he had so often spoken—the needs of which, he felt, must be met in order to allow it to fulfil its destiny of re-establishing the supremacy of France in Europe. Except for his creed of the bourgeoisie, his ideas were still those of the Moderate Liberals of the eighteenth century—at home, a Golden Mean, abroad a brilliant foreign policy. During the critical months of July, August, and September, 1840, he obtained extraordinary credits for the army and the navy. He increased the fortifications of Paris. He raised the salary of officers and improved the *matériel* of the war forces of France. Aided by the enthusiastic co-operation of the Duc d'Orléans, the armies that later won victories in the Crimea and Italy received their first training and development. Assisted by General Bugeaud, with whom he did not always agree, he made the colonization of Algiers a permanent policy.

These are things that are often obscured by the storms of political hatreds and passions in which France has had no rival until recent times. These are facts that should always be remembered along with the wild plunges and failures of the man whose enemies dubbed him *un Napoléon en miniature.*

CHAPTER VIII

MONSIEUR THIERS AND MONSIEUR GUIZOT

THE return of Guizot from England and his subsequent appointment as a member of the new Council had one inevitable and logical effect upon the retiring President; Thiers became a member of the Dynastic Opposition. In fact, after October, 1840, there was no other place in the Chamber where he could go, for Guizot was firmly entrenched in the confidence of the King, and the policies of the new President no longer coincided with those of Thiers.

As early as March, 1839, serious differences of opinion had appeared, and these had made of the two leaders bitter rivals. When the Coalition had proposed to draw up a political programme, Thiers had declared for a reform in the electorate. Such a change would have admitted a greater number of the professional classes to the vote and would have constituted a step towards the attainment of Thiers' cherished ideal of "a representative monarchy by the élite of the nation." So great, however, had been the repugnance of Guizot to the suggestion that, to save the Coalition, it had been agreed to leave the matter as a subject for future discussion and study. Again, Thiers had found his rival completely opposed to the bellicose and blustering diplomacy of the preceding Cabinet. And now, when the new Ministry had come into the plenitude of its powers, Guizot as a member, although not its head, used all of his influence to undo the foreign policy of the Cabinet that had preceded him. Such a programme necessitated, for Thiers, a defense of his actions. Consequently, from 1840 to the disastrous days of February, 1848, with one intermission, the Chamber of Deputies was dominated at one moment by the persuasive eloquence of Thiers, and, at the next, by schoolmaster Guizot. And the battle, long and relentless, was waged over the two questions that separated them: the necessity for reforming the Government and the resumption of a more active foreign policy.

To keep himself and the Council in power, Monsieur Guizot worked to control the two hundred thousand electors of France by the distribution of government favours and by trying to maintain the practice of government functionaries sitting in the Chamber, while Monsieur Thiers made himself the patron of almost every platform to which the King and his Ministers were opposed. Through his friend Duvergier de Hauranne, who was always proclaiming his eighteenth-century principles, he contracted a close alliance with Odilon Barrot and other leaders of the Left Centre while, by espousing the cause of Montalembert and the Young Catholics who were demanding the fulfilment of the promise of Liberty of Instruction, he gained the adherence of an important section of the Right.

Determined as he was, however, to oust Guizot and to transform the Monarchy, he was not the avowed enemy of the King. Within a year and a half after his retirement from office he had gathered a force behind him that might have reduced Louis Philippe to the point of dismissing his favourite yet when, in July, 1842, the young Duc d'Orléans was killed in an accident, Thiers hastened to

Neuilly to the side of the bereaved King, and offered to call a truce. Realizing the danger that the dynasty would now run with an old King on the throne and the heir only a child of five years, he persuaded Barrot's Left Centre, the Young Catholics, and the Legitimists to desist from their warfare and to support the monarch's wise plan for a Regency in the event of Louis Philippe's death before the little Duc d'Orléans should come of age. In August, 1842, it was Thiers and not Guizot who undertook to defend the Regency Bill from the attacks of Lamartine, Ledru-Rollin, and other parliamentarians of the Extreme Left who saw in the situation the possibility of blocking the Monarchy. And then, having won a victory for the King, he fled the denunciations of the Extremists who were laughing to scorn his previous protestations of Liberalism and calling him a turn-coat. Evidently, Monsieur Thiers was still a Monarchist.

After the affair of the Regency, he went to Austria to study the battlefields in preparation for his monumental history of Napoleon. Upon his return, he devoted himself almost entirely to research. He pored for hours over great maps and kept his secretary copying notes or receiving dictation at a furious rate. His conversation was entirely about armies, navies, imperial administration, commissaries, and military tactics. What he had learned in the morning he tried out, at night, on the admirers and followers who crowded his salon. In summer he entered his study at five o'clock in the morning. His library where he worked was long and well-lighted. On the walls hung huge reproductions of Italian masterpieces. Atop the bookcases were busts of great men. Down the middle of the room ran a long oak table on which he could spread maps of great size. He developed a passion for topography. In this room he worked until late afternoon when he rested, and then prepared to go to the theatre, to attend a soirée, or else to receive at home his host of admirers. For a little while Monsieur was playing again his other game. For the moment, he was a man of letters, but soon political circumstances and the ambitions of Madame Dosne called him back into the arena of public life.

While Monsieur Thiers was flourishing in such pleasant pastures, Monsieur Guizot was experiencing difficulties. His party was holding its own, and that was all. Bound to a foreign policy of concessions, the progress of Louis Philippe and his Cabinet had not been an impressive one. At almost every corner the King gave the sidewalk to one of his fellow-rulers in Europe. When the British Government objected to a wise proposal to establish a Franco-Belgian Customs Union, Guizot's companions in the Council abandoned a project which might have been of great economic advantage to the country. Again when Queen Victoria announced that she could not approve of the match, the Ministry, at the King's behest, meekly halted its negotiations for a marriage between the Duc d'Aumâle and a Princess of Spain. These incidents made silence too painful, and, in 1843, as the opening of a new session of the Deputies drew near, preparations were begun by the Opposition to resume their attacks and Thiers abandoned the truce that he had made with the King.

The fact that the Ministry had been able to find a majority to support them in such measures had been due almost entirely to a practice of parliamentary corruption. It was this system, "le système Guizot," that aroused the Deputies of the Opposition to begin their fight in earnest.

In January, 1844, Louis Philippe opened the Chambers with an Address that could only have annoyed the opponents of the existing régime. Taking his cue from Guizot, the King proceeded to felicitate himself and the country on the happy situation of France, on her progress under the salutary influence of parliamentary institutions, and on the extension of her influence beyond her borders! The Opposition listened in silence but when the discussion of the Reply began, their attack broke loose. Gustave de Beaumont, the friend of Alexis de Tocqueville, proposed that a phrase should be inserted into the Reply expressing the hope of the Chambers that parliamentary practices would be developed further under the wise guidance of the King. Following Beaumont, Thiers arose and broke the silence that he had so long observed. He compared the government of France under Guizot and his colleagues to that under Molé where the principle of "representative government" was entirely lacking. It was in this speech of January 16, 1844, that the first mention of corruption and of the need for reform was made from the tribune of the Chamber of Deputies. He concluded by announcing that, in the near future, he would discuss the foreign policy of the Cabinet.

Thiers had opened the attack, and the subsequent actions of the Ministry only tended to increase the suspicions that he and the other leaders of the Opposition had aroused. The weakness of the Council in the affairs of Tahiti and Morocco where, again, the Government bowed before England, met with little favour in the country, while Guizot's vacillating and tricky policy in regard to the Catholics and Public Education revived the demands for a literal observance of the guarantees of the Charter. By June, 1846, the Ministry had to inform the King that the Deputies were not *maniable,* and Louis Philippe responded by dissolving that body and calling upon the country to return a new Chamber.

Once again, but for the last time, the elections were well managed by the Government: superior functionaries were the Ministry's candidates for Deputies' chairs. Guizot's system of manipulation was now manifest to France. Against this practice, Catholic and Liberal alike protested and asserted that under such a system the Chamber could not represent the opinion of the country. The organs of the Opposition blared forth their demands.

L'Univers demanded Liberty of Education and "clean government." Electoral Reform and Labour Legislation became the cry of the *Réforme* and the *Presse*. Although each one understood these things differently, the entire Press of the Opposition united in denouncing the "reign" of Guizot. Above the bedlam might be heard the shrill tones and sharp phrases of Thiers, who played a whole orchestra of newspapers. It was not long before similar cries were heard in other quarters.

In response to encouraging statements from him, from Barrot, and from the newspapers, Labour began again its demonstrations. The small *commerçants* of Paris, Beziers, Toulouse, Bordeaux, and Rouen leagued against the united competition of larger houses. At Nantes, carpenters, iron workers, butchers, and riveters were airing their grievances. In Lyons, labourers had established their own paper, *L'Echo de l'Industrie,* in which they demanded a hearing of their complaints.

Throughout the country there was evidence of a spirit of unrest and of criticism. In many sections of the country the cry was one for reform and for investigation. Even the popular writers of the day had taken up the matter. French Romanticism was weary of mediæval and religious themes and Romantic writers were beginning to find their interest and material in the life of the common people. Hugo and Béranger wrote and sang of them and of their lot. Eugène Sue related their sufferings and laid many of them at the doors of the Church. Georges Sand waxed lachrymose over the virtues of the *Compagnon de la Tour de France,* a typical journeyman-carpenter, and narrated his superiority to his aristocratic employer. Literary society was becoming interested in workingmen's clubs and protective organizations and had already forgotten cathedrals, martyrs, and mediæval saints. And this new Romantic movement penetrated into scholarship where even historians were treating of the rise and triumph of the lower classes. Earlier, Thierry had been the historian of the bourgeoisie and its rise. But Michelet, like his literary contemporaries, went lower in the social scale and was at work on his dramatic history of France in which he challenged, in turn, Kings, Bishops, and nobility with the question: "What have you done with the people, and what have you done for the people?" Lamartine, too, was about to complete his historical panegyric on the Girondists. As able a political scientist as Alexis de Tocqueville had described, in a work of superior merit, the experiment in democracy across the Atlantic. This work, first published in 1835, was having a large sale and was being widely read. And for those who went beyond Republicanism, Louis Blanc, Socialist and more practical successor of the Utopians, was outlining in his *Organisation du Travail* the doctrine of the Right to Work and its solution—the National Workshops or eventual Government ownership of Industry. These writers and others like them were aiding in the desire for Reform or even Revolution.

A change was coming over the social mind of France but it was a change of which most of the leaders in the Chamber did not realize the full import, and which had slight effect on them. Thiers had scorned the earlier Romantic movement with its mediæval trappings and had expressed his preference for the Renaissance, and his sympathy for this new "Romanticism of the Lower Classes" was no greater. He disliked Republicanism and was not interested in such experiments, and he refused to take Socialism seriously. He often called it "a state of nerves." He still remained confined within the limits of his eighteenth-century heritage, his creed of the Middle Class, and his enthusiasms for the campaigns of Napoleon. Like Thiers, Guizot, the rival who had replaced him in the King's confidence, was blind to the latent power of these new forces. He was deceived, even, in regard to the stability and strength of his own influence, and when, in August, 1846, his party won the elections, he believed that his position was secure. Perhaps the fact that neither the Radicals nor Monsieur Thiers and his colleagues had come out so well in the elections prevented him from seeing the other side of the picture and made him ignore the definite alliance of Thiers, Duvergier de Hauranne, and Odilon Barrot on the basis of a moderate Reform.

The original pact of a Reform party came from Monsieur Thiers. In 1845 he had made a brief visit to England and had met there a number of the British Liberals. This sojourn had undoubtedly left its mark upon him. Shortly after his return, Thiers, ever able at discovering compromises and *vias medias,* found a few fundamental principles on which himself, Duvergier, and Barrot could agree. The platform called for a general reduction of the tax qualification for the franchise, a consequent increase in the number of electoral colleges, and a greater representation from the larger towns. Although he was the author of their programme, it is very doubtful that he approved whole-heartedly of their associates. While he agreed with Duvergier and Barrot in essentials, he was afraid of Barrot's friends, Paguerre, Marie, and Marrast, who sat farther over on the Left than Thiers cared to go. And, likewise, he disapproved of the methods that they adopted to spread their ideas.

Restrictions for which Thiers himself had been in great part responsible prevented the Opposition from holding political meetings. Accordingly Barrot and his group proposed to escape the law by following the example of the British Liberals. They decided to organize petitions and to hold banquets. The first of the Reform Banquets was held at Château Rouge, Paris, on July 9, 1847. At this affair Barrot and Duvergier made toasts in which they inveighed against the Ministry and its practices. Their remarks approached very near to the point of attacking the Monarchy itself. With this demonstration Monsieur Thiers refused to be associated. And, when the banquets spread to the provinces, he took occasion to make his dislike of them evident to everyone.

If, however, he was unwilling to attack the Government by means which he regarded as unwise and almost illegal, he did not refuse to perform his part in the Chamber, as a member of the Opposition. Now that Guizot had broken with Palmerston over the question of the Spanish Marriages, Monsieur Thiers praised him and lauded the English parliamentary tribune. He became intimate with Palmerston's new envoy at Paris, Lord Normanby. To discomfit Guizot, he appeared in the Chamber in the rôle of an enthusiastic supporter of the Liberals who were again becoming active in Europe. Where, before, he had regarded the Swiss with an uncertain eye, he now acknowledged a penchant for this courageous and independent people. A few years previously he had led the attack on the Jesuits in France, but now, with Pius IX and his liberal intentions proclaimed at Rome, Monsieur Thiers became ultra-Catholic and cried out: "Courage, Saint-père, courage." One day he exclaimed during a speech before the Chamber: *"Italiens, soyez unis! Peuples, princes, soyez unis! Piémontais, Toscanes, Romains, Néopolitains, soyez unis!"* But ten years later this same Deputy was a bitter opponent of the unification of Italy. As the life of the July Monarchy neared its close, Monsieur Thiers, in his sphere, was guilty of the same rash impulsiveness for which he reproved Barrot and Duvergier. He had condemned their banquets as "very impolitic," but he himself had allowed his zeal for reform to carry him into new liberal enthusiasms, many of which he regretted and abandoned when the débacle came. But, that was not all—by his actions and words he aroused the hopes of the Extremists. On the day when the Monarchy fell, Madame Adelaide is said to have met him and addressed to him these words: *"C'est vous qui nous a perdu, Monsieur Thiers."* If there is a grain of truth in these words, there is also truth in the statement that Thiers, without wishing to do so, paved the way for the Republic and for the Second Empire.

Meanwhile, the popularity of the Banqueteers had been increased by other circumstances. Government scandals, trials of officials on charges of corruption, bad harvests, floods, and failures at the *Bourse,* had made more people attentive to the toasts that were being given. And, incidentally, the toasts changed as other *Réformistes* took them up in the provinces. Dupont de l'Eure, Garnier-Pagès, and Ledru-Rollin gave to the banquets more of a Republican tinge than Monsieur Thiers cared to see.

By the end of the year, the country was in the mood to demonstrate its hostility to the Ministry. At this point, Guizot, now President of the Council, should have resigned. In fact, some of his intimate friends urged him to do so. But, to Guizot, the struggle had become a personal one with Thiers, at whose door he laid the ultimate responsibility for the banquets, and he was too proud to yield to the forces that had been marshaled by the little Deputy. Instead, he proposed now to silence the Opposition by prohibiting the Reform Banquets and by submitting a scheme of his own for electoral reform. To the first proposal Louis Philippe agreed, but he refused his assent to the second for he had been hurt by the fact that some of the Opposition had declined to drink the King's health at the banquets. The Ministry must, then, either resign or go ahead. Unwisely, Guizot decided on the latter plan. When, therefore, the year 1848 opened, the Cabinet was prepared for war to death with the Opposition.

A quarrel between the partisans of Guizot and the Opposition in regard to the customary Reply to the Throne, was followed by the refusal of the Ministry to allow the electoral committee of the twelfth arrondissement in Paris to hold a banquet. Barrot, Duvergier, and their followers were resolved to defy the Government, provided Ledru-Rollin, the most radical of the Republicans, did not attend the affair. Over this question of banquet or no banquet the Opposition divided, and the Conservatives, led by Thiers, advocated, in place of such a defiance, a general resignation from the Chamber, an act which would necessitate convoking one hundred and fifty electoral colleges. But this suggestion was not the counsel that the hotheads desired; Barrot and Duvergier were deaf to such pleas. On February 13, in the *entresol* of the Restaurant Durand, 2 Place de la Madeleine, the Opposition held a consultation. It was an odd assortment; all phases of the Opposition were represented, the Left Centre, the Republican Left, and the Legitimists. The meeting was opened by Barrot, who held forth at great length opposing the plan of resignation. Chambolle replied to him and defended the scheme. He relates that, after his speech, he was perplexed to discover that, of the three former ministers present, two of whom had advocated the plan, not one of them arose to defend it. He approached Thiers and asked him for an explanation of his silence. The reply that he received mystified him even more, "*They* asked me not to take part in the debates today, and I have given my word not to do so." Thiers was still hoping that secret negotiations which Rémusat had opened with the Government would be successful. At the very time of the meeting, he had reason to hope for a reconstitution of the Ministry in which he might even find a place. For this reason, Thiers had remained silent and had not spoken his approval of any of the proposed schemes of action.

For his silence, however, he was ill repaid, for the Rémusat negotiations failed. To make matters worse, another move that had been set into motion by hardier spirits succeeded. In spite of the protests of Thiers and Rémusat, the Barrot-Duvergier group finally came to an agreement with Duchâtel, Minister of the Interior. He consented to allow the Opposition to make a test case as to the legality of the banquets. The proposed affair should be held in the Champs Élysées, whither the Opposition might go in company with the National Guard. The Banqueteers were to enter the hall, and then, at the first order from a *Commissaire de police,* they would retire. The *Commissaire* was then to lodge an order against them, thereby bringing before the proper tribunal the matter immediately at issue between the Opposition and the Ministry.

This was the disastrous compromise of February 20, 1848. It was a mistake which both the Government and the Opposition regretted before twenty-four hours had elapsed, for, once it became known, the Extreme Left set about to carry the arrangement further than either the Government or the Barrot-Duvergier group desired. Without consulting their colleagues, Marrast of the *National,* Ledru-Rollin who had been piqued by the cautious reserve of Barrot in regard to his presence at the banquets, and Garnier-Pagès, drew up an elaborate programme for the event. On the following day, their unauthorized arrangements were printed and issued in what appeared to be an official form. The programme, as published in the *National,* called upon the entire population of Paris to participate in the demonstration, and assigned to the various units of soldiers, National Guardsmen, students, political clubs, Deputies, journalists, and workmen, places where they were to join a mammoth procession that would escort the *convives* of the Opposition to the banquet hall. The announcement was couched in the form of an authoritative order.

In reality, it had not emanated from the Government, nor from the group of Deputies who surrounded Barrot and Duvergier. It was the *National* that, after eighteen years, was attempting to dictate to Paris again. Immediately, the Prefect of Police, acting on Guizot's order, announced that the existing law against unauthorized processions would be enforced in the case of all those who attempted to attend the banquet in a body. At the same time, Duchâtel, Minister of the Interior, appealed to Rémusat and requested him to use his influence to persuade his more rash friends to abandon the idea of the banquet entirely.

Upon receiving this request, Rémusat hurried to Thiers with whom he concerted to prevent the disastrous affair. Together they went to the house of Odilon Barrot where they found Duvergier and a group of *"enragés."* These men were in favour of holding the banquet in spite of the new turn that matters had taken but, after much argument, they finally consented to call a meeting of their cohorts and give Thiers and his companion an opportunity of expressing their views. This meeting, like the previous one, took place at 2 Place de la Madeleine, and, this time, Monsieur Thiers was not silent. "Messieurs," he said, "I perceive the *bonnet rouge* under the banquet table. As to the battle of which you talk, and which you seem to foresee, I do not desire it. Do you know why? It is because I do not wish to be the vanquished, and I desire even less to be the vanquisher." After his address, he drew Barrot aside and lectured him: "My friend, here is one of those occasions when you must know how to take a decision. Your party does not dare recede from its position. Take it out of its embarrassment. Mount the Tribune and say that, in view of the recent unforeseen resolutions of the Government, the proposed manifestation would only be an occasion for bloodshed, and that you are unwilling to take such an extreme measure for the defense of a right, no matter how well founded it is. Say that you will continue to demand this right by other methods, and that, in consequence, you call upon all good citizens to remain at home. You will have all of the Chamber for you; you will prevent the mob from coming tomorrow: you will save order, and you will put the majority under obligations to you. A few of your friends will protest. I offer to share the responsibility with you, and I promise to say whatever you wish."

Barrot's reply to this counsel was given in the most obscure and vague terms. He feared the criticisms of Lamartine and Ledru-Rollin. Had not Monsieur Marie proclaimed before him: "You have made a rendezvous with the people of Paris tomorrow: it would be cowardice not to come to it, but the people are not cowards, they will be there"? And when Barrot appeared to yield to Thiers the officers of the National Guard, that was permeated with Republicanism, turned from him with disgust and announced that they would keep the rendezvous. It was quite evident that the originators of the plan were losing control of the situation and that the entire affair was passing into the hands of the Radicals. In an effort to win them back and to satisfy the moderates who were working with Thiers and Rémusat for a reconstitution of the Ministry, Barrot and Duvergier decided to register in the Chamber an act to impeach the Ministry. In many ways, this plan was almost as foolish as the earlier banquet proposal. Such an action would keep the public in its excited condition: what Paris needed most was time to quiet down. On the morning of the 22nd of February, Messieurs Rémusat and Thiers set out again to interview Barrot and to make a final attempt to bring him to reason. But when they arrived they found, to their dismay, that the plan for impeachment had been already accepted by his followers. Barrot himself was not cordial and responded to their questions with some heat. During the discussion, reports to the effect that the excitement was spreading throughout Paris, began to pour in, but the Deputies who had gathered there would do nothing to quiet the city. Rémusat relates that they behaved like madmen.

Exhausted by the excitement that prevailed at Barrot's house, Thiers left it to reconnoitre and to inform himself of the real condition of Paris. What he discovered appalled him. "I crossed the Place Louis XV, the Place de la Madeleine, to the Ministry of Foreign Affairs, and I returned by the rue Saint Florentin. Children and workers were tearing up the streets with an unimaginable promptitude: they were beginning to build barricades three rows deep." Opposite them stood troops, drawn up in order, silent, and obstinate. The memories of June, 1831, and of April, 1834, came up before the little statesman. Those days were but a prelude to a more awful day. In the barricades of that evening of February 22, 1848, Monsieur Thiers beheld and recognized the setting of the sun of the July Monarchy.

CHAPTER IX

EXEUNT LOUIS PHILIPPE AND THIERS

When Thiers made his exploration of Paris on that last night of the July Monarchy, he was confronted with a situation that was quite different from that which prevailed on the eve of another French Revolution in which he had participated. In 1830, the capitalists had thrown the workers on the streets and thereby begun the movement that culminated in the departure of Charles X and the rise of a Bourgeois Monarchy in its stead. But in 1848, it was the workers who took the initiative and who drove the King of the bourgeois from the capital.

In Paris, during the months that preceded February 1848, a new Opposition, more subtle than that in the Parliament, was preparing. It was this Opposition that Guizot and Thiers failed to consider, on the eve of the crisis in the Chamber. It could be found principally in three sections of the city, the Faubourgs Saint Antoine and Saint Martin, the Latin Quarter, and the Boulevards. In the Faubourgs dwelt the labourers who had experienced two hard winters, frequent clashes with their employers, and who were being worked upon by the various Radical influences in the city. The Latin Quarter, home of the student youth of Paris, was decidedly touched with

in making their way. When they arrived at the Palace, Thiers was met by the Duc de Montpensier and the Duc de Nemours who ran up to him and said: *"Ménagez le Roi."* He was conducted immediately to the King's apartment, where, he relates, he was much affected to find himself in the royal presence again.

Louis Philippe was not in the best of humours. He greeted Thiers with a question, "Have you found me a Ministry?" The Deputy replied that he had just received His Majesty's commands. At this the King flared up, "Ah, you do not wish to serve under my rule?" The response was angry, "No, Sire." Thereupon, the King suggested that they both try to be reasonable. He asked for a list of possible ministers. Thiers suggested Rémusat, Duvergier de Hauranne, and Barrot. At the mention of the latter, Louis Philippe was not pleased. He then asked what their platform would be. Thiers replied that it would probably be electoral reform, by the extension of suffrage to fifty or one hundred thousand more voters, and the dissolution of the Chamber. The first stipulation the King accepted, but he objected to the dissolution of the Chamber, for, he said, a new Chamber would give them bad laws. From this topic, the King turned to the more immediate question of controlling and fortifying Paris. *À propos* of this matter, he announced that he had appointed Bugeaud to the chief command. This intelligence alarmed Thiers, for, because of the part that the General had played in suppressing the revolts of 1831 and 1834, old Bugeaud was very unpopular. The King, however, would not heed the protests of the man whom he desired to be his minister, and said, "Go, *mon cher,* and talk with Bugeaud." To Louis Philippe's mind, only one thing more needed to be done that night and Paris would be quiet; the King must announce to the public the nomination of Thiers and Barrot. To this plan, the former objected, arguing that they had not yet constituted a Ministry. But, at the King's insistence, he finally consented to an announcement to the effect that Thiers and Barrot had been asked to form a Cabinet. As Thiers sat down to draw up the message, Louis Philippe took the paper from him, and said: "No, I will be your secretary."

When the announcement had been written and dispatched to the *Moniteur,* King and prospective minister parted. The latter set out to find a Ministry during the early morning hours. As he went on his way, he was not happy, for the interview at the Tuileries had convinced him that his sovereign was not really cognizant of the situation, and that he would never sincerely accept the reforms that were being demanded. With the belief that Louis Philippe would use him and his friends to extricate himself from difficulty, and, then, once secure, dismiss them, he set about his miserable task of collecting his colleagues.

It was now about three o'clock, when, obedient to the King's wish, he went to the Place du Carrousel to interview Bugeaud. It would be a trying scene, for Bugeaud was eager to become Minister of War, while Thiers was equally persuaded that he could not be appointed. He admired the ability of the old General, but he feared his unpopularity. He found the veteran war-horse in a rage, "*déclamatoire comme d'habitude.*" Here he had been appointed as Commander for two hours and he had not received a single order! He had not sixteen thousand men, and those that he had were weary and demoralized from standing with knapsacks on their backs and in the mud for two days! There was no fodder for the horses. However, "*J'aurau plaisir de tuer beaucoup de cette canaille et c'est toujours quelque chose.*" At Bugeaud's, the news was not encouraging, and from his headquarters, Thiers went to the house of Barrot. When he had received the latter's promise to accept a ministerial portfolio, he proceeded to his own home.

At six o'clock in the morning the men whom he had summoned as his future colleagues began to arrive at the Place Saint Georges. When they entered, Thiers was carefully shaving, as was his habit, and he was as deliberate as usual about his toilet. This irritated Barrot, who said that Thiers and the King wasted time throughout that famous day of February 24. When Monsieur was carefully and neatly arrayed, the informal Council began its deliberations.

Barrot opposed Bugeaud's command. The others regretted it, but they were all in complete agreement in regard to the conditions for their acceptance of the King's commission. These were, the dissolution of the Chamber, the adoption of Rémusat's plan for electoral reform, and a complete indifference as to foreign affairs. If these terms were accepted by the King, Thiers would become President of a Ministerial Council that was to include Barrot, Rémusat, Cousin, La Moricière, Duvergier de Hauranne, Billaut, Dufaure, and Passy. This group were so completely in accord, that they might have saved the Monarchy, had it not been for other factors of which they were already cognizant, and over which they were unable to establish their control.

Just as they were setting out for the Tuileries, they learned of the effect of the announcement of Bugeaud's nomination. As they had feared, it had stirred up the more Radical sections of the Left. The *Mairies* of the arrondissements in the labour sections, Latin Quarter, and Boulevards had been seized by the populace. Flocon, Pyat, Louis Blanc, and Ledru-Rollin, who had made an effort to restrain the zeal of their excited followers, had lost control of them. At the same time, Thiers was informed that supplies and ammunition were lacking. It was with heavy hearts that the candidates for a new Ministry resumed their journey to the Palace at seven o'clock.

Paris presented a very different aspect, and one much

more ominous. Barricades were everywhere. The mob, however, seemed to be friendly to the little group of Deputies. The crowds allowed them to pass through, crying *"Vive Barrot," "Vive Thiers,"* but they also cried *"À bas Bugeaud,"* and at that Barrot began to weaken. When they arrived at the Louvre, they found steady firing going on between the infantry that was stationed there and the Republicans who had established themselves in the house opposite it. In order to get his party by this barrage, Thiers had to go up to the officers and order them to cease firing. When, finally, they were able to pass and had reached the Tuileries, it was seven o'clock. The Deputies noted that there was hardly a sign of a guard in the courtyard. There, they met the Duc de Nemours and the Duc de Montpensier, who had been talking with Bugeaud about the lack of ammunition. The Princes told Thiers that they had sent to Vincennes, and that the troops would bring it up by the most direct road. At this, Thiers held up his hands in despair, for the road would take the troops through the very heart of the riot, and the people might be able to seize the precious cargo. This is exactly what happened. Had the ammunition been brought up by river, it might have arrived safe and in time.

When they reached the King's Cabinet, there was a delay, for Louis Philippe was not yet up. At last, he came in; he looked hard at Duvergier de Hauranne of Reform Banquet fame, and said: *"Je les accepte tous. Verrons aux choses."* Thiers then informed the King of their terms. To the plan for the dissolution of the Chamber, Louis Philippe replied: "Impossible." To the question of Bugeaud's removal demanded by Barrot, he, at first, demurred, and, finally, consented to a compromise that would associate La Moricière with him. At the same time, he agreed to the suggestion to use the National Guard in Paris, and to concentrate the other troops outside the city, to be used in case of an emergency. The Council urged this policy because they felt that the National Guard was more popular, and its use by the Government would not have quite so much the appearance of an act of hostility against the people. These matters settled, Thiers then brought up the question of reform. The King hedged, half promised, and then, to the consternation of the Council, he arose and turned towards the door leading to his private apartments. Thiers arose, made a few steps forward to follow him. Louis Philippe slammed the door in his face. To add to the perturbation of the gentlemen whom the King had left, two of them announced that they had glimpsed through the half-open door Guizot, who was surrounded by the women of the royal family. Guizot does not tell of his presence, but others relate it, and the evidence is sufficient to establish the fact. Three times Louis Philippe went into that room, and each time he returned from it more irresolute than before.

Had Thiers desired to overthrow the Monarchy, here was the opportunity. He and his colleagues were not even constituted as a Ministry, for all of their terms had not yet been accepted, and the King had left them without a word. They could quite reasonably have put on their hats, and gone home to a breakfast that was long overdue. Instead, after they had recovered from their surprise, they debated what to do to save the Monarchy. The most immediate thing was to quiet the populace; this could only be accomplished by giving to them the proof that the King had consented to make concessions. Of this, the people were ignorant, for the *Moniteur* had been barricaded, and the proclamation that the King had written early in the morning, in the presence of Thiers, had not been circulated widely. As it was necessary to spread the news, Barrot consented to be a "walking placard," and to go out on the Boulevards. The next thing was to give the people a proof of the King's pacific intentions; this was done when Thiers, after deliberation with his friends, sent an order to Bugeaud to cease firing. Had the news of the Thiers-Barrot combination been spread earlier, disaster might have been averted, but it was too late. While Barrot was cordially received, he was not heeded, and, when Bugeaud, in obedience to orders, grumblingly withdrew his troops to the Place du Carrousel, the mob was free. It seized the Hôtel de Ville, and then began its march on the Tuileries.

In the meantime the King had resumed his conversation with Thiers. The latter suggested that the King retire to St. Cloud with the regular troops, leaving the National Guard in Paris. Then, in case the Guard could not settle matters alone, Louis Philippe, with reinforcements from the provinces, could march on Paris on the morrow. The King appeared to consider the matter for a moment; then went again into that fatal room, from which he emerged irresolute. Upon his return, he announced his intention of reviewing the National Guard. Had he reached this decision alone, or had he been advised by the retiring President who sat in the royal apartments? The review was pathetic. With Thiers holding the bridle of his horse, he rode along the ranks of the Guardsmen, crying out that he had granted the reform. Suddenly he stopped the proceedings and returned to the Palace, discouraged and grey. He sat down at his desk with Thiers at his side. Monsieur Crémieux broke in upon them. He informed the King that the mob was nearing the Palais Royal, which was quite near the Tuileries, that Thiers' name was not strong enough to stop the mob, and that only Barrot could save him. Louis Philippe looked up at Thiers. The latter assented, and the King wrote out Barrot's nomination.

It was now about eleven o'clock and there was a brief time of suspense while they waited for news of Barrot. Meanwhile, the latter's mission had failed and, fearing to draw the crowd that was following him to the Tuileries, Barrot set out for the Ministry of the Interior. About the same time, news reached the Palace that the insurgents had reached the Palais Royal, and that Arago, Lagrange, and other leaders had conceded to the people. Monsieur de Reims, who then arrived, informed Thiers that his family was safe, and also that the only resource that remained seemed to be an abdication in favour of the Comte de Paris. The Duc de Nemours who had been watching the conversation, called Thiers over to him. "What is the news, what are you hearing?" he asked. "About the safety of my own family," Thiers replied. But Nemours persisted: "What about the people?" "Nothing good," was the reply. "Can your informant be relied upon?" "Perfectly," responded Thiers. At that, the Prince went to Monsieur de Reims and questioned him. The latter finally told the Prince that he regarded an abdication in favour of the Comte de Paris as the only possible resource left them. At this, Nemours looked at Thiers and said, "What say you, Monsieur Thiers?" The reply was decisive: "I cannot venture, I canot bear to talk on such a matter." Nemours and Montpensier then approached the King to tell him that a terrible sacrifice was necessary. Louis Philippe looked up at Thiers and asked, *"Cher ami, que dites vous?"* Thiers did not speak. After a few minutes' talk with his sons, the King went back into the room where the Queen, the Duchesse d'Orléans, the ladies of the Court, and Broglie and Guizot were gathered. Finally, he issued from the Chamber, accompanied by Marie-Amélie, the Duchesse d'Orléans, and other members of his family. When he returned to the Cabinet, he could hear the voices outside crying: *"L'abdication! l'abdication!"* The Queen turned and said, "You do not deserve so good a King." Thiers, unable to endure the scene, left the room. He had reached the hall when someone ran after him, calling, "Come back! Come back! We want your advice for the King." As he turned, he caught sight of Émile de Girardin crying with the rest: "Abdicate! Abdicate!" He saw Louis

Philippe sign his abdication. Then he slipped from the room. He stayed in the vicinity of the Palace until the King and his family had escaped by the very route that he had suggested. Then the little man stumbled blindly out of the courtyard. He fell into the hands of a mob that insulted him and threatened him. Later, he found himself at the Chamber in the Salle des Pas Perdus. Some of the Deputies tried to make him go in, but he turned on them and said: "No, I will have nothing to do with you, your veniality, your subservience, your selfishness. I will never again enter that den of iniquity." And he left them. He did not know that the Duchesse d'Orléans who had remained behind, was, at that very moment, in the Chamber. Only Barrot, of the two, saw her, and Barrot expected Lamartine to move the Regency. To his surprise, Lamartine did nothing of the sort, but moved for a Provisional Government, declaring the Monarchy dead.

In the meantime, Thiers, bewildered, had wandered out to the entrance, and there he met an acquaintance.

"He came up to me, led me aside and told me that he would be murdered by the mob, if I did not assist him to escape. I took him by the arm and begged him to go with me and to fear nothing. Monsieur Thiers wished to avoid the Pont Louis XV, for fear of meeting the crowd. We went to the Pont des Invalides, but when we got there, he thought he saw a gathering on the other side of the river, and refused to cross. We then made for the Pont d'Iéna which was free, and we crossed without any difficulty. When we reached the other side, Monsieur Thiers discovered some street boys shouting on the foundation of what was to have been the palace of the King of Rome, and, forthwith, turned down the rue d'Auteuil, and made for the Bois de Boulogne. There, we had the good fortune to find a cabman who consented to drive along the boulevards, to the neighbourhood of the Boulevard de Clichy, through which we were able to reach his house. During the whole journey, and especially at the start, Monsieur Thiers seemed almost out of his senses, gesticulating, sobbing, uttering incoherent phrases. The catastrophe that he had just beheld, the future of his country, his own personal danger, all contributed to form a chaos amid which his thoughts struggled and strayed increasingly."

"This was the rôle that I played in this terrible catastrophe. Called when all was lost, I came, for my honour's sake, to offer my useless presence to a dynasty whose elevation I had beheld and whose downfall I would have prevented; I came, and I carried away with me only pain and sorrow."—Thiers: *Notes et Souvenirs,* p. 60.

CHAPTER X

THE MAKING OF A THIRD NAPOLEON

WHEN, on February 24, Louis Philippe set out on his flight to England, the former statesmen of the July Monarchy experienced a shock. As the year 1847 neared its end they had become anxious, but few of them, except Monsieur Thiers, had felt any real fears for the safety of the dynasty. Now, in February, these men who had laboured at the manufacture of a Middle Class Monarchy found themselves dispossessed of both their ideal and their power by the brief riot of a day. Shaken by the swiftness of the calamity and grey with fright, many of them passed the night of February 24 in fear for their own lives. They tell us how they barred their gates and fastened tight their iron shutters in preparation for a siege. They describe the cries of the angry mobs that rushed past their houses shouting the ominous words *"République," "Suffrage Universel,"* and *"Ateliers Nationaux."* On that awful night they believed that the reign of the Bourgeoisie was over and that Labour already triumphant was inaugurating its bloody rule.

Monarchy had fled, Bourgeois had hidden himself; both had left Paris to a new and enlightened guidance. A few newspaper Radicals, an angry mob, and Lamartine, poet-statesman, proposed to inaugurate an era of Freedom and real Democracy.

But in France, in 1848, such a purpose was a dream impossible of realization, and the Socialistic Republic that these men envisaged was destined inevitably to become a ridiculous farce. For France had taken the plunge into Democracy too suddenly; her new leaders, self-appointed, were too unversed in its principles, and most Frenchmen had not yet learned the trade of an active citizenship. True, they had talked and dreamed of a Republic, but none of them had more than a speaking acquaintance with it. As for Socialism, one Frenchman later remarked that few Deputies, or even Ministers, had ever read Saint-Simon, Fourier, or Louis Blanc. It was only a minority, and, at that, not a very experienced minority that undertook the task of creating a Provisional Government. This very circumstance robbed the Revolution, at its outset, of the national character that was essential to its success.

In France, by accident, of course, revolutions appear to have a strange way of repeating themselves. The revolt of 1830 has often been called a "Newspaper Revolution." The same epithet may be applied to the February upheaval of 1848. It was the Paris journalists who first assumed the direction of affairs. Once again, the *bureau* of the *National* became an important centre, and Editor Marrast assumed the rôle of spokesman for a self-appointed Committee that prepared a list of Provisional Governors. These committeemen, mild Republicans, selected Arago, Marie, Garnier-Pagès, and Lamartine. Such a choice, however, was not to the taste of the gentlemen of the *Réforme* who immediately issued a rival list that was far more radical—Marrast, Flocon, and Louis Blanc.

For a moment, it looked as though Paris might be torn between *National* and *Réforme,* but agile Lamartine saved the day when he brought about a fusion of the two factions. At six o'clock a Provisional Government was announced, and at the appropriate hour of midnight a Republic was proclaimed.

Two days of compromises ensued; promises here, encouragements there, proclamations everywhere. Painfully aware of their own insecurity, the Provisional Governors gave commitments in all quarters. While Ledru-Rollin was accepting proposals for National Workshops, Lamartine was trying to establish communications with the men of the former régime who could be relied on and whose patriotism was greater than their monarchistic preferences. To pacify noisy Socialists and their Italian sympathizers, red rosettes were pinned to tricolour flags, and busy Ministers, at frequent intervals, interrupted their labours to greet Liberty Tree Planting delegations. For these incessant ceremonies, the eloquence of Lamartine was in great demand. To the celebrators, he was courtesy and assurance, but, at his desk, we are told, he was a much harrassed and very anxious Provisional Governor. For France he foresaw divisions and other perils ahead. These he must avoid. At the same time, he had another important duty—he must quiet an uneasy and restless Europe.

There was a Republic in Vienna and a separatist problem at Pesth. A rash Pope had bestowed a Charter upon Rome, and his delighted subjects were preparing to run away with him. At Frankfort, a Diet was trying to proclaim independence from Austrian hegemony; while, in Berlin, there was a noisy demand for a promised Constitution that the King had not yet promulgated. These problems would give the Holy Allies enough to do and keep them from turning their eyes to France, if only Lamartine could so limit the course of the Revolution at home that Frenchmen would not be inspired to attempt again to liberate Europe. Aside from the Central Powers, Lamartine really had nothing to fear from the remaining nations in Western Europe. In Belgium, Uncle Leopold, son-in-law to Louis Philippe, was biting his nails at the disaster to the House of Orléans, but that was all that he could do about it. While, from England, wise Palmerston had sent a typical bit of advice to Normanby, his Minister at Paris: "Maintain your official relations with the men who, from hour to hour (I do not say from day to day), may have the direction of affairs. . . . We want the friendship of France and commercial relations with her."

It was the necessities of the Holy Allies and the opportunism of Palmerston that rendered France secure from foreign intervention and that gave Lamartine the time to turn his attention to the pacification of his own country.

When a semblance of order had been established in Paris, the men of the former Monarchy began to crawl rather shamefacedly from their places of refuge. Although they had not authorized him, most of them saw in Lamartine and in his conservative Republicanism the best answer for the moment. Even Monsieur Thiers proclaimed that a great light had dawned upon him. "I am not an *émigré* who dreams of an impossible past. I accept the revolution, and I am not in favour of any of the three possible restorations. The time for Kings has passed." In spite of these February protestations, another revelation would be vouchsafed to Monsieur a few months later. In fact, this traveller took the road to Damascus several times, and each time he experienced a different vision. But there were others more conservative and, too, more stable than was Thiers at this time; it was they who rallied to Lamartine's support. De Falloux, Royalist and Catholic, proclaimed his adherence while, from the pulpit of Saint Sulpice, the white-cowled Lacordaire preached loyalty to the Provisional Government. Many parish clergy even undertook to substitute for Lamartine at Liberty Tree Plantings, and provided incense and holy water in lieu of that statesman's poetical eloquence.

These acceptances augured well for the Republic, but could its able leader last? Perhaps if he had been the really predominant influence in the Government, those Catholics, Legitimists, Orléanists, and Moderate Republicans who were, above all else patriots, would have continued to rally about him. But these men, his temporary supporters, were by no means confident that Lamartine would be able to control his Government. They doubted as well that France really desired the sort of Republic that had been proclaimed at Paris.

Of this last fact Lamartine himself was uncertain, and he wished more than all else to give the country the chance to express its approval or disapproval. Over this matter all of his colleagues, however, were not of the same mind.

Among the Provisional Governors, his most serious antagonist was the Minister of the Interior. Ledru-Rollin, extreme Republican with a dash of Red, proud, impulsive, and hot-headed, was determined to make the Revolution more radical. Even if France did not desire it, Paris Reds should take the lead at the cost, if necessary, of manipulating the elections. Oddly enough, in 1848, he followed a practice for which, in 1847, he had so roundly condemned Guizot. In virtue of his office, practically all of the electoral machinery was in his control. Consequently, on March 8, a Circular was issued from his Department, addressed to the commissaries of the Government in the provinces. This document declared that the Central Government had unlimited power in the matter of elections and it advised those men whose Republican sympathies had been proved and recognized to exercise a very strict supervision over the elections. Ledru-Rollin's Circular embarrassed Lamartine with his more conservative supporters and aroused France to a pitch of excitement. Where the provinces had been quiescent, they now became aroused at what they believed to be the danger of a Jacobin dictatorship from Paris. Associations for the liberty of elections, manifestations, and signed protests bore witness to the anger of Frenchmen in many sections of the country. Finally, the election date was postponed, and it was not until the last of April that the citizens were allowed to register their wishes by electing deputies to a Constituent Assembly.

This delay was of great consequence; it gave time for the spread of dissenting opinions which manifested themselves during the Election Days in Paris, Limoges, and Rouen where there were serious riots. Over eighty per cent of the male population voted, and the majority that was returned represented the Moderate Republicanism of the *National.* Even some of the men of the former Monarchy gained seats in the Constituent Assembly. In short, on the morrow of the elections it looked as if the wise and generous attitude of Lamartine had been vindicated.

The success of the Moderates was a very clear indication of the sentiment prevailing in the country two months after the February Days; it was evident that the provinces were not entirely behind all that the new Government had done. The language of the Provisional Governors had not been clear concerning certain matters that were close to the hearts of peasant and small bourgeois proprietors. These last who were, after all, the mainstay of the nation, knew that, at Paris, the abolition of private property had been mentioned as a theory and had never been officially disclaimed by the Provisional Governors. Again, there was that ominous Commission of the Luxembourg where, under the ægis of Louis Blanc, an effort was being made to work out, in the face of great odds, the difficult plan for National Workshops. Compromises, vague assertions, and lapses in official utterances had alarmed property-owners, some of whom believed that the menace of Communism was real. And, as the month of March had advanced, from Paris there came the frequent cry for World Revolution. The men of the French provinces did not want France to become the deliverer of other nations, and they took alarm when the more pacific utterances of Lamartine were nearly drowned in the clamour of the mobs of Frenchmen, Belgians, Germans, Poles, and Irish who had flocked to Paris to aid in establishing Socialism in France and then, with France, to incite uprisings in their own countries. The provincial, however, wanted peace and prosperity. He was not a friend of these reckless harbingers of a New Era and the Paris Governors, several of whom appeared to have gone over to them.

Once again in French history, therefore, Universal Suffrage failed to result in a Radical Democracy. As one leader of the extreme school remarked: *"Il est évident que la France n'est pas propre au suffrage universel."*

On May 4, the Constituent Assembly was convened, and, on May 9, it created an Executive Council. Arago, Garnier-Pagès, Lamartine, and Ledru-Rollin were its members. The last named, because of his radical affiliations, had been chosen by a bare majority. As a matter of fact, he owed his seat in the Council to the gracious intervention of Lamartine. This narrow escape, together with his general unpopularity in the Assembly, made Ledru-Rollin all the more intractable and, as a result, the combination of the *National-Réforme* groups began to disintegrate. Moderate Republicans gathered around General Cavaignac and Editor Marrast, while the followers of Ledru-Rollin, who were almost exclusively Parisian, formed a party known as the *Réunion de la rue de Castiglione.*

Hardly had the Assembly organized itself than another party, destined to play an important part in the history of that body, made its appearance. From its earliest beginnings this *Club de la rue de Poitiers* was a force that had to be taken seriously. It could boast of the largest representation in the *Constituante* next the *National,* and it possessed the greatest number of experienced statesmen. In fact, the *rue de Poitiers* became the pivot of French politics during the tumultuous sessions of the spring of 1848. Monarchist leaders of the July Monarchy were to be found in its fold; Berryer, Molé, Rémusat, and General Bugeaud. These men, together with Montalembert and Falloux of the Catholic Party, were first united for one ostensible purpose—to stem the tide of Radicalism. It soon became evident, however, that they did not despair of bringing about a monarchical restoration in France. Berryer was their first leader, for Thiers was discredited. The equivocal statements of Monsieur A. T., as he was often called, had aroused their suspicions, and he was not a Charter Member of their organization.

To his family, this sort of political ostracism had come as a very disagreeable surprise, but Monsieur Thiers affected, at least, an indifference to politics. He had been shocked by the force of the Revolution, and, never insensible to force, he had collapsed momentarily before it. When his old electoral district of the *Bouches du Rhone* offered to propose his name, he issued a circular in which he implied his desire to abstain from political life. To a friend he wrote; "I shall renounce the living world and pass the remainder of my life in a corner working on a history of the world. . . . I shall not write it, but I shall have the pleasure of studying it."

It is very unlikely that, in the winter of 1848, Thiers really knew what he wanted to do. Whatever his real desires, he was defeated in the April campaign, but the migration to Rome and the "renunciation of the living world" did not take place. For Monsieur Thiers was not a scholar and he had not the real spirit of the cloister; he was only a romanticist who dreamed of being a historian just as he dreamed of being all other things. The fact that, at this time, he resumed the writing of his

History of the Empire, tended a small botanical garden, kept a miniature zoo, and indulged his artistic fancies by purchasing bad examples of Chinese art, is all of a piece in the strange pattern of this man. Such a person, so full of the action of life, could not remain secluded and protected from contacts with the great events that were transpiring. Besides, how long could Madame Dosne have endured a quiet lodging in a little house in Rome? Such a plan was not to her taste, and so, shortly, that Major-General herself issued the call to arms: "Let the Republic wear itself out or perpetuate itself. You would be in a bad way if it fell today, for there are too many pretenders. Courage. If the Republic lasts, you will direct it one day."

Madame Dosne was not mistaken. In fact, she rarely made a political prognostication that was not fulfilled. Eighteen months after this letter had been written, her son-in-law was actually, for a time, the power behind the only President that the Second Republic was allowed to have. It was the danger from the radical elements that brought Thiers and Louis Napoleon into the political limelight.

When, in May, the Prussian troops destroyed the hopes of the rebellious Poles, the workingmen of Paris arose in revolt to drive out the Assembly that had refused to come to the aid of Poland. A show of force by the Conservatives, and their Middle Class supporters from the neighbouring provinces, suppressed the trouble. This disturbance of May 15 showed the party of the *National* that its members had much in common with those who were affiliated with the *Club de la rue de Poitiers*. Both groups had been expressing the same views about the same things. Above all, both of them feared the experiment of the National Workshops to which they laid the blame for the continued unrest in the country. In them there were, they declared, more workers than work to be done, and the numbers of inactive men that lounged about the shops became easy prey for radical agitators and soapbox orators. It is true, riots and demonstrations were multiplying. And these conditions had a marked effect upon the second elections, campaigns for which were just starting. In this contest, Pierre Leroux, Caussidière, and other Radicals were working in Paris when, in the provinces, suddenly and almost without warning, the names of Molé, General Charngarnier, and Thiers appeared on the lists of the more conservative candidates.

The return of Thiers was not entirely unexpected. The shock of the February Days had worn off, and for a month or more a number of his former associates had joined in the instances of Madame Dosne that he propose himself for election. When, finally, Dr. Veron offered him the support of the *Constitutionnel,* Monsieur consented. On June 9, he was elected from the Departments of the Seine Inférieure, the Orme, and Mayenne. He decided to sit for the Seine Inférieure. On the same list of successful candidates were the names of General Charngarnier, Victor Hugo, Pierre Leroux, Caussidière, and Louis Bonaparte.

In general, the June elections alarmed the Government. They meant too slight a gain for the Republicans, and too great a gain for their enemies—both Socialist and Monarchist. As a matter of fact, from June, 1848, it became clear to more than one foreign observer that the future of France lay in the choice of one of these two. As if to hasten the approach of the inevitable conflict, financial matters became more difficult: Government taxes to bolster up the supplementary funds caused repeated strikes of workers and riots of the unemployed. Industry was rapidly becoming paralysed.

Strengthened by the elections and alarmed by the general unrest about them, Conservatives became more insistent in their demands for the closing of the National

Workshops which they regarded as the root of all the evils in France. Finally, a Commission was appointed to investigate the question and, on June 21, the Government yielded to its recommendation that all workers between the ages of eighteen and twenty be enrolled in the army, and that preparations be made to send them into the provinces. When these proposals became known, the workers organized for resistance. In the meeting place of the Deputies anxious groups gathered to discuss ways and means for protection and defense of the Government and Constituent Assembly. Bourgeois delegations were sent to Paris from the provinces, and urged on by these provincial envoys the Conservative Deputies finally called Cavaignac, staunch Republican and excellent soldier, to assume the charge of defending the Executive and the Assembly. Thiers, haunted, perhaps, by the memories of February, urged that the army, the Government, and the Assembly be removed from Paris. Fortunately the advice of cooler heads prevailed; and Cavaignac, ably seconded by Bedeau and La Moricière, fought stubbornly through the June Days.

On June 26, the insurrection of the Paris workmen was finally crushed. Out of the riot, Paris emerged safe and calm; the Socialist danger was over for a time at least. From the June Days came Cavaignac, able and loyal servant of France, with a continuation of his dictatorial powers granted him by a grateful Assembly. Out of the mêlée, too, came others, not yet into power but into political comradeship. The insurrection of June removed the last barriers that divided the Conservatives of France. It reunited the men of the Monarchy.

Shortly after this crisis, an odd pair were received into the fellowship of the *Club de la rue de Poitiers*. They were none other than Thiers and Duvergier de Hauranne, monitor of the old days and former whipper-in of the Reform Party of 1846.

"La cause de l'ordre et de la vraie République triomphe."

With these words Cavaignac had announced that the end of the June uprising was in sight and that the Assembly could now begin the task for which it had been convened. So it was that under auspices by no means democratic, a dictatorship and a powerful Monarchist party, the Assembly set about to create the permanent machinery for a Republic.

Cavaignac was sincere in his Republican faith and did his utmost to protect it in the debates that followed the presentation of the proposed Constitution. His temporary allies, the Monarchists, however, had other designs. They purposed to make the Constitution as much of a plank back to Monarchy as circumstances would allow. But there was a third force that was beginning, at this time, to exert a far more subtle and less definable impression upon the document as it was taking shape. This party is known by the name of Bonapartism, and its leader was one of the strangest and most enigmatical figures in French history.

Once, in February, Louis Napoleon, son of Louis and Hortense, had been driven from the country. Again, in the spring of 1848, he had declined a seat to which he had been elected. Now, in September of that same year, he returned to Paris, accepted a second election, and took his seat in the Assembly. Once seated, for seven whole weeks he watched Monsieur Thiers, the *Club de la rue de Poitiers,* and other conservatively-minded Frenchmen preparing the way for himself without, at first, realizing exactly what they were doing.

The right of Louis Napoleon to take his seat in the Constituent Assembly had been conceded with extreme reluctance by the members of that body. He entered into their midst, a mysterious and, at first, silent figure. He appeared to have no definite force behind him except the evil fascination of the name Bonaparte, a vague and unsubstantiated reputation for Socialistic tendency because of certain pamphlets that he had written, and the allegiance of the touchy editor of *La Presse,* Émile de Girardin, who offered the support of his paper in revenge for slights and charges that Republicans and Monarchists had heaped upon him. The only remarkable act of this nephew of Napoleon *aux grands moustaches* had been to establish for himself a residence on the Place Vendôme where he could gaze upon the statue of the great Napoleon. But although, on his part, there was a complete absence of show, Louis Napoleon had made his entrance into the Assembly at an important time, at the very moment, in fact, when the nature of the Presidency had been introduced for discussion by the Committee on the Constitution.

As it finally evolved, the Republican Charter of 1848 paved the way for the coming of the Second Empire. It was nothing more than an odd compilation of every similar document that the French had produced. It abounded in pious political aphorisms and it gave good advice to the world at large. It defined the structure of the future government of France along moderate lines but, at the same time, it offered a sop to the Radicals by incorporating into its social doctrines the least important theories of Louis Blanc and his coterie, minus, of course, the National Workshops. As a reflection of French political opinion in 1848, it is perfect. It is a true witness to that inherent confusion of doctrines, lack of cohesion, and unwise and ignorant statement that was so typical of the French salons of the middle nineteenth century.

The Charter consecrated definitely one revolutionary principle by providing that the Assembly, elected for a term of three years, should be chosen by universal suffrage. By the same method, the President was to be named. The Chief Executive might appoint his own Ministers who were to be responsible to him and not to the

Legislative, but he could not suspend or dissolve that body. Assemblymen might be re-elected, but the President could not succeed himself nor could he be succeeded by any of his kin. Finally, in order to give the new system a chance to get under way, it was decreed that, during the first two years of the coming Assembly, the Charter should not be altered.

This constitution has been called by Frenchmen "the unworkable Charter of 1848." As a matter of fact, it was not so much the document itself as the nature of the Revolution of 1848 and the state of mind of the political parties that led to the deadlock which, in 1851, gave Louis Napoleon his cue for a coup d'état.

At the moment that the Charter was being discussed by the Chamber, however, few of its creators had Louis Napoleon in mind. The *Club de la rue de Poitiers* acknowledged frankly that the Constitution was a poor thing but were consoled by the fact that it did not exclude the possibility of a monarchical revival. Monsieur Thiers called it an honest but unsuccessful attempt to avoid anarchy or despotism: it was not his idea of a Golden Mean: with his partisans he had laboured hard for that but had not entirely succeeded. On July 21 he had been appointed to examine the work of Marrast's Constitutional Committee. He had consulted here and there, seeking, even, the advice of Lord Normanby, British Minister to France. From his palace at Laeken, Leopold, King of the Belgians, had encouraged him, believing, perhaps, that his exiled relatives might find in Thiers the instrument for their return to France. Leopold had written him; "The eyes of Europe are upon you." It is true, Thiers was the man in France best known to the foreign powers. This fact was undoubtedly why the *Club de la rue de Poitiers* allowed him to make for it the first public utterance defining the attitude of its members to the Republic and to the Constitution that was then in the making.

The occasion for this speech, one of the most notable and adroit that he ever delivered, came on September 13. There were many who expected this return to the political arena to be a spectacular one; they were not disappointed. As he stood there facing his audience, there were before him many new and unknown faces, but Monsieur Thiers was not new to them. In fact, he was so familiar that he was hateful to many of them. In the minds of the newer generation he represented Middle Class Rule, Industrialism Triumphant, and Capitalism without Mercy. At least, that is how their papers describe him. His neat, dapper clothes, his small, round, well-fed body, his large glasses through which shrewd little eyes peered out, and, above all else, that confident little smile of his, annoyed them. No doubt, he knew what was in the minds of his hearers of the Radical Opposition: very likely that whetted his desire for the conflict. He was again in his beloved tribune. His shrill voice carried him just as far as in the old days; the cannon of February had not been able to silence that! His own dreadful fear was gone; Cavaignac, with his supreme powers, was near him. His confidence in himself thus re-established, he warmed to his theme.

His colleagues, Monsieur Thiers asserted, had not desired the Republic but they had accepted it, and they would not conspire against it. This statement was greeted with laughter and calls. And so, he altered his tone; the eyes were no longer kindly: there was a glint of steel in them. But, he resumed, to his colleagues "Republic" did not mean the vain theories of Proudhon nor yet Communism which would only create "a society enslaved and indolent." As for National Workshops, "the Right to Work is a marvellous invention that proposes to give forty sous a day to every labourer who is out of a job." But this, Thiers asserted, was not Liberty as it was understood by the *rue de Poitiers*. Their ideal was Liberty so guarded from the control of courts and street rabble that it could truly assure the success and happiness of each individual.

In the delivery of this important declaration there had not been the slightest attempt to imitate the poetic flights of Lamartine. There was no toleration for Humanitarians and their Romantic followers. Cold, hard logic, a dash of satire, and above all else that strangely irritating and fascinating presence with its compelling intensity of argument, won the day. This discourse of September 13 was believed by contemporaries to have turned the tide in the Constituent Assembly against Socialistic measures and to have led the Assemblymen to insert into the Charter of 1848 only meaningless phrases concerning social and economic reforms. It was shortly after this triumph that Thiers, at the request of General Cavaignac, published a lengthy pamphlet entitled *De la Propriété* against Socialism.

When the Radical element had been safely eliminated from the Constitutional problem, the nature of the Presidency became the burning question of the day. Immediately to this theoretical problem there was joined the more material one of the Presidential candidates. It became impossible to propose a theory without a definite candidate attached to it. Where before Cavaignac and his Republicans had been in accord with the *rue de Poitiers* over the question of Socialism, on this most important matter of all the two parties broke away. Had Republicans had their way, and succeeded in confining the power of election of the Executive to the Constituent Assembly as chosen in 1848, the General would have been named President. But, by the month of October, 1848, France, as a whole, was not as Republican-minded as it had been in June. The increasing influence of the *rue de Poitiers* dimmed the brightness of Cavaignac's chances, and the final decision to confide the election to the nation at large made his success doubtful.

This decision, furthermore, resulting as it did from the rivalries of Republicans and Monarchists, served, indirectly, the cause of the Bonapartists. It presented Louis Napoleon with the occasion to propose himself to the people of France. At first, neither Cavaignac's party nor the Monarchists were far-sighted enough to appreciate the danger. Instead, each section of the Assembly set about preparing its own campaign and paid no heed to Louis Napoleon who, with the aid of an Englishwoman's money, began to give lavish dinners at the Hôtel du Rhin.

By October, 1848, Paris was seething with intrigues. On October 22, Monsieur de Lasteyrie called at the Place Saint Georges. He came on a mission from Monsieur Montalivet, the trusted minister of Louis Philippe now in exile at Claremont. Lasteyrie proposed that Thiers' Moderates bring forward Monsieur Molé as a candidate for election as Chief Executive. But Thiers, piqued, perhaps, by the omission of his own name, opined that France "*n'accepterait pas ces vieux portraits de famille.*" Then Charngarnier, through his Legitimist supporters, made overtures to Monsieur Thiers. First the tricolour of Orléans and then the white flag of the Bourbons climbed the hill to the Place Saint Georges. This was too much for the loyal mother-in-law. The proposal of Cavaignac by the Republicans she accepted as a foregone conclusion, but why not, she argued, the candidacy of her son-in-law as well?

It appears that the wishes of Madame Dosne found some response among a few of the Monarchists. Molé was doubtful of his own success and suggested the name of Thiers. For a few days, at least, the object of these manœuvres took his own candidacy seriously. But by November he, like Molé, had abandoned hope and he made a semi-official statement to that effect when he announced to Monsieur de Falloux: "I thought for a time of the Presidency. But I must renounce it. Perhaps we had best allow Louis Napoleon to be elected, or, even, elect him without ourselves assuming his livery. If I failed, it would be a serious check to the party of order. If I succeeded, I should have to marry the Republic, *et, en verité, je suis trop honnête garçon pour épouser une si mauvaise fille.*"

This decision left only three real rivals in the running; Ledru-Rollin for the Socialists, whose influence was waning, Cavaignac for the Republicans, and Louis Napoleon, provided he could find a party. Thiers' renunciation, however, did not remove him and his family from being drawn into the web of plot and counter-plot that was being woven in Paris. On the contrary, the Place Saint Georges became the field where the knights of Cavaignac and the more muddy vassals of Louis Napoleon vied for the favour of Monsieur Thiers and the *Club de la rue de Poitiers*.

The Republicans, Legitimists, and Orléanists had not been the first to storm the Château of Madame Dosne. In her journal, under date of November, Madame records the visit of a Monsieur de Chabrier whose family had obtained a patent of nobility during the First Empire. The Bonapartists knew their quarry, and had sent their envoy to Monsieur Thiers well armed with arguments and an inducement. The inducement was the promise of a ministerial portfolio, or the Vice-Presidency, in return for Thiers' support of Louis Napoleon. This was a tempting offer, but there was a flaw in it. Thiers would not be a mere concert-master. If the Napoleonic Symphony was to be played, he desired to direct the performance. And, again, Monsieur T. was not sure that he wanted that number on the programme. His verbal response, which could not have been composed on the spur of the moment, was ambiguous and suggestive: "If Louis Napoleon becomes the head of the Republic, I shall not be his Minister. But, if the resolutions of his Cabinet are wise and honourable, I shall gladly support his Ministers, just as I would do in the case of any power that can assure order, security, and loyal government."

Chabrier talked to Jerome and to Louis Bonaparte. Shortly afterwards, it was Monsieur Thiers who found them their man. It was none other than Odilon Barrot, his colleague of a day in February. Barrot agreed to organize for Louis Napoleon his government if he was elected or, as a wag put it, Barrot was to be guest-conductor and Thiers was to direct from the wings. By this time, it was within a fortnight of the Election Day, and it began to appear that the cause of Bonaparte had won over certain of the statesmen and politicians of the former Monarchy.

So much, however, could not have been accomplished without the consultation of Thiers' colleagues. As time wore on, Count Molé who was, undoubtedly, the most respected member of the *rue de Poitiers,* was becoming mildly favourable to Bonapartism. He saw that, in the provinces, the cult of Louis Napoleon was making headway. The small shopkeepers and industrialists feared even Cavaignac's Republicanism and regarded it as the Jacobinism of 1793. They favoured a Conservative Government but they feared an Orléanist, and how could an Orléanist Prince be brought so soon to France? To Molé's mind, Louis Napoleon seemed more and more the man to fill the gap for the moment. But Thiers still distrusted the Prince's vague utterances and appeared unable to forget that he had once written a Socialist work entitled *L'Extinction du Pauperisme*. Finally it was decided that Molé and Thiers should attempt to sound out both Cavaignac and Louis Napoleon. Then the *Club de la rue de Poitiers* would know what to do.

The honest old General left no doubt in their minds; he was a loyal servant of the Republic and he would not consent to any of the compromises desired by the Monarchists. To the apparent despair of Monsieur Thiers, they now turned to Louis Bonaparte.

At the moment when this move was made, that Prince was hard at work on his political Manifesto. Thiers requested Chabrier to let him see it. The request was granted, and after perusing it, Monsieur Thiers reported to Molé that Monsieur Bonaparte could not write, that what he had written was very disturbing, and that his French was execrable. Also, the text revealed the alarming fact that Louis Napoleon was not as much of a Moderate as they supposed him to be. But, some of them argued, could not this man be more easily controlled than Cavaignac? Finally, Monsieur Thiers suggested that the Prince try to write a better message. Frantic discussions followed, and poor Monsieur de Chabrier was kept running between the Place Vendôme and the Place Saint Georges with little scraps of paper in his pocket. Finally, on November 16, Thiers met the man of mystery himself. Louis Napoleon read a new version of his message to his visitor, who promptly opined that it was *mal fagoté* and persuaded the Prince to consent to having his proclamation written by Monsieur Merruau. As a matter of fact, the document was composed under the direct supervision of Monsieur Thiers while Monsieur Bonaparte is reported to have shuddered when the version that emanated from the Place Saint Georges was read to him. After a few exhibitions of temper, the Prince reluctantly consented to eliminate such annoying expressions as *République généreuse* that appeared to the Conservatives to promise too much to the Radicals. Then it was that half in joy and half in fear, the *rue de Poitiers* gave its official support to this scion of the House of Bonaparte.

On December 11, France was informed that Louis Napoleon had been elected by an overwhelming majority. Several days later Monsieur Thiers was telling the

President-elect what clothes he should wear on the Inauguration Day. He advised him to wear a *costume civil* and to cut his long moustaches; Louis Napoleon donned the frock-coat but continued to allow his moustaches to grow.

CHAPTER XI

TELEMACHUS SENDS MENTOR INTO EXILE

LOUIS NAPOLEON had received the Presidency on the basis of a bargain. The wise and crafty statesmen of the former Monarchy had voted for him only on the understanding that his Ministry would represent their party with all of its various shades of political opinion, Orléanist, Legitimist, and Catholic. It had been one of their number, Monsieur Thiers, who had presented him with the head of his Council, Odilon Barrot, and had virtually manufactured the rest of the Cabinet for him. Monsieur Thiers had been generous with his advice as well, and had talked to his reluctant protégé as a schoolmaster to his pupil:

"Beware, above all else, of an indefinite policy, and do not hesitate to rely upon the party that has given you the election. My natural sympathies are for the House of Orléans, but if, by a good administration, you establish order in France, if you govern as I think you should, without weakness, since that which is closest to my heart is the happiness, repose, and glory of my country, you will find me devoted to your cause and willing to put aside the dictates of my own affections for the greater interests of France at large."

And to such a pious homily the poor pupil would reply disconsolately: "I do not want to be a party man."

But where else could the President find support? Neither the discomfited adherents of the defeated Cavaignac nor the Socialists to whom he had already made occasional overtures would trust him. Even, as yet, his small group of Bonapartists could not be called to power: they were too heterogeneous and their origin was too questionable and obscure. Morny was the natural son of Queen Hortense, Fould was the brother of Louis Napoleon's Jewish banker, and Rouher, soon to be called to power, was still under the tutelage of Guizot. "It was, indeed, unfortunate for me that I could not begin with a Republican Ministry," the Prince-President later remarked, "and that I was obliged to give myself over to the men of the *rue de Poitiers*."

Tied to the apron strings of the wise old nurses of a previous régime, what could he do? Monitor Thiers regarded his Telemachus with a fishy eye and remarked: "This prince is a numb-skull. I fear, indeed, that we have only arrived at the pilot-ship, we are not yet in port." Meanwhile, his pupil tugged at the ropes that bound him. Some day, perhaps, he would be free of them. Homilies and catechisms when delivered in such incessant doses will cause the most submissive child to revolt, and this particular child had already shown that he could be an *enfant terrible*. In short, nearly everything in the political entourage of Louis Napoleon tended to limit him and to keep him from the power which he was so eager to grasp.

If, however, there was a lack of harmony between the President, his supporters, and his Cabinet, there was also a serious rift between the Government and the Constituent Assembly. In that body, Cavaignac's defeat had aroused the Republicans, and Editor Marrast, the President of the *Constituante*, soon became a "serious and most pressing difficulty" for the Government. Jealous of the exclusive sway that the *rue de Poitiers* seemed to exercise over the President, both Moderate Republican and Radical decided to prolong the life of the Assembly and not run the risk of an election period. In reality, the tasks for which the *Constituante* had been called were completed, but a trumped-up need for organic laws and electoral regulations served as their excuse to remain in power and to block every move of the Government forces. Finally, on January 29, the President, backed by the *rue de Poitiers* and the Ministry, ordered General Charngarnier, Commandant of Paris, to mass the Army of Paris and the National Guard around the Chamber, and to force Marrast and his fellow diehards to promise a vote of dissolution for the Constituent Assembly, all reason for whose continued existence was now passed. This move, speedily and efficiently carried out, was successful, and the President made the most of the affair by an impromptu progress through the Boulevards where he was wildly acclaimed by thousands.

The *affaire* of January 29 was the first experiment of Louis Napoleon with a military *coup d'état* in Paris. It should be remembered that it had been approved and supported by Monsieur Thiers and his allies of the *rue de Poitiers*. Less than two years later, the Prince-President would employ the same measures against them.

Apparently the success of this *coup d'état* gave the President the courage to assert his own wishes in other ways. From that time on, Louis Napoleon began to show his teeth. He protested against the practice of the Cabinet of holding secret meetings at Barrot's home, far from his own eyes, and he forced that body to show him all their papers and documents. At the same time, he took umbrage more and more at the proprietary remarks and airs that Monsieur Thiers was giving himself. He wished to be free of Cabinet and Mentor, but he could not rid himself of both of them at once, and so he decided to begin with his Ministry that he detested.

Above all else, the President desired to know what was going on and to direct the foreign policy of the Republic. It was here that Barrot, for very good reasons, was weakest. When Republicans in the Assembly howled down the plan to give more assistance to a Pope in exile at Gaëta and proposed, instead, that French arms support the newly established Roman Republic and Charles Albert of Sardinia against Austria, Barrot was inclined to yield to them. But the *rue de Poitiers* with its Catholic members, Falloux, Montalembert, and Monseigneur Dupanloup, supported the idea of the restoration of Temporal Power at Rome. When this deadlock occurred and paralysed Barrot for further effort, it was Louis Napoleon who took matters in hand. Adroitly, the President persuaded Baron Hübner, Austrian Ambassador, to urge his Imperial master to renounce the plan of invading Charles Albert's domains. This appeased the Republicans, while the Catholics were quieted temporarily by the ambiguous statement that the French expedition to Civita Vecchia would restore the Papacy. Louis Napoleon was careful to add, however, that the object of the expedition was to protect Rome from the Austrian menace, to safeguard French influence in Italy, and to insure the liberty of the people.

When he made such vague but well-meaning pronouncements the President had a very definite object in mind. He desired to embarrass his Cabinet with the majority in the Assembly and thus to assure himself of the support of that majority in the forthcoming Legislative Body that was soon to convene. At the same time he wished, by his statements, to impress France with the fact that he was, at heart, a Liberal. Whether he realized it or not, by April, 1849, Louis Napoleon had inaugurated that policy of playing between Conservative and Liberal, a game that would bring him inevitably to the point where, caught between the two, he would declare to the nation that the Constitution was unworkable and that the rivalries of parties made it impossible for him to remedy matters except by another *coup d'état.*

For the time being, however, the Prince-President was strengthened in his relations with the Conservatives, his Cabinet was losing the confidence of parts of the nation that it had enjoyed, while the personal popularity of the Chief Executive was considerably increased. Madame Dosne relates that, during a drive through Paris, the President was "greeted by confusion of cries: *'Vive l'amnestie! à bas les Ministres! Vive le Président! Vive l'Empereur!'* "

Strengthened by the increasing popularity of the man whom they insisted on calling *their* President, and united by a pact in which the various cliques of the *rue de Poitiers* had renounced their differences and had, thereby, even added to their number a few of Louis Bonaparte's personal adherents, the Conservatives swept the new Legislative Assembly that opened on May 28, 1849. The "Dictatorship of the *rue de Poitiers*" seemed to be supreme. The protests and interpellations of Ledru-Rollin and his group of Republicans were not able to prevent the passage of laws that were far different from the dreams of Louis Napoleon when he had spoken of hoping to found in France a "generous" Republic. Press Laws and regulations against Radical Clubs were passed. Finally, to fulfil completely his engagements to the Conservatives, the President allowed Monsieur de Falloux, Minister of Public Instruction, to present a proposal that would allow the Church to participate in public education. A commission was named to examine this proposal. Among its members was Monsieur Thiers. Falloux relates that, at that time, no one displayed a greater ardour for the Catholic cause. No doubt Thiers saw in it a possible check to the Radical danger that had so recently threatened France and that he, with his usual clear vision, had divined was not yet entirely over. Perhaps, said he, if France and Louis Napoleon are bound up with the Catholic cause, there will be less danger from this idea of a "generous" Republic. In fact, in 1849, Monsieur Thiers was grasping at any policy that would limit the course of the Revolution. Consequently, he found himself drawing nearer and nearer to the interests of the Church, and when the French expedition to Italy began to arouse dissensions in the Assembly, Thiers, again, displayed himself as an ardent Catholic.

The Barrot Cabinet was persisting in its attempts to "liberalize" the purpose of the French Army that was now in Italy. At the same time, the Catholics and Monsieur Thiers continued in their determination to ruin the Roman Republic and thus to save the Pope. On June 12, the Republicans under Ledru-Rollin made an effort to force the Government to show its real intentions by filing a demand for the impeachment of the Prince-President and the Ministry. They charged that the Executive and his Cabinet had violated the Constitution by interfering in the Roman affair. Ledru-Rollin even appealed to Paris to rise. Sizable crowds appeared on the Boulevards, but the attempt failed due to the prompt action of the Government. The June rising, however, was not without benefit to Louis Napoleon; it enabled him to appear again before the country as its saviour and the preserver of order. Nevertheless, when the summer elections had been held, it was found that the supporters of a more liberal régime had made gains, while the *rue de Poitiers* had obtained a very small majority.

These developments gave Louis Napoleon food for thought. He desired to remain in accord with the Catholics and their fellow-Conservatives, but he was determined to appear to the country as a Liberal. And now, by the recent elections, the character of the Assembly was somewhat transformed and it was not quite so necessary for him to play up to the *rue de Poitiers*. This situation undoubtedly led the President to alter his attitude to the Pope. He summoned his Cabinet and read to its members a letter that he proposed to send to Edouard Ney. It contained a statement that Ney was to make to Pius IX, calling upon him, in virtue of the fact that the French Republic had restored him, to secularize his administration, to adopt the Code Napoleon, to create a "representative constitution," and to grant a general amnesty to political offenders. The Assembly was *en vacances*, but Monsieur Thiers happened to be passing through Paris. The President, therefore, summoned his Mentor to dinner and a conference. Mentor accepted the conference but declined the dinner because he knew that he would have some unpleasant things to say. He called his pupil's policy inconsistent (as it certainly was), and referred to the political offenders for whom Louis Napoleon was demanding an amnesty as "ruffians who would become the terror of Italy." He accused the President of coquetting with the "Montagnards," as he called the Republicans. But the letter to Ney went through, and its recipient published it in Florence. The Catholics protested that the President of France had dared to dictate to the Roman Pontiff. For another reason, Monsieur Thiers defended before the Assembly the dignity of the Pope and persuaded that body to accept the Pope's promise and to approve the presence of the French expedition as being in the service of the Pope and without any conditions attached thereto. This vote of the Assembly was a virtual repudiation of both the policy of the President and of Barrot. Resulting from this and other discussions, Barrot and his colleagues resigned their posts on October 31.

The retirement of the Ministry had been foreseen by the *rue de Poitiers*. Early in the summer, Thiers had remarked: "A little later Molé and I will be asked to form a Cabinet." And now, it appeared, the time had come; in fact, Thiers believed that the situation was desperate and that now, if ever, was there a real necessity for a strong Ministry chosen from the Right. The President had given evidence of too great a desire for independence, and the Liberal representation in the *Corps Legislatif* had increased.

On the day following the resignation of Barrot, the two leaders of the *rue de Poitiers* were summoned to the Tuileries. According to their own accounts, they found a much worried President. While the interview with him did not result in the formation of a Ministry of the Right, it had certain important consequences. The Conservatives promised again to support Louis Napoleon provided he would aid them in the passing of "certain wise and necessary measures." The first was the Falloux Law concerning Public Education, and the other was a proposal to stem the rising tide of Liberalism by the abolition of universal suffrage.

In the words of Alexis de Tocqueville, Monsieur Thiers and Monsieur Molé "made up their minds to remain the masters of the Government without becoming its Ministers. . . . They were eager enough for power, but not for responsibility." Perhaps that is why the Cabinet that supplanted Barrot's Ministry had no official head. The President himself presided over its deliberations. It was composed of his friends. By a strange irony of fate, the leaders of the *rue de Poitiers* had consented to an extra-parliamentary Ministry—a practice against which at least one of them had been fighting ever since 1824.

The mild acceptance of such a ministerial combination was an abrupt change of front on the part of Thiers. And, in fact, the whole attitude of Monsieur Thiers was changing. By October, 1849, he perceived that France might not reach the harbour of safety under Louis Napoleon, and he began to realize that he himself would not be able to control his *enfant terrible* much longer. More and more he displayed his distrust of the existing state of affairs. Even his spectacular success in carrying the Falloux Law through the Legislative Body failed to comfort him. He appeared to be disgusted with his surroundings. An acquaintance relates that he found him sorely changed and describes him as "more ill-bred and devoid of tact." He adds: "I do not know if the Republican régime has increased these defects, but his language and coarse expressions are intolerable."

In truth, Monsieur Thiers and his immediate associates were becoming impatient of waiting for their opportunity to give France what they regarded as a good government. They were now fearful that Louis Napoleon would end by serving, consciously or unconsciously, as a plank to Radicalism or Empire, and not to Monarchy under the chastened House of Orléans. From now on, they voted for the Government when it proposed measures that coincided with their ultimate purpose. They were no longer the party upon whose support the President could count. Above all else, they were determined to save themselves and the system of order for which they stood, even if it be at the cost of abandoning the man whom they had rather reluctantly elevated to the Presidency. Their greatest concern was to check Radicalism and disorder which, they asserted, was so prevalent in the provinces. It is not unlikely, indeed, that they purposely exaggerated the condition of affairs outside of Paris. If the President would not help them, they would pursue their designs without him, and check him and the Radicals whom he had always tended to favour. And the means for this limiting of his power they had already prepared in a proposal to revise the unworkable Constitution.

For some time past, the majority of the Right had been in the habit of meeting, between sessions of the *Corps Legislatif,* in the Salle du Conseil d'État to deliberate together. They had formed an inner council of twelve to direct their discussions. This presiding group became known as "the Burgraves" after the then popular play of Victor Hugo in which the old *sermoneurs* play an important part. The Burgraves included Berryer, de Broglie, Thiers, Montalembert, Molé, and Léon Faucher. It was about the middle of February, 1850, that the question of the necessity for a revision of the Constitution was first mentioned in their midst. It was Monsieur Thiers who first presented it and exposed the actual situation with his usual lucidity. The revision, he asserted, would mean that they must face the possibility of the return of the Monarchy in the near future. But before that could be accomplished, there was another matter that must be settled. He was himself, he declared, a Monarchist, but until the rivalries of the House of Charles X and that of Louis Philippe had been settled, the possibility of a restoration remained remote. Furthermore, he expressed the fear that the existence of the Bourbon Legitimists and their continued assertion of their superior claims would always be an obstacle to those who desired the return of the Orléans family for, to the Radicals, Monarchy would always mean Bourbon Monarchy. But, he announced, he had in his pocket a suggestion for their consideration; he suggested not a revision of the Constitution but the reduction of the electorate. Such a measure, he argued, it was within the rights of their party to propose, and it would have the advantage of eliminating a great number of voters from the very classes whose power and tendencies they feared.

After several days of discussion, the Burgraves accepted Thiers' plan: Léon Faucher carried the matter to Baroches, Minister of Justice, and, after a consultation with the President, the request of the Burgraves was approved by the Government. On May 8, an extra-parliamentary commission was appointed to work out a plan for the abolition of universal suffrage and, ten days later, Léon Faucher presented to the *Corps Legislatif* a proposition that was virtually the one that Monsieur Thiers had submitted to the Burgraves, and to its author fell the honour of forcing the bill through the Legislative. He concluded his address with glowing words of admiration for Louis Napoleon whom he apostrophized as "the great man who had discovered how to keep *la multitude, la vile multitude,* in order!"

In such wise, three million electors were deprived of their rights in order to preserve the power of the Conservatives. As if to make a show of their recently gained security, the last days of the *Legislatif* before the summer recess were spent in passing a series of laws that set limitations on electoral campaigning and that provided machinery for weeding out Republicans from petty local government offices.

After the struggle for the Electoral Law of June, 1850, was over, Monsieur Thiers wrote to a friend: "Behold us in the midst of a régime without name, without future. I am fighting in the camp of good sense." His fight now took a decidedly definite turn. The latter part of June found him in England. Messieurs Molé, Thiers, and Victor Broglie had come on a pilgrimage to the bedside of Louis Philippe while Messieurs Berryer and Saint Priest took the train to Wiesbaden and visited Charles X. It looked as if the leaders of the *rue de Poitiers* once they had abolished universal suffrage, had turned their backs on the Prince-President.

The Orléanist delegation found their former master on his deathbed. Thiers relates, with genuine emotion, the few brief conversations that the old King and his former Minister had together. They parted with affection and real sorrow. There were, however, other conversations that Monsieur Thiers had during this brief sojourn at Claremont. He talked with ex-Queen Marie Amélie and with the widowed Duchesse d'Orléans, mother of Louis Philippe's heir. To them he exposed the deplorable condition of France. He must have said more for, after the death of Louis Philippe, the Prince de Joinville wrote him: "If you ever come to feel that you need us, we are ready. You have only to say the word."

Following the visit to the royal exiles at Claremont, Thiers went to Baden to join his family, to rest, and, very likely, to meditate on the relationship that he had just renewed. He confessed to Mignet, his most trusted friend, that the sight of the old King had revived all the former affection that he had had for the House of Orléans. In reply to this confession, Mignet wrote: "Now the time has come to save the last hope of representative Monarchy. It lies in the family of the dead King. The Bourbons of the July Revolution must never unite with the Bourbons of Legitimacy."

There was the difficulty for the Monarchists of 1850. In fact, the Count of Chambord, heir to the claims of the House of Bourbon, had just pronounced that a fusion of the two parties with the men who led them was impossible. Lost for a time in these perplexing meditations, Monsieur Thiers and his colleagues were suddenly rudely interrupted by the startling performances of Monsieur Bonaparte.

While the two monarchical factions of the *rue de Poitiers* had been spending their vacation in sounding out their princely favourites, the Prince-President had been making a progress through France and feeling the pulse of the nation. The practice of a Chief Executive embarking on a stump-speaking tour for himself was a new departure in French political procedure. At first this extraordinary *tour de France* was not an agreeable experience for the man who was making it. At Lyons, in Burgundy, and in Alsace, Louis Napoleon met with hostile cries that were obviously occasioned by the revision of the suffrage and by the repressions of Republican activities by the *Corps Legislatif*. These unpleasant occurrences were not without their effect upon the President, and when the month of August was half over Louis Napoleon had experienced a change of heart. He had consulted with Préfets and sous-Préfets, and these gentlemen had said things that had impressed him. They had told him that he was now strong enough to stand alone provided he stood on a more liberal platform. Some were even urging him to demand of the Assembly a prolongation of his powers. To this end they promised an impressive number of petitions. Practically all of them told him that, if he wished to be re-elected, a revision of the Constitution was absolutely necessary.

The traditional and, apparently, immutable hatred of the provinces for Paris was apparently working to the advantage of the President if only he would separate himself from the group that had tried to control him in the Capital. As well, the talk of the Republicans was working to the disadvantage of Monsieur Thiers and his coterie, and the provincial was coming to regard that political coterie as absolute Monarchists who desired to establish a dictatorship from Paris. By the end of August, Louis Napoleon had reached Normandy where he himself began pleading for a revision of "the fatal Charter of 1848."

Upon his return to the Capital, therefore, the President was in a new frame of mind. And what he found in Paris did not please him. General Charngarnier, loyal Orléanist and Commandant of the city, had organized at the Tuileries a public requiem for Louis Philippe. Undoubtedly Louis Napoleon wished the former King a peaceful rest, but he desired far more that eternal peace should descend upon the activities of the House of Orléans and its partisans. When the *Corps Legislatif* reconvened, it found a changed President with a determination, a purpose, and a method that were new to them. Monsieur

Thiers and the *rue de Poitiers* perceived that a crisis was imminent and realized that it might be Louis Napoleon, and not themselves, who would precipitate it. This eventuality, they felt, must be prevented at all costs. The question was: where to seek safety? It was Monsieur Thiers who persuaded them that in Charngarnier, in his popularity, and in his power—for he had the Army of Paris behind him—lay their salvation.

At first, it was proposed to elect Charngarnier President of the *Legislatif*. But Thiers advised against this plan when he learned that the Government would view the General's election in the light of an act of war against the President. Monsieur Thiers did not wish to provide the *casus belli* himself.

On January 2, 1851, Charngarnier precipitated matters when he ordered his troops to pay no heed to civilian authorities. A week later, Louis Napoleon demanded the General's resignation.

This act of the President's provoked an angry session in the *Legislatif*. Baroche defended the action while Thiers attacked it. His friends relate that it was a scene never to be forgotten. Monsieur Thiers kept wiping his forehead with a small, fine pocket handkerchief. He was exciting, holding, and enchanting an Assembly by calling up before them the dangerous precedent established by Charngarnier's dismissal. Their own divided condition, he informed them, was a temptation to the *Élysée*. By this time, the *Legislatif* hung suspended on his lips, and then it was that the orator made his famous pronouncement, a pronouncement that was all too true—*"L'Empire, c'est fait."* Swept off its feet by this dreadful prophecy, the *Legislatif* voted no confidence in the Ministry.

Its successor was as unparliamentary a Cabinet as one could wish for. The President sought to explain away its unsatisfactory character by declaring that it was only a temporary affair. The truth of the matter was that, by the last of January, 1851, it would have been impossible to have formed a Cabinet that was truly representative of the Assembly for there *was* no majority. The pact that had united the *rue de Poitiers* had begun to disintegrate: Orléanists and Legitimists, reflecting the minds of their respective pretenders, were too jealous of each other to effect a fusion, and the Right could rarely summon a sufficient number of votes for any positive measures. There remained the Republicans who were stronger than in the past, and the growing party of the *Élysée* that had come to count for something since the summer tour of the President. The parliament was divided into four almost equal parts. Everything was at a deadlock: its refusal to increase the salary of the President led to his selling his horses and carriages at public auction and borrowing from the Spanish Ambassador. Monsieur Thiers was in despair when a communication reached him via Belgium from England.

On February 10 King Leopold sent off to him a letter requesting him to give the bearer, who was in the confidence of the exiled Orléanist Princes at Claremont, a statement as to the situation in France. Monsieur Thiers, as usual, asked for time for deliberation and then, a little later, dispatched by this same messenger (who was probably a valet to the Orléanist Princes and brother of Monsieur Thiers' valet) a long communication. It was addressed to the Royal Family at Claremont. At the writer's request, it was returned to him by the same channels after it had been read by the ex-Queen, the Duchesse d'Orléans, and her brothers-in-law.

This letter, which is to be found at the *Bibliothèque Nationale,* begins with a detailed account of the state of affairs since the dismissal of General Charngarnier.

This most recent development, he writes, means that the Empire is ahead of France. To prevent its accomplishment, he tells the Princes, there is only one remedy, and that is the candidature of the Prince de Joinville in the Presidential elections of 1852. Neither Monsieur Thiers nor any of his colleagues is willing to descend into the street to incite riots: they will only use legal means. And there are legal means by which Joinville might return to France; it is not impossible that the Assembly could be forced to vote his recall. Be ready, then, be patient, and await the crisis that is almost certain to come. There have already been times when both the Right and the Left have been desirous of finding a rival candidate for the election of 1852, and these times will recur. When they do, he writes, the allies of the House of Orléans may act in Joinville's favour, but on a condition; namely, that the Prince, if elected, will be President *de bonne foi* and will promise not to attempt an overthrow of the existing order for the benefit of his nephew. "Perhaps, however," adds Monsieur Thiers, badly in need of arguments, "after four years as President, Joinville will find France desirous of Monarchy. In that event, he will, of course, be released from his engagements. But if, by chance, France should still incline towards Republicanism, the Prince, at the end of his term, will have added four glorious years to the history of his House and spared France the Empire with all of its attendant evils."

This epistle and its arguments are not convincing reading today and, apparently, in 1852, they made the same impression on the members of the House of Orléans. Was it not possible that Thiers was trying to use them simply as a means to be rid of Louis Napoleon whose elevation he now regretted? On March 8, the reply of the Princes reached the Place Saint Georges. Their Royal Highnesses were grateful to him, they believed in his loyalty to their cause, but Joinville must be free from all previous engagements. "We have no faith in the Republic, and we cannot promise to assist in its establishment."

Louis Napoleon, it happened, was completely aware of Thiers' conspiracy and of the temporary setback that it had received. Obviously, he could now manœuvre with a freer hand and hobnob, for a change, with men who were more liberal.

By March, 1851, the President had been convinced that the Electoral Law of 1850, limiting the suffrage, had been a great mistake, and he had virtually promised the Republicans to have it repealed. With this promise in mind, he tried at last to appoint a definitely liberal Ministry with Barrot's brother at its head. Monsieur Thiers balked this effort. To gain time, the President named what he called a "Ministry of Reconciliation" in which Léon Faucher, Orléanist, accepted a place on the condition that the Electoral Law would stand.

The new Cabinet agreed with the President to propose a measure for pacification or temporization by prolonging his term of office. In return for this support, Louis Napoleon promised the Conservatives to secure their re-election. This arrangement was, on the part of the President, a master-stroke; it split definitely the Monarchist party. Berryer and his Legitimists favoured the extension of the President's term because they believed that any sort of revision of the hated Constitution would be more favourable to the Bourbons; Molé and Broglie inclined towards it because such a change would give Louis Napoleon ten years more and then the Comte de Paris would have attained his majority. But, the Thiers-Dufaure group had made up their minds to reject every proposal because they still believed in the possibility of recalling Joinville and of electing him. The unfavourable reply of March 8, had not put an end to communications between the Place Saint Georges and Claremont. In fact, they had become more frequent. On May 28, Monsieur Thiers again crossed the Channel. The ostensible purpose of his journey was to visit his friend Ellice and to see the London Exhibition. The trip lasted five days, two of which were taken up with conferences at Claremont.

In July, 1851, Louis Napoleon decided to take advantage of the rift in the Monarchist ranks and in the Assembly. He multiplied the number of officers in command of Paris troops; he imported his own friends, generals and staff officers from Algiers and from the provinces. By a second tour, he tried to strengthen his own influence in those sections of France where he had not been enthusiastically supported, and, upon his return, he revised his Cabinet. The situation began to look ominous. On November 4, he sent a message to the Assembly in which he virtually commanded them to undertake a revision of the hated Constitution claiming that, as matters stood, he could not fulfil the promises that he had made to France. The reply of the *Legislatif* was to suggest to the President of the Assembly that he use his constitutional right to call out troops to protect that body from Louis Napoleon. This suggestion was heartily supported by Monsieur Thiers and, in the hope of passing it, he managed to reform temporarily the Monarchist majority. But this momentary success was the actual cause for the loss of a motion that might have delayed, at least, the *coup d'état* that soon followed. The Republicans were more afraid of Thiers and his reconciled Monarchists than they were of Louis Napoleon and his party of the *Élysée.* On November 17, the motion was voted down.

From that time on, it was common belief that the Prince-President, in order to bring about a revision in favour of which he had worked up the country, would use force against the Assembly. But now that the time had come to stage his show, the President hesitated. He was, essentially, a timid and a stubborn man; he did not wish to resort to force unless he had to do so to save himself. Twice already he had withstood the urgings of his friends.

It is most likely that it was the behaviour of the Orléanist faction that finally brought the President to the point of setting into motion plans that had, probably, been prepared some time ago.

Ever since his visit to England, Monsieur Thiers had been actively working along the lines that his letter to Claremont had indicated. Funds had been collected by him, by Lasteyrie, and by Guizot, for an electoral campaign in behalf of Joinville. Thiers had corresponded steadily with Claremont and with his political sympathizers. He had even resorted to a code and to the use of pseudonyms and false addresses. By late autumn it looked as if Joinville was coming around to Thiers' view and was almost persuaded to his plan of accepting honestly the Republic and then seeing how matters stood. At that time, Duvergier de Hauranne wrote to Monsieur Thiers: "For two months there has existed a contract between the Prince de Joinville and ourselves, and this contract cannot be broken except by the consent of the two parties concerned. We would think it wrong of the Prince if, after having allowed us to use his name, he deserted us without ceremony; and he, on his side, would have good cause to complain if, after having used his name, we selected another candidate."

Evidently, Monsieur Thiers and his group had given their word; now they could support neither another Orléanist, as General Charngarnier, nor the proposal to prolong Louis Napoleon's term as President. Committed to a disastrous policy, they pursued it with their usual intensity. If they did not descend into the streets to incite riot, they did almost the same thing and organized a general conspiracy. Palmerston even believed that, during the last of November, plans for an Orléanist coup reached a definite organization and that while Messieurs Thiers, Charngarnier, and the Burgraves were making final preparations in Paris, the Prince de Joinville and the Duc d'Aumâle were on their way to France. At any rate when, a week after the famous day of December 2, Palmerston sent his dispatch to Lord Normanby, he enclosed a Memorandum which he gave as affording a reasonable explanation why Louis Napoleon brought off his coup d'état earlier than was expected.

But this extraordinary story is not necessary to explain the resolve of the Prince-President. To himself and to his party it was perfectly evident that each day delayed was a day lost for the Empire and a day gained for the cause of the Monarchists. All had been in readiness for several weeks and the mere utterance of a single word set presses working on parts of proclamations that were, in their separated state, jargon to printers, and police stations collecting from their beds those who had stood in the way of Napoleonic Destiny.

One of the most dramatic of the episodes that occurred during the early morning of December 2, was the scene that was enacted at the Place Saint Georges. No incriminating evidence was found by the police. Even today there is not a scrap of paper belonging to Thiers or to his mother-in-law that has any important references to the days immediately preceding the *coup d'état*. The *Commissaire de Police* found Monsieur Thiers sitting on the edge of his bed clad only in his night-shirt. At first, Monsieur tried oratory, but that availed nothing. Then, he resorted to threats: "Do you know that I am armed and that I should be perfectly justified if I treated you as a malefactor?" But when the *Commissaire* indicated by an ominous gesture that he, too, had a weapon, Monsieur Thiers subsided and began to put on his clothes.

The plans made by Rouher, Maupas, and Baroche worked without a hitch, and most of the Deputies who had been arrested arrived at Mazas prison about the same time. As he was descending from the calaboose, Monsieur

Thiers, Monarchist, met General Cavaignac, Republican. Cavaignac, as he passed him, remarked: "*Eh bien,* you have been crying for a strong Government. Now you have it."

On December 8, Thiers was given the choice of his place of exile. Not wishing to embarrass the family of Orléans by a retreat to England, he selected Belgium. On the same day, after writing a public protest against the treatment that he had received, he, with Rémusat, Chambolle, and Lasteyrie, crossed the frontier.

CHAPTER XII

MONSIEUR BONAPARTE AU POUVOIR; MONSIEUR THIERS *EN RETRAITE*

Many years later, after his greatest labours for France had been performed, Thiers passed in review his active life and set about to record the philosophy that his many experiences had taught him. In this *Plan d'un Ouvrage de Philosophie,* which was never completed, one finds these lines: "Young, active, enthusiastic, I made mistakes, not through wickedness of heart or falsity of mind, but through a natural impetuosity: and it was rare, indeed, when I was not quickly punished for them. That often happens in this world while we are awaiting the final justice reserved by God for all human beings who are responsible for their acts."

In December, 1851, he paid heavily for his rashness.

The exiles passed the first days of their expatriation in Belgium. The faithful Mignet came at once to join Thiers and to reassure him about the safety of his family. To his friend Monsieur announced that he would return to his studies. "This persecution shall not deprive me of my peace of mind nor of my perseverance in my ideas," he added. Leopold, King of Belgium, wrote him a kindly letter but informed him that, for diplomatic reasons, he could not receive him. The French Government, however, felt uneasy at the proximity of Thiers to the Belgian Court. Consequently, in February, 1852, Monsieur crossed the Channel.

In England his spirits revived, for there was a pleasing dislike of the *Coup d'État* in London. He was fêted as a hero by his friend Ellice; he met the young Queen under whose spell, he averred, he had fallen. There was Disraeli with whom he talked politics and literature, and there were many other statesmen and men of letters whom he entertained sumptuously at his hotel in Bond Street. Macaulay presented him with all his works and, in haste, Monsieur Thiers ordered from Gorschler all of the volumes of the *History of the Consulate and Empire* that had yet appeared. He confessed that his contact with the brilliant, metallic historian had aroused in himself the desire to complete his own *History*. One night while at dinner at the house of Baron de Rothschild, Disraeli tendered his good offices to obtain the cancellation of the decree against him, but Monsieur Thiers thanked him and said that he would not accept a recall unless all of his friends were allowed to return at the same time.

His talk against Louis Napoleon was bitter and imprudent. Walewski, Ambassador of France to the Court of St. James, who was already seriously alarmed by the coldness of England to the new régime, wrote that it was absurd to allow Thiers to remain in London. "Here he is doing us a great deal of harm, but, in Paris, he would be under the hand of the Government." A few days later, the Ambassador even offered to intercede for him, but Thiers declined his overtures. To William Nassau Senior, who was continually plying him with questions, he declared: "Constitutional Monarchy is the form that suits us best. We are unfit for a Republic; we cannot breathe under a Despotism. What we need is a King who will fill the place and leave us to manage our own affairs." What is this but the old Orléanist programme? If, in the same breath, he denied to Senior that he was a partisan of the House of Orléans, it was simply a part of his policy not to embarrass the exiled family at this time, by any reference to it.

As time wore on, he found that exile was not a dull experience and recalled, to his delight, that other men of the classical times had suffered the same experience. "I may say that I bear my exile with greater patience than did Cicero, and that while I admire his rare political sense, his incomparable sagacity, and his striking wit, I find that his sorrow over his exile was excessive."

As a matter of fact, for the first time in his life this modern Cicero was free to wander at will over Europe and to indulge that insatiable curiosity. He visited Germany and marvelled at the beauties of Cologne Cathedral. (As far as one knows, Monsieur Thiers never uttered a word of praise for the Cathedrals of his own fair land.) The climax of his travels approached when he reached Italy. He explored Saint Ambrose at Milan and exhausted his priestly guides. But, once in Florence, all the rest of the world faded before him. There, the *petit homme d'État en vacances* found happiness again in the cradle of what he often called *ma chère Renaissance*. "When old age has, at last, removed us from vain pleasures and has ripened our taste, when the deceptions of life have left nothing in our souls but the cult of noble things, it is here that one must come to contemplate beauty in the masterpieces of all the geniuses of all the centuries. . . . Yes, here, indeed, is the Christian Athens in its incomparable elegance. . . . Every step that I make confronts me with new ideas for that History of Civilization which has been vegetating instinctively in my head for thirty years."

November, 1852, found him, again, in London and established comfortably at Bath House. He went the usual round of country houses. He discussed Free Trade with John Bright who had opened a subscription for the translation and distribution of Thiers' discourse on that subject.

Then, when, at last, he learned that the time of his recall was approaching, he paid farewell visits to the Orléanist Princes at 23 Northumberland Street and went to salute the widowed French Queen at Claremont.

On New Year's Day, 1853, Thiers' recall became effective. Telemachus allowed Mentor to return. It was, however, undertood that Telemachus did not want a Mentor, and Mentor announced that, as for himself, he was through with politics.

When Monsieur Thiers returned to Paris, the President, by the use of plebiscites, had made himself Emperor in fact as well as in name. Ostensibly, the basis of power was the will of the people. Universal suffrage still remained, but the *Corps Legislatif* was controlled by the practice of official candidatures whose campaign and political expenses were paid by the Government, and hedged in by a Senate that could revise its acts and a *Conseil d'État* whose duty it was to discuss for it what the *Legislatif* would be asked to vote upon.

It was a real and, for the moment, efficient system of oppression that Napoleon III had put into operation. At the same time, however, he had attempted to throw out sops to the people and to liberal opinion. To the bourgeois, he gave satisfaction by means of a wise policy that safeguarded and, even, developed their economic interests. From their number he selected advisers, able men, Talbot, the founder of the Paris, Lyons, and Mediterranean Railway, and Didion, President of the Chemins de Fer d'Orléans. The Compagnie Générale Transatlantique was established in order to facilitate trade with America and Algiers, and the Emperor began to enter into negotiations with Englishmen for the reduction of tariffs. As a further aid to the economic development of France, the Crédit Foncier and the Société Générale du Crédit Mobilier were inaugurated. Such measures were proving the worth of the Second Empire. Before its establishment, Louis Napoleon had declared to the French people: "The Empire means Peace." In the early 'fifties many Frenchmen were persuaded that the Emperor had come among them to bring peace and prosperity, to modernize the country, and to bring to it the material benefits of the Industrial Revolution.

When, in 1855, the Great International Exhibition was opened in Paris, France seemed to be on the way to rival England who was, by that time, her ally. This was the greatest accomplishment of Napoleon III, and had he confined himself to such pursuits all would have been well. But the Emperor was an upstart and a Bonaparte. Underneath this laudable ambition for the increase of French prosperity there lay another desire far less worthy and far more impossible of attainment; Napoleon III wished that, under his leadership, France should assume the direction of Europe.

Like another and earlier ruler of France, this Emperor, too, had his Great Design. He burned to obliterate the treaties of 1815 which, he believed, had dishonoured his House and his country. At heart a sentimental liberal, he desired to assist, often blindly and foolishly, the oppressed nationalities and, in this way, aid in undoing the work of the victors of 1815. In justice to him, it may now be remarked that his intentions were not always warlike. He hoped to accomplish his ends by peaceful means; he always attempted first to resort to a Congress of the European Powers. But Louis Napoleon was not an able statesman and many of the men upon whose assistance he relied were worse than the Emperor. Consequently, most of his Congresses failed of their purposes and he must needs resort to war in which he always fell short of the mark. And what is more ludicrous than a conqueror who has appeared to fail or to desert a cause at the moment of victory?

For mere show and for friendship, he fought beside England in the Crimea and nearly exhausted the funds and patience of France. In the Congress of Paris that followed, he failed signally to be the shining light. To retrieve himself in the eyes of his subjects and Europe, he fulfilled a pledge of some years' standing given to the oppressed Italians, only, at the moment of victory, to withdraw because he realized, suddenly, what the consequences of an Italy, united and too liberal, might be. From this second effort he emerged to find himself more distrusted than ever. Italians and many French Liberals whose hopes he had aroused, regarded him as a traitor to the common cause. Again, to recoup, he embarked on that quixotic and cruel enterprise for the establishment of a Mexican Empire under the gentle and well-intentioned Maximilian. Out of this effort he brought disaster and sorrow to his own country and to others, and opprobrium to himself. In foreign affairs, an evil genius seemed to pursue this variable dreamer, a genius to whom his enemies in France always allied him. This is one aspect of the early Empire, but there is more to it than a mistaken and poorly managed foreign policy.

An upstart he was and, true to his kind, he preferred show and relied too much on externals. This third Napoleon gave to his reign a metallic brilliance. Baron Haussmann and Company set about to beautify Paris and to rebuild it. With the Emperor's consent, he even appealed to public credit in order to carry out his extravagant enterprise. He bought up old property, destroyed old Paris, and laid the city out in spacious squares and magnificent boulevards. Other towns, Marseilles, Lyons, Bordeaux, Tours, followed his example. But underneath this apparently æsthetic and noble activity of the Ministry of Public Works there was a nasty tangle of financial chicanery that became, in time, a public scandal. Thanks to his Civil List of a million pounds sterling, the Emperor and his associates dazzled their people and foreigners with their brilliant costumes and handsomely appointed establishments. The Empress Eugénie set the mode for the two worlds. The life of the Court at Paris was the talk of the two Continents. It was a surface brilliancy maintained by a steady round of spectacular fêtes, charades, and plays, in which the celebrated quips even of Madame de Castiglione were banal and dull. The official world of France was playing desperately at Louis Quatorze.

This picture, however, was not true of all Paris. The upstart Emperor found, from the very first, domains that he could not conquer. In these quarters there were people who were not dazzled or deceived by the performances of the Imperial Court. The salons of the Faubourg Saint Germain remained stubbornly closed to the partisans of the Empire. At Madame de Lieven's, Madame d'Argout's and Madame de Girardin's, old France laughed at the new. Even the Emperor himself could not control the elections to the Academy and to other learned societies, and, under their guidance, the real genius of France still flourished. Victor Hugo, exiled for his diatribes, continued to possess a great deal of public favour, and the genius of Augier, Dumas fils, Flaubert, and Sainte-Beuve held sway. Renan was engaged in his linguistic and theological studies, and the great Taine was beginning to evolve his new psychology. But only in rare instances did they penetrate into the circle of the Imperialists. Of all her family, Mathilde Bonaparte appeared to be the only one really able to appreciate this new generation of Frenchmen. Aloof and proud, these men were preparing a greater France that was destined to be born of the mistakes of her present master.

It was with parts of this silent social opposition that Monsieur Thiers was associated during the years of his political retreat. His view of the situation reflected, very likely, the attitude of many of his friends; "Among the revolutions of my time, I beheld one of them compromise the cause, not of persons but of principles, to which I had been devoted. While always hoping that this cause would one day arise from its defeat, without hesitation I accepted retreat and submitted myself to the decision of the Superior Wisdom that presides over the fate of States."

With such an easy philosophy, Monsieur Thiers found himself just as happy in retreat as he had been in the greatest days of his public life. He became one of the leaders of Paris society and his hôtel on the Place Saint Georges was frequented by many of the men of the Old Political School, and by scientists, writers, playwrights, and players. He gratified his social tastes freely and took a brilliant part in the racy conversations of the *élite* of the city. Foreign visitors sought interviews with him and begged for invitations to his receptions where Madame Dosne and Madame Thiers presided. And often if the master of the house failed to do so, Madame Dosne herself supplied the caustic commentary on the Emperor that was always expected.

While, during this time, he observed to the letter his vow of abstention from politics, Monsieur Thiers kept himself always informed of events. And while he had no personal use for the Emperor, he remained a loyal patriot and desired the success of France, even when her armies were engaged in wars of which he did not approve. From time to time, his advice was sought by the Government through Prosper Mérimée, his friend. But as his counsel was nearly always the opposite to the policy that the Government had adopted, it was never followed. He abominated the Crimean War which, he declared, was "a war to give a few monks the key to a grotto," and he believed that France was fighting to no real advantage to herself and only to the greater profit of England. But when that war had reached its middle point, he became alarmed for his country. He went to the Champs de Mars and watched the manœuvres and, in the evening, he exposed to his callers the blunders that he had seen and explained how they could be remedied. At this time he was studying the heroic period of Napoleon I, and he was constantly drawing invidious comparisons between the great Emperor and "L'Empereur IIIe" as Madame Dosne called the present ruler. When, in 1859, the Italian War began, Monsieur Thiers was almost in despair, for now he saw the danger of a weakened Austria, and the complications that would follow a united Italy. Free as he was, at this time, from a personal concern in the affairs of France, his judgments were calm, sane, and remarkably accurate: many of the prophesies concerning the future of Europe that were uttered in his crowded salon by the wise man of the Place Saint-Georges were soon fulfilled. For the great revival that his popularity would soon experience, this period of retreat was an important preparation. Ever so slowly, a new Monsieur Thiers, the man of leisure, the philosopher, the sage, was making another conquest of France.

Such a restless nature as his, however, would not have been satisfied for long with the rôle of critic and prophet that he was playing. His whole mechanism demanded an absorbing task and an outlet to that instinctive feverish activity that was always burning within him. It was the completion of his *History of the Consulate and the Empire* that provided him with the distraction that he needed. "Writing," he remarked, "is a poor thing after action. I would give ten successful histories for one successful session or for one successful campaign."

In 1856, therefore, Monsieur Thiers was a reluctant historian in spite of his momentary enthusiasms for History. What interested him most, probably, were the contacts that historical investigation afforded him. Nevertheless, it is an undeniable fact that, during the years of his political retreat, Monsieur Thiers proved himself to be a better history writer than he had been in 1824. During the Restoration, the *History of the French Revolution* had been written in the heat of political passion. But, during the Second Empire, Monsieur Thiers declared that he had no personal ambitions and, certainly, he had no desire to write a panegyric of the Bonaparte family. Even the idea of the Empire was not repugnant to him; his only real hatred was the man at its head. Consequently, in 1856, Monsieur Thiers was in a different frame of mind; and he approached his work on the later volumes with a changed spirit and a more detached attitude. In short, his retreat brought him a step nearer to becoming a real historian.

His earlier work had ignored causes and had dealt, in great part, with events. In 1856, however, he said: "It is difficult to represent to oneself the opinions of the spectators of events. We can now estimate their relative importance, we know what their real causes were, we can see how long these causes had been at work before their action became perceptible to contemporaries. An historian is like the surgeon who performs an autopsy; he can trace in the body that he is dissecting the marks of a long-standing disease; he can tell us that, years before, when the man was apparently vigorous, he had been suffering from an organic malady which was slowly but surely turning against him. I can now see that, in 1808, the fall of Napoleon was inevitable."

Although Monsieur Thiers tried to be the surgeon of the First Empire, his judgments were by no means always exact. With greater care then ever he arrayed his documents, he visited his battlefields, and consulted his human evidences in the persons of the men who still survived. He undertook tremendous labours that would have absorbed all of the attention and strength of any one normal man, but Monsieur Thiers was always in touch with the affairs of the Second Empire, with their relation to the rest of Western Europe, and concerned with his relation to them in the past and in the present. And these external influences have left their marks on the last volumes of the *History*. As Napoleon III decreased in stature, Napoleon I became magnified by the contrast. The *History* became a better autobiography of Monsieur Thiers' state of mind than an historical account of the First Empire. Napoleon I is the hero because, in part, of his unworthy successor. The second hero is Metternich, who became so prominent in the later volumes partly because the middle nineteenth century had thrown both the Prince and Thiers out of politics and into each other's arms.

Thiers and Metternich had made contacts before the *Coup d'État* and not through diplomatic correspondence alone. In 1838, the intrepid little Frenchman had bearded the lion in his den at Como, where he had been rebuffed. Again, in 1850, the two had met at Brussels, thanks to the well known penchant of Leopold of Belgium for the would-be historian. The interview had taken place in August. And the two had spent an entire morning together discussing what Thiers had written concerning the years 1809 and 1810. Princess Metternich records that the whole thing was so full of errors that she thought it useless for her husband to offer advice. But Metternich does not appear to have shared her impressions. He was, however, careful. He asked for written questions and promised to give written answers. Thereupon Thiers posed twelve questions: ten of these Metternich answered at once; the other two he promised to answer after he had consulted the Archives at Vienna. During his sojurn in Belgium, Thiers was entertained at Laeken by the Royal Family. The Austrian Princess, evidently, was not impressed any more favourably than she had been at Como. She writes that Thiers was well received as the friend of the unfortunate Orléanists, but she adds: "he was late to dinner and was dressed in ill-matched clothes. A black cravat and grey breeches, a fact that was generally considered a breach of etiquette."

After this second encounter the little Frenchman had returned to Paris where he had experienced great events, the *Coup d'État* of 1851, and a year of exile. Upon his recall, he had resumed his historical studies inspired, as he asserted, by the example of Macaulay.

In 1857, his work had reached the critical year of 1813. Arrived at this point, he felt again the need of Metternich's help. Another interview was arranged, this time not by Thiers himself, but through the good offices of a mutual friend, the Princess Grassalkovitch. Thiers had sent the former Chancellor of Austria a copy of the fifteenth volume of his work. The gift had delighted the old statesman and, from his Château on the cliffs of Johannisberg, he had pronounced on its accuracy. Encouraged by these reports, Thiers let it be known that he was contemplating a trip to Germany. Would he be received at Johannisberg? A cordial invitation was the response to his question and, in July, Monsieur Thiers made the pilgrimage to Metternich's retreat. Revolution humbled, for the moment, by the rude experience of recent years, sat at the feet of the Old Régime and drank in its wisdom. It was a grateful and highly flattered Thiers who sent his host the following note of appreciation. No doubt both the writer and the recipient had their tongues in their cheeks when they surveyed this masterpiece of true Gallic flattery:

"Just arrived, I hasten to thank you for your charming hospitality and to assure you that I spent the most agreeable hours of my life at Johannisberg. I realize that you, with your fame and pleasant 'intérieur' have nothing to regret. The world, however, such as one may expect it will become in a few years, offers no temptations to me who have not seen as many or as great things as you. Already I desire only peace and the time for study, and I shall be very angry if I have to renounce either of these. The new generations are going to conquer the world, and heaven knows what they will make out of it! Now that you will permit me, I am going to discuss with you sometimes the human affairs that were the occupation of your life-time, and I shall reason at your side in the guise of a disinterested philosopher.

"From the heights of Johannisberg you have, my Prince, a wonderful view of the course of the Rhine; from the heights of your intelligence you enjoy an equally magnificent view of the course of human events. I shall come again to enjoy both of them."

Metternich appears to have been flattered by this epistle and replied in kind.

Two years passed, interspersed with occasional communications between these two strange friends. They were eventful years for Europe and very busy years for Monsieur Thiers. He remained loyal to his muse of History: he abstained from politics. But it would have been impossible for him to have refrained entirely. Friends of his would not have permitted it, and his own restless nature forbade too rigorous an observance of his rule. Through these friends, some of whom were friends of Napoleon III and Ministers, he was kept *au courant* even with what was transpiring in the Emperor's innermost circle.

Thiers, in his seclusion, was secure; but Napoleon III had no such comforting assurance. Already, in 1859, he was suffering the consequences of his policy of espousing the cause of the oppressed nationalities in Europe. Italy's hopes he had aroused and yet he had tried to protect the throne of Saint Peter and yearned for the friendship of Austria. Already he was on the verge of another European crisis. Unless Austria could be persuaded to accept a new state of affairs, Europe would experience another costly war. But the Austrian Emperor was young and proud.

It was a difficult problem, and the little man behind the desk at the Place Saint Georges came into it. Walewski was a power in the Emperor's circle, and, in the earlier days, Thiers had befriended Walewski. Again, in 1859, Walewski sought his aid. Negotiations with Austria, in regard to the Austrian Princes ruling in Italy, seemed to be failing. But it occurred to Walewski, and to others, that Thiers and Metternich were friends. Might not this friendship provide a new channel of approach to the Emperor of Austria? Metternich was old, but his words still had weight. Would Monsieur help—would Monsieur Thiers advise the Emperor of the French? To this request Monsieur gave an emphatic negative, but, after a second call from Walewski, he did consent to write Metternich about the affair. It is Thiers himself who tells us of the foregoing situation in a footnote written at the end of his copy of the letter to Metternich. This letter was dispatched by special courier on March 9, 1859:

"At Paris we are still concerned with the condition of Europe and especially with the state of our relations with the Austrian Court. I do not need to tell you, my Prince, how much the more intelligent of us desire a satisfactory arrangement. In the retirement in which I live and am happy to live, I have done what I could for the cause of peace between our two countries. I have had, in previous times, relations with several of the Ministers, and politics has not interfered with these friendships. In spite of the fact that I am not accustomed to meddle in affairs that do not concern me, I feel that I have not been indiscreet in expressing to them my opinion in regard to a matter that concerns the greatest interests of my country." France, he writes, today desires friendship with Austria. But although she recognizes the treaties of 1815, she dislikes them, and those arrangements that have been made since 1815, she abhors and does not recognize. The great difficulty is the question of Austria's interests and actions in regard to her Princes who are ruling in Italy. At present, they are under the guarantee of Austria. Would it not be possible to place them under the collective guarantee of Europe? In this way, while Austria would be safeguarding her incontestable rights and privileges, she would be responsible, in case of a crisis, to the European powers. This, wrote Monsieur Thiers, is the only way in which to preserve the European equilibrium, and the only means by which Austria may be sure of remaining friends with Europe.

Some weeks later the reply came. It was a disappointment, for Metternich refused to present his friend's views and concluded with a repetition of his vow to observe "the detachment which I maintain from this stage on which the present painful drama is being enacted, a drama for which I cannot find a satisfactory description."

And so this mild negotiation failed. It was the last bit of correspondence that passed between these two strange friends. Metternich died in November, 1859, and Monsieur Thiers completed without his aid the last volumes of his enormous undertaking. It was hailed as the master history of the First Empire, and the strange heir of the great Emperor, Napoleon III, was moved to propose a prize as a sign of his gratitude. Unwilling to be won, Monsieur Thiers, however, declined to accept the award and requested the Academy to use the sum to found a triennial prize.

Meditation and past experience had matured and developed Monsieur Thiers. But, during the last years of the Empire and the momentous days that followed its disappearance, there were other influences that came to play on him.

This second half of the nineteenth century witnessed the growth of a spirit of scientific investigation. Romantic inquiry, literature, and history had lost their hold. Material progress had come, at last, to France, and many of her citizens were turning from dreams to realities. Faith in the advantages of a return to the past was waning, and in its stead there came the creed of the new generation who believed that the future greatness of the country lay in commerce, industrial expansion, and colonies. In the realm of the intellectual world, a corresponding change was taking place.

It had been the teachings of Auguste Comte that had dealt the first blow to idealism, revelation, and metaphysics. And now the discoveries that were being made in astronomy, physics, chemistry and biology, where Pasteur reigned supreme, were increasing this tendency. Consequently, along with the industrial expansion that the Empire had inaugurated, there developed in France a materialistic and determinist attitude which destroyed the conceptions of the more idealistic thinkers of the Restoration. Monsieur Thiers himself was not untouched by these new influences. In fact, he was prepared to receive them and to be affected by them.

During the Restoration he had displayed eager but sporadic enthusiasms for the realm of science. Sainte-Beuve relates in detail Thiers' early passion for mathematics, and his friends assert that he snatched as many hours as he could from hack-writing to devote himself to solving problems of calculus. Later, his travels and his studies for the *History of the French Revolution* aroused in him a lively interest in geography and exploration. He even thought seriously of writing a History of China. So great did this new enthusiasm become that, in 1829, he made preparations for a tour of the world on board a French cruiser. It was only the crisis occasioned by the appointment of the Polignac Ministry that caused him to abandon this ambitious project. And now, in the 'fifties and 'sixties, with the avenues to a public career practically closed to him, he returned *en connaisseur* to these interests and made contact with currents of life and thought that were other than political and that left their marks upon him.

His world was aroused, some of it to the point of hostility, by the first discoveries of Pasteur. This controversy piqued the curiosity of Monsieur Thiers, and he requested an interview with the master at his laboratory. His request was granted, but soon, it is said, Pasteur became embarrassed and annoyed by the assiduity of his new acquaintance, and handed him over to the care of Duclaux, his assistant. Thiers' second tutor, was, at first, flattered by his eagerness to learn. After a short time, however, Monsieur Duclaux became tired of his task and told Monsieur Thiers that he was too inquisitive and that he never waited for one question to be answered before posing another. And so this venture ended with some hard feelings on both sides. For a time, after this episode, Thiers flirted with other sciences. He frequented the Observatory and, under the patient tutelage of Leverrier, he dabbled in astronomy. In 1862, along with many of his fellows, he was captivated by Darwin whose works had just been translated into French. In Taine, Renan, and their followers, he found an attitude of questioning and criticism that he tried to practise and that, later, he attempted to embody in an ambitious philosophical work that was designed to assemble and co-ordinate all of the new learning that had come to light in his own time. This work exists only in outline. It may be found among his papers and it bears the title inscribed with his own hand, *Plan d'un Ouvrage de Philosophie.*

The influence of these greater and more persistent contemporaries of his increased in him an intellectual attitude of which, due to his eighteenth-century heritage, he had already shown symptoms. Monsieur Thiers became materialist, determinist, and follower of a philosophy that admitted of a God but not the God of orthodox religion.

By the closing years of the Empire, therefore, he found himself more in sympathy with the world intellectual. His early dislike of Mysticism, Romanticism, and the Romantic historians, of whom Michelet and Barante had been the leaders, now seemed to be justified. As in the natural sciences so in Philosophy, Religion, and History, Realism and Objectivity were the watchwords of the day. These were the influences that made Monsieur Thiers what he became in later life, and their earliest manifestations may well have affected the character of the *History,* the final volumes of which were received with such tremendous applause.

If, however, Monsieur Thiers participated in the intellectual revolution that was taking place in France, he was singularly untouched by another development with which he was destined later to come to grips.

During the first years of the Empire, Socialist effort had been under a cloud. Workers asserted that they were tired of fighting in revolutions that were always turned to the benefit of the bourgeoisie. With the discrediting, in 1848, of Louis Blanc's sincere experiment, the problem of the worker became one of minor importance to Frenchmen. Two developments, however, brought about its revival. One was the great industrial expansion that took place under the ægis, even, of the partisans of the Empire: the other factor came from beyond France—the spread of Marxianism and the formation of the International Association of Workers. When these movements began, French labour took heart again, and when, in 1862, French and English workers met in London, Socialism was revived in France and Marxian doctrines supplanted the nationalist theories of Louis Blanc.

With these new ideas Monsieur Thiers showed not the slightest sympathy and very little understanding. Once, in 1848, he had written a book against Socialism and he declared that he had not changed his opinions. Staunch bourgeois, he defended the Right of Property, and the absolute power of the employer over the employed. He desired, he averred, the comfort and welfare of the labouring classes, but he had met them too often on the boulevards, in the midst of riots, to have anything but distrust and fear of them *en masse*. "Force and justice, these are the only resources of society against the disorderly passions that are fermenting among certain people," he wrote. "That is what we must mean by Liberty." And, later, he pointed with pride to the mines of Anzin of which he was a director, where, he boasted, there were adequate living quarters, an average yearly income per family of three or four thousand francs earned by father and children, and schools, doctors, and a pharmacy provided by the Company. "Some of them are grateful," he wrote, "and others complain. This condition of welfare leaves their arguments without force provided one employs a vigorous discipline to control them."

In politics and in social problems, Monsieur Thiers, who, from painful experience feared the "multitude," remained shut within the narrow walls of his Middle Class creed.

CHAPTER XIII

ACHILLES EMERGES FROM HIS TENT

ELEVEN years after its founding, the Empire whose establishment had been hailed by Louis Napoleon as the guarantee of peace in France and in Europe, had proven itself to be quite the opposite. Under the unwise leadership of the Emperor, France had played a part in a number of military ventures in the Crimea, in Italy, in the Far East, and in Mexico. Such an ambitious policy had cost the country much in money and in men, and had brought Napoleon III none of the popularity to which he aspired, nothing, in fact, except opprobrium. France was weary of his war policy; so, too, was Europe.

The net result of these enterprises had been to leave France almost without a friend on the Continent. Napoleon, erratic and uncertain, had become again an object of suspicion and jealousy in England. Russia, too, never kindly disposed to the idea of the Second Empire, resented the words of encouragement that its head had given to the Poles. Italians felt that his sudden desertion at Villa Franca had blocked the attainment of a real Italian unity, and the Pope, who was reasonably alarmed at the approach of the House of Savoy to Rome, laid the blame for it at the Emperor's door. Even Prussia was suspicious of him. At the same time, however, that country was cautious. The Court at Berlin did not criticize him openly; Bismarck had already seen that Napoleon III, friendless, might serve, in a peculiar fashion, the needs of Prussia.

Of his rather desolate position the Emperor of the French was thoroughly aware. He had taken stock of his accomplishments and had been bewildered and frightened at what he had found. More than all else he realized that it was not only the dislike of Europe that endangered him; his situation was rendered even more insecure by the indifference of fully one half of France. Once again he aroused himself from that lethargy that was beginning to settle so heavily upon him, and prepared for an effort to regain, in his own country, the enviable position that he had enjoyed in 1852.

To do this, he must win that other half of France that was so indifferent to him. It could give him statesmen of experience, men of the former régime whom he had sent into exile in 1851. These men were better than any of those whom his own party of the *Élysée* could muster. But they were separated from him by that barrier that Persigny, Rouher, Plon-Plon, and Morny had raised around him. And, too, they could bring him that new France whose members were observing a policy of nonparticipation and who were quietly looking towards the Future and not to the Present, the Emperor himself. The bourgeois whose wealth he had helped to make had deserted him, and were out to increase their possessions even at the cost of the Empire. And the workingmen, ever increasingly distrustful of him, had preferred their own unions and the International to his Utopian schemes. In short, the country was wearying of Louis Napoleon; he had remained aloof from them too long. After eleven years of acquiescence and abstention, Frenchmen were becoming impatient of him and desired a change.

Ever so slowly political life began to revive after 1860.

In spite of the fact that, under the Empire as it then existed, politics offered little in the way of a career to one who was not allied to the Government, the men of the former régime began to bestir themselves. Outside of the *Corps Legislatif*, so meticulously guarded by the practice of "official candidatures," a new liberal opinion was gradually forming. The Emperor perceived this change and desired to win the returning statesmen over to himself and so to turn a new Opposition into an Imperialist majority.

Until the year 1863, such Liberal Opposition as existed in the Legislative Body had been under the leadership of a group of men called *Les Cinq*—Ernest Picard, Jules Favre, Émile Ollivier, Darimon, and Henon. They were able men but not experienced politicians. The representatives of the older liberal parties, as Cavaignac and Carnot, had not been of any real assistance to them, for these more venerable Republicans had stood for election only for the purpose of refusing to take the oath to the Empire and so registering a protest against the Empire. The Moderate Liberals, the survivors of the *rue de Poitiers*, Thiers, Broglie, Rémusat, and their friends, had continued to observe a more logical policy: they had abstained completely from public life. By the time, however, that the Mexican affair was under way, they began to consider the possibility of a return to political activity. While the failure of the Emperor had not aroused their sympathies, it had awakened their concern for France. In the spring of 1863, it was the Duc de Broglie who first gave utterance to these sentiments when, at his house, he gathered together a group of his former associates. He proposed to them that they accept the Constitution and recognize the validity of the plebiscites of 1851 and 1852, in order that, banded together, they might fight "for the enlargement of public liberty and for the safety of France in Europe."

The result of the Broglie conference was a resolve on the part of those who attended to propose themselves as candidates in the autumn elections. If chosen, they would take the oath to the Constitution, and promise not to conspire against the Empire. They agreed, however, to pursue a steady and unrelenting opposition that would be in conformity with the laws that were then in force. This decision brought back into political life Broglie, Berryer, Jules Simon, Marie, Rémusat, Odilon Barrot, and a number of other men of the July Monarchy.

It was not until after the announcement of this new Liberal Union that Monsieur Thiers emerged from his tent. He had not taken part in Broglie's conference, although he had approved of its purpose. He had given as his reason the fact that he was engrossed in the completion of the *History*. To intimate friends, however, he had divulged another explanation. He still clung, he wrote, to the same plan of procedure that he had followed during the July Monarchy; he wished to be free and he did not desire to be closely associated with any group of the Opposition. When he felt the need of a party, he preferred to create it on the spot and entirely along his own lines: "to re-establish bit by bit the *régime constitutionnel*, to prevent follies that may result disastrously. That is my programme." And, in the pursuit of such an end, he was not sure how far Berryer with his Legitimism and Marie, who was a Republican, would follow him. Consequently, this modern Achilles made his return to the battlefield alone.

In many respects it was a new Thiers who reappeared in public life after twelve years' absence. He had learned a great deal from watching the mistakes of others, and he had formulated a philosophy of life which had mellowed him and given him a more tranquil mind. And, in 1863, he appeared in a new light to many Frenchmen. Before, Monsieur Thiers had been tolerated by quite a number as a luxury; now these same people believed that he was a necessity. His rashness and extravagant actions in the past had been forgotten in the general depression of the present. He was revered as a sage, a veteran of long experience, recognized as one of the foremost men of letters of his day, and credited with a reputation for sound judgment. Many of the observations and prophesies that he had made while he was *en retraite* were now being realized.

His supporters, too, were new. During the years of his retirement, he had become the idol of the younger generation. From time to time, he had attended *réunions* of young writers, artists, and students of the Sorbonne and of the Law School. On these occasions he had chided them gently for their impatience and extreme views, and had preached to them the doctrines of common sense and of caution. It was to the youth of France that this statesman, experienced in revolutions and grown old and wise in the service of his country, appealed. An unwise move on the part of the Emperor's political family brought Thiers support from another quarter.

In September, when the electoral campaign opened, Persigny took up the cudgels against him. He wrote to Baron Haussmann a letter which was published in the *Moniteur*. This letter denounced Thiers as the upholder of "a régime which, for eighteen years, produced nothing but impotence at home and feebleness abroad, *en un mot, le régime parlementaire.*" He opined, as well, that Thiers' election would be a serious check to the policies of the Emperor. Although Thiers had announced that he did not desire his election or failure to be interpreted as a defeat or victory for the Emperor, Persigny's letter brought him new adherents. Until September, Democratic papers had opposed his candidacy because, in 1850, he had worked so hard for the restriction of the suffrage. But the attacks of Persigny and Haussmann brought even the *démocrates* to the Place Saint Georges. One day, during the campaign, he was visited by three delegates from the *Comité Démocratique de la Butte de Chaumont,* a section of the Labour Party. These gentlemen questioned him as to the truth or falsity of Persigny's remarks. If he was elected, would he be hostile to the existing régime? The reply was typical: "I like questions that are nicely put. For that reason this one pleases me. Yes, in the *Corps Legislatif,* I shall be the enemy of the Empire and the Emperor, but I do not want, at any price, to owe my election to a *malentendu.* I shall be the enemy of the Emperor and the Empire, but only within the limits allowed by the Constitution."

When they heard this statement, the simple gentlemen of the radical committee assured him of a large number of labour votes.

Now that his election seemed to be almost a certainty, Monsieur Thiers was hounded by his Imperialist enemies. Persigny and Haussmann showered France with scandalous pamphlets about him, but the object of their unkind attentions shook off their insults with a shrug of his shoulders, and remarked philosophically: "I am an old umbrella on which it has rained without damage for forty years." Nevertheless, proud and sensitive as he was, he never forgot the slights of these two henchmen of Napoleon III. The war that they carried on against him rendered impossible any *rapprochement* between the Emperor and the man who might have saved him. It was a foolish game that they were playing, and Thiers was a dangerous man to have as an enemy. Baron de Heeckeren, a member of the Senate, commented: "The Emperor is crazy. He now wishes to engage with Thiers in a contest of tongues. His goose is cooked. He will not last five years."

The election of Monsieur Thiers to the *Corps Legislatif* was a stirring event. He found few whom he knew, but all the members knew him. More than all else he discovered, outside that body, an element of French society whose sentiments he shared and whose desires he could proclaim. He expressed the hopes of that silent and hitherto unrepresented Opposition of scholars, students, and professional men who, without him, had been unable to overcome the fear of the people and the instinctive defiance of the selfishly-minded bourgeoisie. At first, for the Left had good memories and disliked him, he had only a few companions in arms, Ernest Picard, Jules Favre, Émile Ollivier, Berryer, and Jules Simon, but, within three months of his election, he became so strong that he was the leader of all Oppositions, divided as they were. In fact there was no rival to his power until 1869, when Léon Gambetta strode into the *Corps Legislatif*.

If to Persigny, Haussmann, and the rest of the clique of the *Élysée*, the recent elections seemed serious, to the uneasy and perplexed Emperor they appeared to afford a chance of escape from his difficulties. Napoleon III decided, at once, to attempt proffers of friendship. The hated Persigny Ministry was dismissed, and the Cabinet was revised. Even a sort of concession was made to the principle of Constitutional Government when the Emperor appointed Billaut as a Minister of State without portfolio, to act as a defender of the Government before the *Legislatif*, and as general consultant in regard to the state of public opinion in France. At the same time, certain of the Liberals began to draw nearer to the Emperor.

A little while before the elections, Émile Ollivier, one of the original "Cinq" in the Chamber, had set out to discover a means for creating an understanding between the Emperor and the Liberals in regard to the extension of liberty in France. Ollivier desired to play the rôle of mediator and negotiator in a Great Compromise which would save the Empire by liberalizing it. His programme, however, smacked so much of compromise and of the divine right which the plebiscite was supposed to have conferred upon Napoleon III, that its originator and his small group of colleagues soon found themselves separated from the Orléanist and Republican wings of the Opposition. Out of this divergence of opinion came a party known as the Third Party. And the fact that this new party drew into its fold a number of liberally-minded Imperialists, tended to weaken rather than increase the prestige of the Emperor who was now faced by divided counsels even within his own ranks. It remained to be seen if the Third Party could gather into its fold those members of the Opposition who were not Republican.

The formation of this group of pseudo-Liberals, pseudo-Imperialists, created a grave question for Frenchmen. With the revival of liberal opinion, it became obvious that the character of the Empire was to be changed. Should this change be in the direction of Ollivier's idea, which would transform it into a sort of Constitutional Government as Louis XVIII had understood the term? Or, should the plan of Monsieur Thiers and the former Orléanists be accepted? In that case, the existing government would become a revised and improved type of July Monarchy. It was this problem that created the occasion for Monsieur Thiers to deliver his first important discourse before the *Corps Legislatif*.

In his own opinion, the performance that he contemplated was likely to have grave consequences for himself and for the Opposition. For Thiers, it meant that he would have to present a tactful yet convincing definition of his attitude to the former Monarchy whose servant he had been, and a new consecration of himself to the interests of his country which, it must be shown, were above all personal and sentimental preferences. For the Opposition, if he convinced them, it would mean a real break with the compromising Liberalism of Ollivier and the acceptance of a definite platform that would admit of no concessions to the Emperor or, even, to his Republican opponents. With a greater foresight than is usually allowed to him, Rémusat opined, on the eve of the delivery of this discourse when he attended the usual dress rehearsal at the Place Saint Georges, that the address would either mark the beginning of the revival or the breaking-up of the Empire.

On January 14, 1864, Monsieur Thiers entered the Tribune and inaugurated a series of discourses that have rarely been equalled in the history of the French Parliament. After the necessary prologue about himself and his previous affiliations, he launched into the theme of his speech—*Les Libertés Nécessaires*. Of these liberties, he declared, there were five without which real Liberty did not exist in a country; Liberty of the Individual, Liberty of the Press, Freedom of Elections (and not the prevailing practice of "official candidatures"), Freedom of Parliament (which included the right to initiate laws and to discuss them as well as to vote on them), and Ministerial Responsibility. This declaration, which was fearlessly made, revealed to many Frenchmen how far they had gone, since 1851, from the fundamental principles of the Revolution. It gave to the bulk of the Opposition a definite platform on which they could meet and maintain their stand. By this performance Thiers re-established his own influence, won to himself a party, and strengthened the determination of the majority not to concede one jot or tittle of their principles.

January, 1864, provided him with the occasion to criticize the internal policy of Napoleon III. The events immediately subsequent to this date afforded him an excuse to attack the foreign policy of the Empire.

Thanks, in part, to the oratory of Monsieur Thiers, the Emperor had been unable to make the number of friends that he had desired among the Opposition in France. In the meantime, however, he had found a friend, a disastrous friend, in Europe; Monsieur de Bismack came with gifts.

In December, 1863, Christian IX ascended the throne of Denmark. Shortly afterwards, he issued his decree incorporating Schleswig, one of the German Duchies, into the Kingdom of Denmark. Immediately Germany, led by Prussia and Austria, protested this action. England, relying on Louis Napoleon's well-known sympathies for "the oppressed nationalities," urged him to side with her in support of the Danes, but the Emperor of the French, influenced by Bismarck, refused the request. Not very long after this announcement, Napoleon III let it be known that his sympathies lay on the German side of the question. Out of the argument, came the wars of Prussia and Austria against Denmark and the ridiculous settlement by which Austria agreed to allow Prussia to participate in the administration of Schleswig and Holstein.

To wise heads, this settlement of the question appeared to be no settlement at all. Many believed that it would lead inevitably to a conflict between Prussia and Austria. Furthermore, with the Italians traditionally hostile to Austria and even, at that moment, inclining to an understanding with Prussia, and with Louis Napoleon apparently completely under the charm of Bismarck, it looked as if the Government at Berlin had an open road to power before it.

It was shortly after the foolish Convention of Gastein, that Thiers arose to warn France and its ruler of the ultimate danger to his own country. Out of a second war, he declared, there would come a new and magnified power on the Rhine unless Napoleon III desisted in his policy of *laissez-faire*. Like the classical city-states, France should seek to prevent the small from becoming great, and the great from becoming more powerful and threatening. Italy and Prussia, he said, were the two new forces that might soon endanger the equilibrium of Europe and the security of his own country.

Even had he perceived the danger of which the leader of the Opposition warned him, the Emperor could hardly have acted upon it without liquidating all of his enterprises. This would have been tantamount to acknowledging to the world that his régime was a failure. The Mexican affair was threatening to embroil him in difficulties with the United States. The Italians were demanding that he obtain Venetia for them as the price of their abstention from Rome, and the French Catholics, backed by many members of the Opposition, were insisting on the maintenance of the complete independence and sovereignty of the Holy See. To the Emperor there seemed to be only one person in Europe who could help him to regain his lost prestige and to cover, with a semblance of honour, the retreat that he must make. That person was Prince Bismarck. In September, 1865, the French Sovereign and the German Chancellor met at Biarritz.

There, close to the Pyrenees, the fate of Prussia, of Italy, and of the French Empire was decided; Prussia would take entire possession of Schleswig-Holstein, Italy would be given Venetia, and France, if she could persuade England to agree to it, might annex Belgium. But to Napoleon's pathetic pleas for a few Rhenish provinces Bismarck was deaf. Still, it was the best that the Emperor could do, and so he did not oppose the plan and indicated that he would probably observe again the policy of *laissez-faire* as far as Prussia and Italy were concerned.

By a strange irony of fate, it was Napoleon III a few months later who gave the signal to the Italians to open negotiations with Bismarck. Only once did he attempt another method of settlement, and that was when he made a rather weak proposal for a congress to consider "the differences that were dividing Europe." Shortly after the rejection of this plan, the French Government publicly declared "its neutrality in the events that are preparing."

By this time, the *Corps Legislatif* was thoroughly aware of the danger that lay ahead and of the magnitude of the war that was about to begin. Since January, 1866, Thiers and his party had allowed no occasion to pass without delivering a warning to France. Every question that had been submitted by the Government had been adroitly turned by the Opposition into a discussion of foreign affairs. In the Parliament the supporters of Monsieur Thiers had increased considerably. In February he wrote that, following his last discourse, even Berryer, the Legitimist, had embraced him and "wept aloud his approval." And when, in March, Rouher, Minister of State, began his speech with the phrase "the dangerous spirit of Monsieur Thiers," the Chamber had forced him to withdraw his words. By April, the majority were in accord with the views of the Opposition on matters of foreign policy. But what could they do if the country would not support them? There was the difficulty. Even in 1866 they could not be sure of the sympathy of the provinces where the peasants did not comprehend diplomacy and where most of the towns, although they were aware of the danger, were held in check by prefects and mayors.

In his alarm, Monsieur Thiers finally sacrificed his pride and, in an effort to bring them to reason, went personally to members of the Imperial Family. His warnings did not mince matters. To Prince Napoleon he said: "Monseigneur, although you have made an Italian marriage, you must be, above all else, a French prince. I am old, but the way things are going, I believe that I may yet go to greet you in exile."

Such arguments produced nothing but a more stubborn attitude on the part of the Government. Although they had won over most of the *Corps Legislatif,* Thiers and the Opposition found themselves blocked by a stone wall which was the Empire itself. It would be the foreign policy of Napoleon III that would, eventually, make them realize that *les libertés nécessaires*—their creed for internal affairs—could only come by revolution and never by remaining within the limits of the Constitution of 1852.

On April 29, the order for a general mobilization was issued in Italy, and, almost at the same time, the King of Prussia announced that circumstances had forced him to do the same thing. Word of these resolutions reached Paris on the following day and Thiers, urged on by the Opposition, made a final effort to arouse the country.

Sixteen years previously he had prophesied, in dramatic fashion, the coming of the French Empire. Now, on May 3, with a cry of alarm and of wounded pride, he proclaimed the creation of a German Empire, equal almost to that of Charles V, and extending the tentacles of its influence into Italy. He knew that his speech came too late to prevent hostilities—"it was like serving mustard after the dinner," as one of his contemporaries put it, but it served the one end that he was striving desperately to attain; the indolent provinces became aroused, at last, over "the disastrous policy" of Napoleon III.

The Emperor and his aides felt the effect of this terrific attack. In an effort to counteract it, the sovereign ran to the provinces and delivered himself of an apologia. On May 6, at Auxerre, the Emperor tried to cover the criticisms of his opponents by protesting that he hated the humiliating treaty arrangements of 1815, and that he welcomed this new conflict that would serve France by obliterating them forever. Thiers responded to this feeble effort magnificently by remarking: "The treaties of 1815 are not the work of our generation which was at school, nor of the Bourbons who were powerless in 1814 and 1815. It is, indeed, extraordinary that the Imperial dynasty should recall these treaties: it should not only declare that it detests them, but it should also make a public act of repentance for them. For this dynasty was the cause of them, and the treaties are themselves the very condemnation of the policy of the Bonapartes."

When it came, the war of Prussia and Italy against Austria caused the Emperor of the French no little difficulty at home. Divided counsels among his own friends made it necessary for him to make decisions. And this it became increasingly difficult for him to do. While his Minister of Foreign Affairs, Drouin de Lhuys, was almost persuading him to save Austria, at the last, by sending an army to the Rhine, other Ministers, Plon-Plon and Rouher among them, continued to advise neutrality and *laissez-faire*. On July 5, the Emperor, assured that Italy would have Venetia, was pro-Austrian. But, on July 14, he expressed his assent to the annexation, by Prussia, of Hanover, Hesse, and Frankfort, and was willing to recognize her hegemony in the smaller states of Northern Germany. The more variable became the whims of the Emperor, the more the Opposition increased its influence in France. Newspapers, even, lost their fear of the law, and began to demand an accounting of Napoleon III for all of his unwise acts. The Emperor, worried in mind and ill in body, was almost desperate. He talked of a Regency. Even his chosen adviser, Rouher, despaired of bringing him to the point of a settled policy. Diplomatically he was beaten in Europe while, in France, many believed that the end of his reign had come. At last, however, he was aroused from his indecisions; he resolved to crush this opposition at home and to demand of Prussia a price for his neutrality and her conquests.

Just a fortnight after Sadowa, which Thiers had called "the defeat of France," the Emperor sent to the Senate a law which threatened a return to the strict régime of 1852. It forbade the *Corps Legislatif* to discuss the Constitution or to amend it, and, at the same time, it withdrew from the Press the right to "comment on the fundamental law of the Empire." Shortly after this decree, Drouin de Lhuys sent word to Prussia that the Emperor of the French would not give a formal recognition of the Prussian conquests unless Mayence and the Left Bank of the Rhine were ceded to France. To this bit of bluff, Bismarck's King gave a sharp refusal. It looked as if Napoleon III was girding himself for conflict with his subjects and with his foreign rival.

For a moment Germany believed that the war might have to be carried into France. But Napoleon protested that he had only meant to make a friendly request and, in the face of Prussia's unfavourable reply, he promised to recognize the changes that had taken place in Germany provided Prussia would not oppose his annexation of Belgium. To this condition Bismarck did not give a formal refusal. Instead, he revealed it to the German Princes and used it to convince them of the necessity of placing the combined forces of Germany under the control of the King of Prussia for offensive and defensive purposes. As Monsieur Thiers had foretold, the Bonapartes again aided the system that was to bring further humiliation to France.

Two extraordinary letters of the Emperor bring to a close the next to last act of that strange performance that is known as the Second Empire. The first missive bore the date of September 17, 1866. It was issued upon the settlement of the differences that had given rise to the Austro-Prussian War. The Emperor addressed to his perplexed and angry subjects what was virtually a confession of *non possumus:* "Public opinion is divided between delight at seeing the destruction of the odious treaties of 1815, and the fear of an unreasonable increase of power to Prussia . . . between a desire to preserve the peace and a longing to increase our own territories. It salutes the liberation of Italy, but it asks for some assurance concerning the dangers that may threaten the Holy Father."

Far from satisfying public opinion, this ambiguous statement only created greater uncertainty and concern for the future. What was the Emperor now contemplating? Was it to be war or peace?

Several months later there was a second mystification. In February, 1867, a decree addressed to the nation guaranteed new liberties to France. But, at the same time, Rouher, the hated opponent of the Liberal Opposition, remained in power, and the promises of February were postponed. What, asked the Opposition, was the real intention of the Emperor? Many agreed with Thiers who is said to have remarked: "It is all over with the Empire. Even the Emperor does not know what he wants."

The twilight of Napoleonic power had come. And, as the curtain descends on this last scene but one, Louis Napoleon appears enjoying for a last brief moment that empty glory that he had always sought. There was a second World's Fair and, at Paris, there was *une joie folie*. "The place," writes Madame Dosne, "is once more filled with strangers who have the manner of saying 'See Paris, and then die.' " The Emperor of Russia, the Grand Turk, the Pasha of Egypt, the rulers of Austria and Prussia were expected. "In the midst of this apparent success, Napoleon III has forgotten his errors." Napoleon had forgotten, too, the humiliation and the danger to France.

But others, the Opposition, had not forgotten these things, and, in the midst of this pretended prosperity and false happiness, Monsieur Thiers and his partisans were busily interviewing these visiting monarchs and their statesmen—even conferring with the victorious Prussians themselves. "It is best to try to arrest the torrent . . . even without hope of succeeding."

CHAPTER XIV

WAR CLOUDS

THE equivocations of Napoleon III had contributed to the general sentiment throughout France in 1868 that war with Germany and, even possibly, Revolution were in the offing. These same uncertainties had also led to the expansion of public opinion in the country. The terms *Imperialist* and *Opposition* were no longer sufficient; within these two categories divergent shades of opinion had begun to appear. Rouher, still in power, commanded one group of Imperialists; these were the Absolutists who clung tenaciously to the system of 1852. But Ollivier's Third Party, that stood for the ideal of a liberalized Empire, had increased considerably in numbers and was becoming daily a more important factor. It was among the ranks of the Liberal Opposition, however, that the greatest changes had occurred.

There, Monsieur Thiers and his Moderates were no longer in complete control. Their own speeches and actions had inspired hardier and more radical elements and these new gentlemen could not tolerate caution and scrupulously observed "opposition within the limits of the Constitution." Instead, they called Broglie, Rémusat, and Thiers by their true names, "Monarchists," and proclaimed the rebirth of the Republican party in France.

This revival of Radicalism had been encouraged by the example of the *Union Libérale*. Under the sane guidance of Brissot, Jules Favre, and Ernest Picard, its doctrines were being spread in the *Corps Legislatif*, while, in the provinces, the fiery oratory of Léon Gambetta and a new set of newspapers were spreading the message. Towards the close of 1868, Thiers himself was forced to acknowledge that public opinion in the provinces was turning Republican. He might also have remarked that in Lyons, Saint Étienne, Bordeaux, and other large industrial centers, Socialism was reappearing. In those cities, this more radical doctrine was being disseminated by the *Democratie* published by Louis Blanc and Félix Pyat, and by the increasing influence of the *International* among the workers.

From 1868, therefore, the Emperor was confronted with a new situation that required, to meet it, a man far more determined and capable than himself. Previously, he had had only a new and not unkindly opposition that was not opposed so much to the form as to the method of his rule. Now, however, he met with a force, divided, it is true, but rapidly growing and, in many places, determined to accomplish his own undoing. It was not long before he demonstrated that he was totally incapable of handling the New France that was coming into being.

In January, 1869, he met his *Corps Legislatif* and delivered before it his customary Address. From the majority, who had been elected as his official candidates, he received the usual support. But, from the Opposition, the attacks were violent and more radical in tone. The newspapers had openly condemned him and had implied, with reason, that the official majority in the *Legislatif* did not represent the opinion of the nation. To this charge, the Emperor believed that there was only one reply that he could make. True Bonaparte that he was, he reasoned that he had been brought to power by an appeal to the nation, a *plébiscite*. Would not another appeal of much the same sort silence his enemies? With such a hope, he dissolved the *Legislatif* and called for new elections in May.

This action, inspired by Rouher, threw the country into a fever of excitement. Madame Dosne complained: "The salons, where no one talks of anything but elections, are like beehives when swarming is in progress. But the honey that they are making has not been culled from flowers." Business was at a standstill, for cautious bourgeois were uncertain of results. Even some factories were shut down, and the workmen who were deprived of labour provided excellent material for radical demagogues.

Here, in the elections, was a real opportunity for the *Union Libérale* to make its moderate policies prevail and to carry the country over the crisis. But, as before, when faced with the reality, these men of the former régime could not agree. With the possibility of power before them, all of their individual sympathies and pretensions revived. One group feared Berryer and his Legitimism, another element mistrusted the compromising tendencies of Ollivier, while still others suspected Thiers, Broglie, and Rémusat of Orléanism. The *Union Libérale* was encumbered by the débris of political opinions inherited from the first half of the century. And it was the Radicals who made the most of these divisions and did their utmost to increase them. Even the Emperor with his almost invariable and fatal propensity to do the wrong thing, allowed Rouher to attack the *Union* and again, as in 1863, Monsieur Thiers became the target for their arrows. Rouher's minions searched the speeches and writings of Thiers to find expressions that might be used to discountenance him in the eyes of the Opposition. They sought to prove that he was not a Liberal because he had spoken of *"la vile multitude,"* and they asserted that he was carrying on a sentimental correspondence with the members of the Orléans family (a fact which was true) and accused him of working for the substitution of Louis Philippe's heir for the House of Bonaparte.

This propaganda told. Rouher and his party were successful but hardly in the way that they desired. While Thiers and "the odious men of July" received a serious set-back in the elections, these manœuvres brought other enemies of the Empire to the fore. Those members of the Opposition who had their faith shaken by such means did not give their votes to Napoleon III; instead, they turned them to the account of the Republicans, and Léon Gambetta was elected from Marseilles. With him, the Democracy marched triumphant into the *Corps Legislatif*. Of the seven million seven hundred and thirty-eight thousand votes cast, only three million three hundred thousand were for the Imperial dynasty.

The divisions of the *Union Libérale* had lost them their predominance, and the victorious war that the Emperor had waged against them was not turned to his own benefit. Monsieur Bonaparte and Monsieur Thiers now had a new rival—Gambetta of Marseilles. In the words of Madame Dosne, "the Kings of the Moment are Gambetta, idol of the soldiers, Rochefort, leader of Labour, and Raspail, orator of the streets." As for the Moderate Liberals, these elections threw them into the arms of Émile Ollivier. As for the Emperor, they drove him into the way of concessions. The period of the Liberal Empire began in August, 1869, when Napoleon III prorogued the new *Legislatif* that he was not yet prepared to meet, and dismissed the Rouher Cabinet.

The transitions of Louis Napoleon were always slow. Upon the retirement of Rouher, the Emperor did not turn at once to the Third Party. Instead, he appointed a midway Cabinet which was put under the direction of Chasseloup-Laubat. A month later, at its suggestion, the

Senate passed a decree that enlarged considerably the powers of the *Corps Legislatif*. It gave that body the right to initiate legislation, to vote on the budget, to amend laws, and to interpellate the Ministry. It also acknowledged the principle of ministerial responsibility. So far was so good but when, in October, the Emperor failed to open the new *Legislatif* on the day appointed, France began to fear that Napoleon III was returning to his old policy of equivocations. Under Rochefort's leadership, the Radicals decided to force the issue, and a serious rising occurred in Paris, a revolt which lost its magnitude when it became known that Gambetta and his followers condemned the use of force. At the same time, however, the Emperor was warned that he was expected to carry his programme of reform beyond the modest limits set by the September decree.

It was this sane but stubborn attitude of the Republicans that really brought Émile Ollivier into power on the second day of January. At last, the party that had openly proclaimed its loyalty to both Empire and Democracy was afforded the chance to accomplish its purpose. No one could doubt its good intentions, and practically all of the Moderate Opposition rallied around the new Minister. Monsieur Thiers gathered his cohorts about him and announced that their opinions were to be found on the Council's bench. Together Third Party and Moderates set to work on a plan of reform which would have amounted, virtually, to a revision of the Constitution of 1852. Freedom of the Press and Freedom of Election were granted in an unsuccessful attempt to win over the Republicans to their side. Finally, as a sure pledge of his liberal sentiments, Ollivier proposed to abolish the exclusive right of the Senate to alter the Constitution.

At once he ran up against the strong objections of the Senators who were imperial appointees, jealous of their rights, and as absolutist-minded as Rouher himself. Alarmed at this threat to their power, these gentlemen warned the Emperor of the danger of such a radical change. With a cunning that does them credit, they advised him to consult the people by *plébiscite* before allowing any more alterations. Counsel of this sort was welcome to Napoleon III. Affairs had marched too fast to suit him: he was displeased at the alliance of Ollivier's party with the Monarchist followers of Monsieur Thiers. Confident that an appeal to France would justify him, he proposed to ask the people to choose between the old Constitution and the changes that the party then in power desired to make.

Neither the Moderates nor the Republicans were blind to the danger of such a proceeding. Falloux wrote to Thiers that this *plébiscite* was a mere subterfuge to justify a return to Absolutism. Both of them took up this cry and spread it throughout the country. Napoleon's wish prevailed, however, and, on May 8, 1870, the *plébiscite* resulted in a vote for the Emperor's system. Conservative Frenchmen, of whom there remained a plenty in the provinces, evidently feared the introduction of more radical elements into the *Corps Legislatif*.

While the jealousy of the Senate and the influence of the Absolutists had been great factors in encouraging Napoleon III to attempt this method of restoring power to the central government, there was another consideration that had played a large part in determining him to take such a step. By May, 1870, the Emperor had found himself in a trying situation as far as his foreign relations were concerned, and he had feared that the proposed alteration of the Constitution would create greater divisions in France at the very time when he might have to act and act quickly. Ailing, involved in quarrels at home and unsuccessful intrigues abroad, this Emperor had set to work on a secret plan to extricate himself from his difficulties and to render his country secure from the dangers to which his own blundering had exposed her.

Ever since the successful conclusion of the war of Prussia and Italy against Austria, Napoleon III had been confronted with two embarrassing problems. The first of these was the new situation that resulted in Germany.

There, in the North, Prussia was predominant. But her leaders were dreaming of supremacy and desirous of extending her hegemony to South Germany. The Emperor of the French was determined that this step must not be taken without a corresponding compensation to France, by which he could calm the fears and satisfy the national pride of his subjects. Not daring to attempt the annexation of Belgium or of the Rhine provinces, Napoleon III resorted to the idea of the purchase of Luxembourg. The occupation of that duchy by Prussian troops had called forth the loud protests of Thiers and his Moderates and, also, of the Republicans. It was in answer to this general alarm, in which the greater part of the country had come to share, that the Emperor opened parleys with the King of Holland. Negotiations were proceeding nicely when Prussia stepped in and refused her consent. Once again Napoleon III was checkmated by Bismarck, and his enemies in France began to use this situation as a weapon against him. At the same time, however, there was a second problem that had aroused hostility to him in his own country and in Europe.

Having won Venetia, the Italians were not satisfied, and desired Rome. On the other hand, the Catholic Party, arm in arm with Monsieur Thiers and the Moderates, demanded the protection of the Papacy and its sovereign rights. And when Garibaldi and his Red Shirts set out to do what the King of Italy desired but dared not do, Louis Napoleon must needs intervene to prevent a popular rising to annex Rome and accomplish the unification of Italy. Garibaldi's failure only served to fire the desire of the Italian patriots. At any time, therefore, the Emperor of the French might have to defend by force the Holy See. If he failed to do so, he would stand in danger of the anger of the Catholics, and, if he took a firm stand, he was sure to incur the wrath of the Republicans. Furthermore, there was another matter that complicated the situation: Russia and Italy were friends and should Bismarck support the Italians in a move on Rome, France would be faced with an alliance too powerful for her to have any reasonable expectations of success.

Confronted with these possibilities, Louis Napoleon had set about to increase and improve his armies. In this plan, the majority of the *Legislatif* had supported him. But, to put successfully into operation his scheme for escape from the problem of a New Prussia and a New Italy, he must have secrecy and quick action. And neither one of these would have been possible with a reformed Constitution and a *Legislatif* possessing enlarged powers.

To the mind of the Emperor, his design, if it succeeded, would restore him in the opinion of his own countrymen and of Europe. It envisaged a triple alliance of France, Austria, and Italy. France would guarantee to Austria the protection of the South German States from Prussian aggression: Austria would allow to Italy a part of the South Tyrol in place of Rome. And thus, Louis Napoleon might avoid the danger of a united Germany under Prussia and of a holy war carried on by himself to protect the Pope.

By the time, however, that the informal negotiations for this entente were under way, reforms had come into the Empire. These created the block that Napoleon III feared. Now, before he could give definite guarantees to the two powers whose alliance he was seeking, the *Corps Legislatif* would have to be consulted. Then, at that moment, publicity would come, and Bismarck now knowing for a fact what he already suspected, would almost certainly appeal to the German Princes to give him the armies that they had promised. Consequently, in May 1870, the projected alliance was merely an informal affair, and when the question of a Hohenzollern candidate for the Spanish throne arose, the Emperor of the French was without a friend upon whom he could depend.

When, on June 4, Leopold of Hohenzollern decided to accept the offer of the Spanish crown, Europe suspected that another coup of Bismarck's was about to succeed. To Frenchmen, the prospect of a Hohenzollern ruling in Spain was alarming: they saw their own country placed, as they phrased it, in a vise between Prussian Power on the Rhine and a Hohenzollern Prince on the Pyrenees frontier.

It was the party of the Absolutists that first signalled the event and that made the most of it by calling for a war to save France from envelopment by Prussian power. At first, the Opposition was silent, as if struck dumb, for the moment, by the sudden fulfilment of the very prophecies that some of their leaders had uttered in the *Corps Legislatif*. They concurred with the Absolutists in the belief that this offer of the crown was the result of a conscious intrigue to hem in and endanger France. At the same time, however, the Moderates of the Opposition and even those Republicans who were nearest to Gambetta, were not desirous of war. They realized that France was not adequately prepared for so great an effort and they suspected that the war cry of the Absolutists was simply an effort to get themselves back into the power which the creation of the Liberal Empire had lost them.

In this opinion, Émile Ollivier, the Minister, agreed. And Ministry, Moderates, and their leaders united to prevent what they felt would prove to be a catastrophe for their country. In place of war which he and his allies did not desire, Ollivier proposed to try to win a diplomatic victory at Berlin, and so to silence the Bonapartists whose papers were already arousing the country with the gospel of Mars. In conjunction with Monsieur Thiers and other leaders of the Centre, he decided to send a strong message to Prussia to admonish its King that Frenchmen would, without hesitation, "do their duty against any foreign power that attempted the destruction of the balance of power in Europe."

This message was loudly condemned by the Bonapartists as unpatriotic and "as savouring of the supine character of the statesmen of the July Monarchy who had conceived it." So great was the excitement that these *enragés* aroused that even after the *Legislatif* had given its consent to the plan, the Ministry began to weaken. Ollivier, alarmed by the reluctance of his imperial master to defy the War Faction, began to lose confidence, and admitted that, perhaps, the message had not been strong enough. To the Moderates, it looked as if the Ministry were yielding to the idea of a conflict. Thiers, therefore, certain of the support of conservative opinion in France, began to draw about him a Peace Party. On July 11, he interviewed the wavering Ministry and tried to reassure them. They responded to his rather drastic ministrations and when, on the following day, it became known that the Hohenzollerns had declined the honour, peace seemed assured. As a matter of fact, the calm that followed was merely the deadly quiet that often precedes a cataclysm.

During the first days of July the complexion of the Prussian Question in France had changed; it had come to have a double meaning to many Frenchmen. Thanks to the manœuvres of the Absolutists the question of war or peace now meant Absolutism or Ollivier, that is to say —the restoration of the old system but recently abandoned or the maintenance of the newly established "Liberal Empire." At the same time, the Absolutist

patches disclosed the capture of forty thousand of the enemy among whom, it was said, was Prince Frederick Charles. Paris went wild with delight and the dim popularity of Napoleon III became momentarily brighter. But this rejoicing was destined to be of short duration. Almost immediately sinister rumours were bruited about and Frenchmen began to ask themselves questions. Why, if France had won a victory, had the Empress Regent convoked the *Corps Legislatif* so unexpectedly? Gradually the truth became known; MacMahon's victory had been turned into a disaster and the forces of Frossard, too, had been beaten; both armies were in retreat. The joy of Paris was turned overnight into a resentment that was as bitter against the Government as it had been against the Teuton invaders.

When, on the morning of August 9, the *Legislatif* was convened, public feeling was running high. Once again the streets of Paris were crowded with mobs that were noisily demanding a victory. 1870 became 1814; another Bonaparte had deceived the nation and brought the invader across its lands. The spirit of the streets had invaded the *Corps Legislatif*, and when Émile Ollivier arose to make his plea, he could not quiet the demonstration that was aroused by his appearance. When calm was finally established, the Opposition proposed the formation of an executive committee "chosen within the Corps, invested with full powers of government, to repel the foreign invasion." This measure was the first direct attack made on the family that had brought such ills to France. Eugénie hesitated to agree to it, knowing, perhaps, its sinister import. Finally, however, she yielded when she accepted the retirement of the discomfited Ollivier and gave the Ministry into the care of General Palikao. Trochu was made Commander of Paris, and Bazaine was placed in charge of the Army of the Rhine.

These concessions only half satisfied the Opposition,

and when the siege of Metz had been begun, the Empress was forced to make definite overtures to the Moderate section of the Opposition and its leader. Through Prosper Mérimée, Monsieur Thiers was actually invited to join the Government. There is some doubt, however, as to whether Mérimée's overtures were countenanced by the distraught Regent. For two days Mérimée pursued that elusive old gentleman for interviews and bombarded him with notes. But Monsieur refused to be caught. He informed Mérimée frankly that he believed that the Empire was at an end. But he added that he would not work for its destruction. Nay, more, he would even aid it with his counsels as a good citizen should do. To assume its livery, however, was out of the question, for the Empress Regent would never accept his conditions. These last, however, Monsieur Thiers was very careful to specify—"a government as impersonal as possible, anonymous, which would not be the result of the triumph, present or future, of any existing party—in a word, a government thoroughly national." To his own friends, however, the master of the hôtel on the Place Saint Georges was more specific. He revealed to them that he would not serve in any government unless the Emperor abdicated, the principal troops were concentrated around Paris, and the entire population armed. Such stipulations were unacceptable to Eugénie and "therefore I cannot promise to attempt, in my own name, an enterprise that is hopeless."

Failing in her efforts to enlist the services of the leaders of the Moderate Opposition, the Empress resolved to retain Palikao. But when the Advisory Council of Defence, that had been demanded by the Opposition, was formed, Monsieur Thiers was approached a second time. His reply was definite: he would not accept an appointment to the Council unless three members were elected by the *Legislatif* and unless that body ratified his own nomination. When these conditions had been met, he forgot the insults that the *Corps Legislatif* and the Imperial Family had thrown at him barely a month before, and entered upon his duties with eagerness.

It was on August 24 that Monsieur Thiers resumed the task that he had begun in 1840—the fortification of Paris. Among his papers at the *Bibliothèque Nationale* there are great *dossiers* of notes on the approaches to Paris, the rivers, the forts, and the victualling of the city. As Counsellor he spent hours on the ramparts personally directing the work of fortification, and other hours studying the training of the new army of which France stood so desperately in need. And daily the secret reports from the front became blacker. To Mignet, he confided his belief that his task was a thankless one and a useless one. "The work has been begun too late, and the high command will never realize until the time for it has passed, the necessity for concentrating their armies around Paris." d'Haussonville writes of a walk that he took with Thiers over the fortifications of Montmartre. They watched green and inexperienced volunteers drilling in the hot sun. Their clumsiness nearly drove his companion to distraction. "And these are to be the defenders of our city." It was a melancholy promenade.

Meanwhile, the fortunes of the Emperor were going from bad to worse. Finally, at five o'clock on the afternoon of September 1, Moltke captured Sedan and the Emperor with it. At once Napoleon III asked for peace terms. But when they came they included the cession of Alsace-Lorraine, and of Metz and Strasbourg. To save the last vestige of honour that remained to his House, the captive Emperor refused to listen to them.

News of this final disaster did not reach Paris until September 3, and then the tumult broke loose. The army which, during the better days of the Empire, had held the Radicals in restraint, no longer existed, and control of the city was nearly gone. By evening the mobs were again on the streets. This time, some of the people were carrying arms, and they were demanding not only a victory but also "the fall of the Empire."

Here was the chance for the Republicans. But their leaders hesitated to take advantage of the situation: Gambetta, Jules Favre, and Jules Grévy feared to saddle the Third Republic, that they desired, with the disastrous consequence of the Second Empire. In fact, this state of mind existed among all of the parties that were represented in the *Corps Legislatif:* no one faction was willing to attempt the establishment of its own régime because of the terrific problem of the continuation of the war with which the new Government would be confronted. Meanwhile, exiles and pretenders, even, were flocking to Paris. It was announced that the Princes of Orléans were on their way to the distressed city. But in their actual state of mind, no one of the adherents of the former Monarchy desired the presence of the Orléans family in France. Even Monsieur Thiers advised that the Princes retire to foreign soil and occupy themselves with recruiting a foreign legion, and forget about usurping a throne. In the alarm of the moment, they believed that postponement of this issue and purely provisional measures were the only safe lines of conduct to follow. This condition was destined to provide France with a government that for several years was neither Monarchy, Empire, nor Republic.

For the time being most of the leaders of the Opposition appeared to favour the plan that had been originally suggested by Thiers—a provisional and thoroughly nonpartisan government. Certainly, this seemed to be the only alternative to anarchy and the rule of the mob. Accordingly, while the crowds were rioting on the boulevards, Jules Favre and his followers decided to call a meeting of the *Legislatif* and make it seize the power. Then, they hoped to have that body name a Committee of Public

Safety of which Palikao, Schneider, and Thiers were to be members.

Upon the arrival of Monsieur Thiers at the Chamber, he found himself again the man of the hour. Since his return to public life, he had resolutely avoided a definite political marriage: consequently both the Left and the Right desired to make him their man. But he remained reserved and non-committal. Jules Favre, Garnier-Pagès, Gambetta, and Jules Ferry drew him aside. They told him of their plan to nominate him, but he refused to serve. He saw clearly that an unfavourable peace would have to be signed and that, he declared, he could never bring himself to do. Also, he said, he was so strongly opposed to the antiquated policy of the existing army staff that he could never agree with them.

As soon as the session had opened, Favre proposed that the *Corps* declare the end of the Empire and seize the power. Against this suggestion Monsieur Thiers protested, and objected to the use of the term "the fall of the Empire." He argued that this expression was too harsh and urged the substitution of the phrase *"vacance du pouvoir."* He then read from the Tribune a counter-motion that was concise and definite: "In view of the circumstances, the Chamber shall name a Commission of Government and of National Defence; a Constituent Assembly shall be called as soon as the situation allows it."

This motion appeared to satisfy all except the Bonapartists who delayed the vote until a mob led by Socialist leaders broke into the Assembly, ejected its President, and forced that body to pass a vote condemning the Empire.

This sudden intrusion of the mob threatened to render any real decision unlikely of accomplishment. If they were to retain their hold on Paris, the Republicans must act and act quickly. Accordingly, Favre and Gambetta hastened to the Hôtel de Ville and from there proclaimed the Republic.

For a brief moment, it looked as though there would be a struggle between the Moderates of the *Legislatif* and the Hôtel de Ville. But Grévy was sent to the Republicans with a protest written by Thiers who had been appointed temporary chairman of the now partly dispersed Assembly. Backed by General Trochu, Commandant of Paris, the Moderates asserted the inviolable character of the *Legislatif* and, finally, through the efforts of Thiers, the Hôtel de Ville agreed to recognize the temporary control of the *Legislatif* and to consent to the formation by that body of a Committee of Government and National Defence. It was also understood that a Constituent and National Assembly would be convoked on October 15. In this wise Paris was spared for a time, at least, the horrors of an insurrection at the very moment when the German forces were marching on the city.

Late on the evening of September 4, the exhausted *Legislatif* adjourned. Jules Favre accompanied Monsieur Thiers to his home. On the way the carriage was halted, and the man who had saved the day in Paris was forced by the acclamations of the crowds to descend from his conveyance and speak to them. With Monsieur Bonaparte a prisoner, Monsieur Thiers was again on the way to becoming the idol of Paris.

On the morning of September 5, the serious business of the new and provisional Government began. Monsieur Favre, as soon as he had assumed control of the important post of Minister of Foreign Affairs, discovered what he had expected all along; France in her extremity had no alliances and no real means of communicating with Europe. But the need for an appeal to the neutral nations was desperate. Germany was advancing rapidly across the country to Paris, and an armistice must be obtained, else France would go down in utter defeat. After conferences with Lord Lyons and Prince Richard de Metternich, it was decided to send an agent to submit the case of France to the Powers and to appeal for intervention. Favre knew that the chances for actual assistance were slim, but he realized, at the same time, that there was only one man in France who had the slightest chance of success. Monsieur Thiers was his logical choice for he was best known to the European courts where he had many friends. Favre himself explained the selection in the following words: "At the same time, Monsieur Thiers carried with him the great party of Moderate men timid and uncertain, whose support, even in time of crisis, is important for a government."

The Minister, accordingly, went to the Place Saint Georges to beg its owner to undertake this difficult task. When he arrived, he found Monsieur Thiers in bed, worn out with the excitement of the previous day and in a panic about the future. He was ill with a cold and a fever, he declared, and he proceeded to bring out a thousand reasons for refusing the appointment. "You trouble me more than I can say by making this unexpected proposition. You know my sentiments; I am not hostile to the Government of National Defence; I desire its success; but I do not wish to be associated with it. You see me in no wise fit to be its messenger. But that is the smallest obstacle to my acceptance; the principal one is the hardness of heart of the cabinets that I shall have to consult." He asked for time for reflection.

Early the next morning, however, Monsieur Thiers appeared at the *Affaires Étrangères*, "alert and well, and eager to serve his country!" Favre and he discussed the journey and the nature of the appeal that he should make. The most pressing necessity was, of course, to obtain, through the intervention of the neutral powers, an interview for Favre with Bismarck. Both the Minister and his envoy, however, appear to have believed, even at this date, that they would be able to obtain armed intervention on behalf of France from one or two of the powers. Haste was necessary but there were delays. Communications with the provinces in the northeast were so disorganized that they were not certain that this envoy extraordinary would be able to reach the coast. Then, too, Monsieur Thiers must have his trousseau. It was not until September 12 that the mission left for Calais. It was a dramatic moment. The train that carried Thiers was the last train to leave Paris for the Channel, and after it had passed over the ramparts of the city, French engineers blew up the bridge to delay the rapidly approaching German armies a few days longer—until, at least, an interview had taken place between Favre and Bismarck. With the noise of this explosion ringing in his ears, Monsieur Thiers started out upon the most momentous, rapid, and extensive tour of his long life, and with the certain knowledge that Paris would be encircled before his return.

At seven o'clock on the morning of September 13, the French mission arrived at London. At noon, Lord Granville called. Thiers immediately opened his attack by denying that the French people had been responsible for the war; he knew that his visitor had frequently asserted the contrary. He even recalled to him the services that France had rendered to England in the Crimea. Granville related to others that he was deeply moved by the sorrow and agitation of the aged statesman who had undertaken a task that would have been difficult for a man far younger than himself. His voice broke, and once, at least, tears poured down his cheeks. Granville was gentle and sympathetic. It was not the same with his second caller. In the late afternoon Gladstone put in an appearance. The little Frenchman relates that this Minister was cold and *difficile*—"an old goldfish"—and that he discoursed piously and at great length on Queen Victoria's maternal affections. All that he was able to obtain from Gladstone was a promise to facilitate an interview between Favre and Bismarck. But Thiers still hoped for more, and in such hope he remained in London seeking interviews in every possible quarter and almost as often meeting with indifference. Disheartened, on September 17 he made his preparations to return home, and as he set out upon this sad journey, he carried with him the painful conviction that a peace, even a cruel peace, was a necessity for France. The case for intervention now seemed almost hopeless. Far greater was his despair when, upon his arrival in France, he received instructions to proceed to Tours—the path to Paris was practically blocked.

Hardly had he set out upon the first stage of his journey than the Government of National Defence was faced with a serious problem. By September 15, the German armies had come close to Meaux and it was certain that Paris would be encircled. Under such circumstances, could the rest of France be administered from a beleaguered city? That was the question that confronted Jules Favre and his colleagues. Finally, it was decided that the Government should remain where it was but that a delegation of three of its members should be dispatched to Tours to administer "unbesieged France." Accordingly, a committee with extraordinary powers was established at Tours as the seat of authority for those parts of the country that were cut off from Paris. Shortly afterwards the young Gambetta left the Capital via balloon, armed with extraordinary powers to raise an army in the provinces to continue the war.

Upon his return, therefore, Thiers found a Government divided in body if not in spirit. He went in haste to Tours where he learned that the conference that he had obtained for Jules Favre with Bismarck had taken place on September 18. Bismarck's terms—the preliminary sacrifice of Strasbourg and Metz—had been declined by Favre who had announced his refusal in a magnificent "Circular to the Nations of the World." France, then, would not yield, and her aged envoy, already worn by four sleepless nights of anxiety and travel, resumed his weary journey in search of a friend for his distressed country. As he set out he remarked that after the cold douche that he had received in London he was more than ever doubtful of the reception that he would have in Austria, but that the courage of Favre had given him new inspiration.

The journey to Vienna was a long, hard experience interrupted by changes of plans and the inevitable confusions of a disorganized officialdom. The original arrangement had been for him to go part way by sea but haste was necessary. Therefore, an entire land route was finally selected. Early on the morning of September 20 he set out from Tours to Mont Cenis. On the evening of the twenty-first he arrived in Italy. The little town of Suze where he stopped en route was celebrating the entry of the Italian troops into Rome—another symbol of the rapidly changing world in which Monsieur Thiers was moving. The town was decorated and the people rejoicing in the streets. The contrast to what he had seen in Tours on the previous day was, he relates, almost too painful. On the evening of September 23 he arrived at Vienna to be greeted by a poster of himself *en pythonisse* saying to a contrite Napoleon who knelt before him: "I told you, *misérable,* that there was only one more mistake left for you to make."

His interviews did not begin until the next day. He found Count von Beust personally sympathetic to him. The Austrian statesman acknowledged that he pitied him in his distress and anxiety. Thiers immediately took advantage of this reception to urge a general alliance of France, Austria, and Russia to limit the ambitions of Prussia. Evidently, in spite of the fatigue and strain, he had not lost his quick and ready wit, for when von Beust interrupted him by referring to the many fair promises and fair words that he must have heard, the little Frenchman shrugged his shoulders and replied: "Oh! I have not been spoiled by them."

From his sojourn in Vienna and his conversations with von Beust and Andrassy, one encouraging thing developed: he was informed that, if Russia could be brought to the point of intervention on behalf of the general interests of Europe, Austria would join her. "In the Tsar and in Gortschakoff lies your hope." With these words, the most cheering that he had yet received, Thiers and his wife set out on their sixty-hour journey to Russia.

They stopped en route in Warsaw where they were the object of the curious gaze of crowds of silent but sympathetic Poles. On the morning of September 27 they reached St. Petersburg. Gortschakoff at once sent word that he would receive the French envoy after he had had time to recover from his long journey. But the reply of Monsieur Thiers was that he would pay his respects to Monsieur Gortschakoff early in the afternoon. Surely enough, at two o'clock, he presented himself at Tsarkoé-Sélo!

Russia herself was sympathetic to the plight of France, and the Russian Minister, himself a man subject to flattery, was not insensible to the great compliment that this venerable French statesman had paid him in journeying so far and so fast for his counsel. The Tsar, however, was friendly to the Prussian King, and the Russian Government had doubts as to the character and durability of the new Republic. Neither the Autocrat of All the Russias nor his Minister would welcome a return to 1793. But the very fact that the Government of National Defence had sent Thiers, whose moderate sympathies were well-known, predisposed them in his favour. Undoubtedly, the wisdom of Jules Favre in sending Thiers was a great factor in determining the sympathy that France met with at St. Petersburg.

Thiers soon found, however, that an alliance was not likely. Russia was determined to wait until she was sure that the French Revolution would not repeat itself. Soon matters took a new turn, and it was Gortschakoff who talked and Thiers who listened and was finally persuaded that, to save his country, he must abandon all idea of an immediate and active alliance with the Courts of Europe and, instead, accept from them a new Commission. "For the present, let us attend to extricating France from her immediate difficulty." Sacrifice first, then negotiations with Germany, backed by the moral support of England, Russia, and Austria. In fact, after a conversation with the Tsar, Thiers virtually found himself forced to assume the position of negotiator with Germany. Alexander II displayed to his astonished visitor a copy of a telegram that he had sent to his Prussian cousin: "Monsieur Thiers is here. He is wise, moderate, he alone can obtain from France the concessions necessary to a peace. Send him a safe-conduct." "But," protested the subject of this message, "you give me the character of a peace negotiator and my Government has not empowered me to act in such a capacity. Present me rather in the rôle that I am now playing—one who knows the internal character of my own country, who has surveyed Europe, and now desires to be authorized to enter Paris in order to try to find *un moyen de rapprochement.*" In the end, this suggestion was adopted and followed.

The St. Petersburg conversation had, in this way, a very important effect in changing considerably the aspect of Franco-Prussian affairs. Monsieur Thiers came to Russia in search of an alliance, and he left that country a peace negotiator in search of a mandate from his own country. The new position that he assumed undoubtedly made him the most important Frenchman in the eyes of Europe, and played no small part in making him later on the pivot of political power in France.

But it was a delicate undertaking to which he had consented: he had virtually agreed to return to France and to enter beleaguered Paris through the German lines—a step that was to be permitted and facilitated by the enemies of his own country in order that he might persuade his Government to accept the idea of concessions and to appoint him as their negotiator. The plan was fraught with every possibility of failure. There was Bismarck's temper and the impatience of the German High Command, both of which he feared. But, more than all else, there was France whose state of mind he found even more disturbing upon his arrival on October 21.

At Tours, he consulted at the headquarters of the War Party which was now led by Léon Gambetta, impractical patriot and nationalist *à outrance*. There his talk of concessions and peace met with little sympathy and, frequently, with harsh censure. Peace only if it would give the country a chance to be delivered by arms, was the attitude at Tours. Paris, at least the Government resident in the besieged Paris, was for an armistice, the immediate calling of an Assembly, and peace negotiations that could be speedily ratified by that new body. Not so, however, with the section of the city that was under the influence of the Radicals. It was this Government, unstable, hemmed in by Germans, in danger from its own Radicals, and becoming daily more suspected by the Tours delegation, that Thiers must reach. Finally, on October 28, his *laissez-passer,* obtained through the good offices of Russia, arrived, and Monsieur Thiers set out to inform Jules Favre of what he had found and to obtain powers to negotiate at the General Headquarters of the Germans at Versailles. As he entered Orléans, great posters announced the surrender of Bazaine. He entered the coach of the local diocesan and drove to Versailles whence he was to be transferred over the lines to Paris.

It was nine o'clock at night when he drove into Versailles in his calêche. The moment was propitious. Certain of the German Princes were eager to end the war and the neutral nations had also expressed themselves on this point. Bismarck, to whom Thiers was presented, was in a mood to consider terms and wished to hold a preliminary conference then and there. But the little Frenchman loyally remembered his duty to the distressed Government within the gates of Paris and replied to the advances of the German Chancellor in these words: "I can only talk to you to say that I cannot talk with you." At last, Bismarck desisted in his attempts and remarked: "We will discuss the matter on your return provided, of course, that you return, for they tell me that a new revolution is on the way at Paris, and, perhaps, you run a risk in going there."

With these words, he was dismissed and conducted to the lines at Sèvres. There, a German officer signalled to the French to send a rowboat across the Seine for their distinguished visitor. At last a small boat, rowed by a French soldier, put out. Monsieur Thiers entered it. Midstream the shells shrieked above them and Thiers remarked: "Do you know what would be a picturesque event in History? Suppose that this boat which is carrying peace and deliverance to the Parisians should be blown to bits by a French shell."

At five o'clock on October 29 he arrived at the house of Baron de Rothschild in the Bois de Boulogne, where the French had established their General Headquarters. Favre, Trochu, and Picard came out to him, and he spent the long night relating the discouraging tale of his experiences and explaining his conversion to Gortschakoff's idea of concessions. As the old man proceeded, the faces of the three gentlemen from Paris became more and more grave. When he had done, they exposed to him that their own power in Paris hung by a thread. The populace, they told him, was impatient and starving, and stirred by Félix Pyat "and his revolutionary friends." A Commune, they believed, was imminent, and the only way to prevent it was an immediate cessation of hostilities around Paris, food, few concessions, and the speedy reunion of France under a Government authorized by a National Assembly. If Paris remained cut off from the rest of the country much longer, a revolution was inevitable. Towards morning, it was agreed that the Government would accept the armistice that the neutral nations advised, provided they would be allowed food in Paris and in the invaded sections, and complete liberty of election in all parts of France for a National Assembly. The afternoon of October 31 found Monsieur Thiers and Roger on their way back to the German Headquarters.

At four o'clock they reached the bridge at Sèvres. It was cold, there was a heavy rain and a high wind. Through the storm the two Frenchmen gazed back on Paris, this time with misgivings. Thiers relates that in their hearts they doubted if the Government that had sent them forth would be there when they returned. The interviews began the next day at Bismarck's temporary residence on the rue de Provence. Monsieur Thiers himself was not impressed with the appearance of their surroundings. Two bottles with candles stuck in them served as candelabra. The German Chancellor was not opposed to the idea of an armistice that would allow the French to convoke a National Assembly empowered to ratify a peace. But he was not sure of the durability of the Government with which he was already treating; he had a complete knowledge of Gambetta and the War Party at Tours and of the Communards at Paris. Consequently, he desired a guarantee for the future. He first talked of the cession of a Paris fortress. For two days more the negotiations dragged on and then, on November 3, Bismarck read to Thiers the news that the expected uprising had come almost immediately after the departure of the two envoys from the city. Exasperated by Favre's peace talk and by the fall of

Metz, the Radicals had arisen, had virtually seized the Government, and imprisoned some of its members. Monsieur Thiers asked to be allowed to send a friend to Paris for news. This was granted and when the messenger returned he announced that order had been restored but that the position of the Government was very uncertain. Thiers at once went to meet Favre at Billancourt. There he learned that his plan would never be acceptable to Paris or to the Government. From Tours Gambetta had already launched an eloquent anathema against it. There followed the disconsolate return of Monsieur Thiers to Versailles and the rupture of the negotiations. Then, disheartened at the failure of his efforts, he proceeded to Tours where his pleas for a reasonable attitude were drowned out by the war cries of Gambetta who was determined to become a second Organizer of Victory. To an extent, Gambetta's efforts were successful in staving off a definite defeat for several weeks to come. It was only after the bombardment of Paris that Favre himself came out to Bismarck again and an armistice was accepted on German terms which included the immediate calling of a National Assembly.

CHAPTER XVI

MONSIEUR THIERS AND THE THIRD REPUBLIC

THE bombardment of Paris by the Germans and the consequent indignation of England and Russia had finally led Bismarck to conclude an armistice with Jules Favre. This arrangement put an end not only to the siege of Paris but also to the Government of National Defence. From Bordeaux, Gambetta announced that this act of the Paris Governors placed them beyond the pale. But Gambetta's excommunication was merely another explosion of his frenzied oratory; the important fact was that the very terms of the armistice provided for the immediate calling of a National Assembly at Bordeaux. And this last duty became, at once, the concern of Frenchmen.

To the minds of most of the voters, the election was more a matter of peace than a question of government. Gambetta and his Republicans from the great towns alone thought of continuing the struggle. The majority desired only a speedy termination of hostilities and a return to the pursuit of their daily tasks. Consequently, France gave most of her suffrages to the Moderates, and to the venerable statesman who had played such a large part in the first attempts to end hostilities and who, it had been amply demonstrated, was most likely to obtain the sympathy of Europe for the plight of France. While the earlier career of Monsieur Thiers had its part in his election, the fact that he was chosen from twenty-seven departments was due, in great degree, to the rôle that he had played during his *tour du monde* in September and October of the preceding year.

Early in January he had removed with his family from Tours to Bordeaux and lodged himself comfortably at the Hôtel de France. Once there, he needed only to wait until the nation's representatives had gathered together and offered him the power. His elevation was a foregone conclusion, for so violent was the Opposition led by Gambetta to Favre and his colleagues, that the election of any member of the Government of National Defence was impossible. On February 13, 1871, the National Assembly met. It presented a surprising character: of the six hundred and fifty members, about four hundred were Royalists. It looked as if the Republic was doomed, and, indeed, that seemed to be the case for a time. Four days later they elected by acclamation Monsieur Thiers as their leader, and gave him the title of Chief of the Executive Power.

In spite of the unanimity that had attended his election, the position of Thiers was not entirely clear in the minds of those deputies who had chosen him. From the very beginning, however, he seems to have had no doubt about his own obligations. To the Royalists, Orléanists and Legitimists, who had not waited until his election to beseige him with requests, he counselled a temporary abstention from political issues. The first duty of the deputies, he told them, was to secure the deliverance of French soil from the Germans. "I accept the power and will hold it until the day when, the work of national reparation having been accomplished, France will be called upon to decide what form of government she desires." Unsatisfactory as this was to *Gambettistes* and *Royalistes,* they recognized the wisdom of his words and accepted them. For the time being his inaugural address, which was not so impromptu an affair as has been supposed, became the constitution of France. Frenchmen called it the *Pacte de Bordeaux.*

As to the future, he may have had another opinion. There is good reason to believe that while he recognized the existence and necessity of the Republic for the moment, he was not entirely convinced as to its desirability or its duration. In his heart, he still believed in his old ideal of *monarchie parlementaire*. But that must come, he wrote, by the will of the nation after the nation had been delivered from Germany. On the other hand, he added, if the Republicans displayed the greater zeal in making peace and regeneration possible, then the Republic might be the best thing. In the meantime, loyalty to the established state of affairs was an absolute necessity.

One hour after the announcement of the formation of the new Government at Bordeaux, England, Austria, and Italy formally recognized it. On the following day Thiers announced his Cabinet which included Jules Favre, Dufaure, Picard, Jules Simon, and lesser lights. Then he took leave of the Assembly and set out for Versailles.

There, in the midst of surroundings that were so reminiscent of the past grandeur of France, he entered upon a five-day contest with Bismarck. Phrase by phrase he debated the fate of his country with the Iron Chancellor whom, now, he found more determined than he had been in October. The interviews began on February 21 when Bismarck opened their conversations with a word that was far from encouraging.

BISMARCK: "When I saw you in October, Monsieur Thiers, I mentioned a sum of money. Today that amount is not enough, for since then we have suffered and expended a great deal. I asked for four milliards; today we must have six."

THIERS: "Six milliards! Why, no one in the world could find that amount. It must have been the military who suggested such a sum: financiers would never have dreamed of asking as much as that."

Thiers stuck bravely to his point. Once, even, the aged statesman buried his head in his arms and sobbed. It was these tears, apparently, that decided the German Chancellor to relent a little. At the last he agreed to £200,000,000 that was to be guaranteed by a German army of occupation until the debt had been discharged.

The negotiations then turned from finance to territory. This was the most critical problem of all. Metz and Belfort were demanded by Germany, but Thiers felt that Metz was relatively a matter of indifference, "for Metz closes nothing while with Belfort one holds the frontier intact." For the retention of Belfort by France he stood firm. This debate lasted nine consecutive hours. Finally, on February 24, Bismarck suggested a compromise: "I have an alternative to propose to you. Which do you prefer: Belfort or the renunciation of our determination to enter Paris?" And Thiers, in despair, cried: "Belfort! Belfort!" This last agreement made possible a settlement by which Thiers committed his country to the indemnity, an army of occupation, a German triumph in Paris, and the cession of Alsace, Metz, and practically all the department of the Moselle. "They wished to take away from us three-quarters of Lorraine," he wrote to a friend in London, "we have saved four-fifths: but we have lost Metz. The choice lay between Metz and Belfort. . . . Finally, I recovered Belfort for us."

Back to Bordeaux he hastened, in terror of what he had done. His family and friends received him as a victor, and, indeed, he was a victor, for the terms that he had obtained were far more lenient than many had anticipated. It is related that when the lovely Madame Thiers welcomed him she called him a hero. To this compliment the little man is said to have replied: *"Mon Dieu,* why did you not give me more tears to shed? Then the terms would have been even better."

Thiers, however, was far too astute to be deceived by the flattery of his entourage. He was depressed, and afraid of the opinion of his country. When, however, February 28 had dawned and he stood before the Bordeaux Assembly, his courage had returned. Fearlessly he faced the indignant protests of *Gambettistes,* Socialists, and Paris Radicals, and exposed to the delegates the sacrifices that they must make. Cold logic and practical common sense characterized this address in which a bit of the schoolmaster appeared again: "We must act like sensible people and not like children, for we are settling the fate of our entire country and of two of our fairest provinces." His arguments prevailed and a vote of acceptance was passed by a majority of three hundred and forty. In this way the war with Germany was ended, and the life of a dismembered France began when the deputies from the ceded lands made their dramatic departure from the Assembly.

By the first of March, the Chief of the Executive Power had concluded hostilities with Germany. But immediately the possibilities of a civil war began to loom larger on the political horizon of France. The vote of the three hundred and forty had not been accepted gracefully by all of those who had opposed it. Some Republican deputies from the larger towns had declared that they could never reconcile themselves to such an arrangement, while, in Paris, Blanqui, Pyat, and their Socialists openly condemned it. In fact, just at the moment when Thiers and Bismarck were arriving at their conclusions, the Paris populace had answered the call of the Provisional Committee of the National Guard by conferring on it a permanent power to prevent the Prussians from entering the city. And, on February 24, they formed delegations from the various metropolitan districts and seized cannon to place them at the Buttes de Chaumont on Montmartre. In spite of these threats, however, they did not attack the Prussians when, on March 1, the victorious army of Germany penetrated as far as the Place de la Concorde. "The most brilliant of suns," wrote Jules Favre to Thiers, "insults our misery and its rays seem to salute our sorrow and the triumph of our enemies."

The German entry into Paris was regarded as an intolerable insult by many of its citizens, and this event plus the fact of a Royalist majority at Bordeaux increased the suspicion with which the citizens of the Capital regarded the Assembly. Favre wrote Thiers that the only thing that would allay this growing sentiment was the immediate return of the Chief Executive and the Assembly to Paris: "People are saying, and with truth, that this mark of confidence alone can disarm evil passions and turn men's minds to their ordinary occupations. If the Assembly will do this and if, at the same time, it will align itself with us by a declaration of its intentions to make a sincere experiment of the Republic, it will render further trouble impossible." But to come to Paris was exactly what the majority in the Assembly did not want to do.

Both the Moderates and the Royalists feared contact with the *"enragés"* in the Capital, and there was only a minority of Republicans at Bordeaux who desired to move the seat of authority to Paris. But to Favre and his colleagues this abstention seemed to be fraught with danger. And, when it appeared that the Chief Executive himself was inclined to remain where he was, Favre wrote a violent protest to him. On March 5, Thiers replied: "You are very cruel to write to me of resignation because of difficulties that neither myself nor my colleagues have created. The Assembly is composed of divers parties and some of them of an intolerable impatience. At present, it is devoted to me, but I know not how long that will last. It is, however, profoundly defiant, not of me but of the general situation. Therefore, I dare not leave it. Nor can I leave my Cabinet which needs to be kept entirely together simply because it represents such a variety of opinion. In such a situation I cannot come to Paris without the Assembly. And it is impossible to bring it there. Nevertheless, it has consented to move near the city; it prefers Fontainebleau."

The truth of the matter was that Thiers had already compromised with the majority. He had given his promise that he would not place them in the midst of Republican Paris, but at its doors. Finally, Versailles was selected. When the Chief Executive had arranged for four trains to be run daily between the Capital and its suburb, and had mounted cannon atop Mont Valérien, he felt that he and his colleagues had done enough.

This decision was the great error that Thiers made. Afterwards, many of his contemporaries declared that the horrors of the Commune would have been avoided if he had resolutely forced his moderate-minded Assembly and his Cabinet to move to Paris on the first of March. As a matter of fact, Thiers does not seem to have grasped the real seriousness of the situation in the Capital. On March 6, he wrote to Broglie: "The troubles of Paris are more a nervous malady than anything else. I am going to collect re-enforcements of fifty thousand men. That will calm the nerves of some and quiet the villainy of others, at least I think it will. But, if it is necessary to fight, we will fight." There is, perhaps, another explanation for his attitude: in the face of a mob Thiers had never shown great courage or even clear-headedness. To defend himself from this charge he resorted to the dangerous practice of historical parallels when he employed with Jules Favre the most ridiculous argument that he could have invented: "If, in February 1848, Louis Philippe had fled Paris, he would have been back there in eight days' time, his dynasty would still be reigning and we would have been spared many terrible trials." In short, the head of the Government himself was afraid of Paris. March, 1871, is not the heroic period of Monsieur Thiers' career.

When it became known that the Government and Assembly would not come to the Capital, the Central Committee of the National Guard took matters in its own hands and proclaimed the right of the people of Paris to defend the Republic against the Bordeaux Royalists. Upon receipt of this news, Thiers rushed to the city and, on March 18, ordered the Governor of Paris to seize the guns that the insurrectionaries had sequestered. At this the National Guardsmen arose in revolt, and at three-thirty in the afternoon of that same day the Chief Executive and those members of his Government who were resident in the city made an undignified retreat to Versailles. Shortly after their departure, the insurrection was victorious and celebrated its triumph by the brutal execution of two Government generals, Thomas and Lecomte.

Within three weeks of his conclusion of peace with Bismarck, Monsieur Thiers had instituted a war with Paris. "Frightful war, because of which my heart bleeds" —was how he described it, but many Frenchmen smiled at his words and some of them, Moloch especially, drew cartoons of this bleeding heart that would not pass the censor today. To these attacks he was impervious and like a *Napoléon en miniature* he set about organizing for the conflict and dictating to the Assembly that had joined him at Versailles. French soldiers returning from Germany found themselves transferred to a great concentration camp at Cherbourg. Soon Monsieur Thiers had an army of one hundred and thirty thousand men at his disposal. Indeed, he might have needed all of that for, by March 25, voices of protest had been heard at Saint Étienne, Lyons, Toulouse, Marseilles, and Limoges.

quarrel of Legitimist and Orléanist, coupled with the neutral attitude of Thiers, meant a new lease on life for the Republicans. And, in August, these gentlemen proposed to insure this advantage by a prolongation of the status quo. With this purpose in mind, the so-called *Constitution Rivet* was passed and gave to Monsieur Thiers the title of President of the Republic. It also prolonged the political life of the existing Assembly, and permitted the President to participate in parliamentary debates.

Wiser and less selfish heads had, however, voted for the measure. These men realized that it was absolutely necessary for Monsieur Thiers to remain in office a little longer. It would give to Germany the assurance that the obligations which France had assumed would be discharged, and it would make possible the completion of the President's plans for the reorganization of the French army, a matter that, to Frenchmen, was of grave importance in view of the measures begun by Bismarck for the formation of the Dreikaiserbund. In July, 1871, the first of the indemnity instalments had been paid, and by March 15, 1872, enough would be paid off to justify requesting the German Emperor to agree to a complete evacuation of French soil by the German troops in the course of the following year. "We wish only," wrote Monsieur Thiers to the French Minister in Russia, "to see France resume her place in the world, possessing the strength that she should always have had and which the Emperor wasted by his foolish enterprises. My desire is peace, durable peace, and reorganization. Nothing more, nothing less."

And to such a happy and reasonable state of affairs, Monsieur Thiers was really bringing his country. But it was done at the expense of his own popularity and influence.

At this time, his letters to his intimates were filled with complaints about the attitude of his friends. To Duvergier de Hauranne he wrote: "I thank you from my heart for your friendly, kind letter which comforted me. I am happy to know that you, the oldest of my friends, agree with me. With the exception of yourself, Rémusat, Sainte-Hilaire, Calmon, and Casimir Périer, the greater number of my acquaintances are behaving badly because of diplomatic posts that are not given, *bâtons de maréchal* that I have refused to confer, and ministerial portfolios that are not forthcoming." His intimate coterie was called, by his enemies, *"la garde personnelle de Monsieur Thiers,"* and, as time went on, they were accused of exerting an undue and malign influence over the aged President. Barthelémy de Sainte-Hilaire was dubbed his alter ego, and the story was spread about that he paid out secret funds to his agents. Sextius Aude, his personal secretary, whom he had first known at Aix-en-Provence, was called his valet, and there was much amusing comment about those fragrant cups of coffee so carefully prepared by Madame Thiers and carried to the Chamber by Aude when the venerable President was about to make an address. The names of prominent women, too, were not omitted from the stories. The well-known friendship of the beautiful Princess Troubetzkoï for Monsieur Thiers was said to have its ardent phases as well as its political significance. Rumour said that this lovely Russian played the same game with the President that Madame la Princesse de Lieven had played, in earlier days, with Guizot—Russia knew the state secrets of France. Ever so slowly a whole legend of scandal crept into the past history of Monsieur Thiers, much of which is relished and believed even in certain quarters today.

Of this talk Thiers was fully aware, but he did not allow it to worry him. What caused him real vexation was the intrusion of party interests into every phase of his efforts to revive and reconstruct France. His own stubborn reserve and the impractical attitude of the Assembly, were beginning to effect a consolidation of the Republic in the course of which the retirement of Monsieur Thiers would come. In January, 1872, the President and his Cabinet actually presented their resignation. When this became known, the Royalist groups forgot their disgust at the presence of Republicans like Jules Favre, Jules Simon, and Ernest Picard in the Cabinet, and united with Republicans in begging the Chief Executive and his Council to reconsider their act. France realized that, at that time, a change in the Government might entail a return of those quotas of the German troops that had already retired.

At this time, Thiers was frequently accused of behaving like a dictator. To a certain extent, this charge is well grounded. From the beginning of the year 1872, he appeared to lean in that direction, so eager was he to carry his policy of regeneration to a successful conclusion. And he would not brook interference from the selfishly minded groups in the National Assembly. In this attitude, the country undoubtedly supported him, but he found increasing opposition from the body of legislators who watched jealously his every act. To General Le Flô, French Minister at St. Petersburg, he wrote: "The country is sensible, industrious, and is making money. But the political parties are pigheaded and stupid. They have just made a magnificent display of their weakness: they ought to allow the government to carry on; they should not always be trying to embarrass it."

In truth, all the blame should not be laid on the shoulders of the Royalist groups. While the Royalists were stirring up the west of France by their pilgrimages and meetings in La Vendée, Gambetta and his Republicans were striving to force a more definite Republican sentiment upon the people of the east and south. At Chambéry and Grenoble that fiery-tongued orator was now proclaiming that the President and the National Assembly should go. The only mandate that the electors had given them, he said, was to make peace, and peace had been made. Ever so slowly, however, the little President beheld a group developing that might save France and unite it by adopting a compromise between Monarchy and Republic. The discussions of the Royalists were wearying him and he feared the intemperate patriotism of Gambetta. More and more he found his greatest support and comfort among men like Jules Favre, Jules Simon, and Ernest Picard. Of these gentlemen he wrote: "The expression Conservative Republic has had an immense success in all sections. Timid folk were throwing themselves into the arms of Monarchy. . . . The idea of a Conservative Republic reassures them and will win them to us. I am, therefore, far from being alarmed by this recent development, and, at the opening of the next session of the Chamber, I will plant our standard on the ground of the Conservative Republic."

Obviously, Monsieur Thiers was becoming tired of his task of combating the two extremes. He wrote to his friends more frequently of his desire to complete the evacuation of French territory by the Germans, to have passed a fundamental law concerning government, and then to retire. This was his state of mind when the Assembly reconvened in November, 1872.

On the thirteenth day of that month he resolutely took his stand before the Legislature. The time had come, he declared, to destroy the provisional and uncertain condition of things. "The provisional state of affairs will be the death of us." To the dismay of the Right, his message appealed to the Left Centre and asked them to raise the question of permanent institutions. "The Republic exists; it is the legal government of the country. To desire anything else would be to desire a revolution worse than any that we have experienced. Let us waste no more time in proclaiming it, and let us devote our attention to giving it its necessary and desirable character. A Committee that was named by you some time ago gave to France the title

République conservatrice. Let us assume this title, and by what we do make sure of its existence." The Right was maddened when these words were read to them. "What of the Pact of Bordeaux?" they cried. The obvious answer to this query was the fact that the reason for the existence of the Pact of Bordeaux was now practically over, and that the time had come to consider the future government of the country.

When he sent his message, Monsieur Thiers had a very definite idea of what sort of a Constitution France should have. He feared that the protracted disagreements of the Royalists would lead France back into anarchy. "On the eve of my message, everyone, even those who refuse to abandon it today, was condemning the provisional state of affairs. If I aligned myself with the almost unanimous sentiment of the country it was because such an act was necessary in order to prevent the possibility of a Chamber more radical and, even, carrying Socialism along with it. Against this danger, I saw only one means of resistance, namely to create a High Chamber, conservative, and an executive power strong and vigorous, sharing with the High Chamber the right to dissolve the Chamber of Deputies. This organization was to be completed by a wise and conservative electoral law." It appears, then, that Monsieur Thiers, in 1872, envisaged the establishment of much the same sort of Constitution that France received after his retirement.

The proposal of November 13 aroused a tremendous uproar in the Assembly. Once again this Achilles who had observed a strict neutrality had emerged to propose a policy that by its definite character alarmed the Right. Royalists were not yet ready to enter into a discussion of institutions which might definitely close the door to Monarchy, and the extreme Left feared the victory of the Left Centre Moderates to whom Thiers had given, at last, a gage of friendship. For fifteen days these groups delayed a decision. Most of their attacks centred on the President himself. One called him a dictator worse than the hero in his famous *History of the Consulate and the Empire*. Another attacked him for too great leniency to Gambetta, while a third demanded an investigation as to whether the existing Government really represented any faction in the Assembly. At last, on November 29, Monsieur Dufaure's request that a constitutional committee of thirty members be named to draft a law regulating the administrative power, was passed by a bare majority of thirty-seven.

Out of this conflict the President emerged more than ever convinced that the safety of France lay in the Republicans of the Left Centre. Very likely he parted with regret from his cherished idea of an eventual Constitutional Monarchy for France. His alliance with the Right was, apparently, over. His reasons were, mainly, the behaviour of the Monarchists themselves. "It is not the Republic that is the cause of our troubles, but the Monarchist group," he wrote. "If it was united, capable of concerted action, I would understand its ambition. But divided, irreconcilable, it has no other result in prospect than destruction and that, purely and simply, is a criminal task. The Monarchy at present would be no better. There would be a Monarch, Emperor or King, who would be opposed by two dynastic parties and the Republic."

As finally named, the Commission of Thirty was composed, in great part, of Orléanists. Its establishment, however, brought France one step nearer the realization of Republicanism. For the President was eager to speed the work of government-building and he hurried them on and opposed them, when he disapproved, adroitly. At the same time, he tried to reconcile the more uncertain members of the Orléanist faction to his idea of a *République conservatrice*. With this in mind he admitted into the fold of his Cabinet two of their number. One other development seemed to come to his assistance when the adherents of the House of Louis Philippe broke with the party of Henry V. At once, Thiers sent the loyal Barthelémy de Sainte-Hilaire to negotiate with the Duc de Broglie who had resigned his diplomatic post to come to France and lead the wavering Orléanists. This unsuccessful attempt at transaction, however, caused the President to lose some of the support of the Left; Gambetta, alarmed at this move, redoubled his propaganda against the Chief Executive. As a result, Monsieur Thiers' Paris candidate was defeated in the spring election. The defeat of Rémusat was the first prediction of the fall of the President himself.

By the spring of 1873, therefore, it looked as if Thiers had aroused a tremendous opposition to himself, and, indeed, the crisis was near at hand. Some of the Republicans had shown that they had some doubts about him. At this first sign the Monarchists took heart; de Broglie, their leader, became the implacable foe of any Republic no matter how conservative.

In the meantime, the Committee of Thirty was proceeding with its constitutional labours and working at odds with the President who had perceived that *au fond* their desire was a real restoration. Even the Assembly had been reluctant to recognize his remarkable services in clearing France of German troops of occupation and debt, and had hesitated to name him Liberator of the Territory of France. And now, once this honour had been grudgingly bestowed, they proclaimed that the real *raison d'être* for his tenure of office no longer existed. Because of this attitude, the Committee of Thirty had shorn Thiers of power; when they denied him the right to appear in the Tribune without previous notification of his intention, they deprived him of his most effective means for controlling the Assembly. Under Broglie's direction, over three hundred members of the Right had prepared and presented a demand for an interpellation of the Ministry on the necessity for the Government to observe "a resolutely conservative policy." To this thrust Thiers' supporters had parried by laying before the Assembly a proposal concerning the organization of public powers and the creation of a second legislative house. In fine, the ground was prepared for the battle and, on May 24, the contest reached its height.

Fashionable Paris likes nothing better than a display of political pyrotechnics, and to the Assembly at Versailles there flocked all the beauty and wit of the Capital. It was in such a brilliant setting that Monsieur Thiers staged his last great performance. On the previous day, Broglie had exposed before the deputies the fears of the Monarchists that Thiers was becoming the protégé of Gambetta with whom he was preparing "the revenge of the Commune." Monsieur Thiers replied by stating that the Duke himself as head of the Opposition of the Right would inevitably become the protégé of three parties—Orléanist, Bonapartist, and Legitimist.

Most of his audience expected him to present a lengthy review of his entire career, "a historical swan-song." But this was not the theme that the President chose. He dismissed himself in short order. "I do not fear for my own memory; for I do not intend to appear before the tribunal of the parties; before them, I withdraw. But I do not withdraw before the tribunal of History; I am worthy to appear before it." It was to France that he devoted his speech, and to the necessity of rallying to the *République conservatrice*. Many a time before, Monsieur Thiers had held his hearers spell-bound and extricated himself from a perilous position but, on May 24, weary of public life, and held at bay by men with whom he had often been in sympathy, he was pleading for the only kind of government that he believed would render his country secure and prosperous.

Amid a storm of applause, the President left the hall

BIBLIOGRAPHY

THE principal sources for the study of Thiers are to be found at the Bibliothèque Nationale and the Bibliothèque Thiers at Paris, and the Musée Arbaud at Aix-en-Provence. Of these collections the most important is the one at the Bibliothèque Nationale. Additional material relative to Thiers may be found at the Archives Nationales in the files of the Ministry of the Interior, Police Générale, and in the papers of the Ministry of Justice, Direction des Affaires Criminelles. The archives of the French Foreign Office contain files relating to the policies of Thiers, but most of this material is duplicated in the collection at the Bibliothèque Nationale. I have consulted as well corroborative material at the Public Records Office, Foreign Office Files, London, and the French and English newspapers of the period.

The list of readings that follows has been intentionally curtailed. There is very little good secondary work in English and most of the memoirs and letters have not been translated. For the period of the Second Republic and Second Empire, I have purposely omitted the mention of many general histories except those of Monsieur De La Gorce whose studies are far superior to any other works that treat of this subject.

HIGHLY RECOMMENDED

Arnaud, R.: *The Second Republic and Napoleon III.* New York, 1930.

Artz, F. A.: *France under the Bourbon Restoration.* Cambridge, 1931.

Bismarck, Prince: *Reflexions and Reminiscences.* London, 1898.

Debidour, A.: *Histoire diplomatique de l'Europe*, 2 vols. Paris, 1891.

De La Gorce, P.: *La Restauration. Louis XVIII.* Paris, 1926.

De La Gorce, P.: *La Restauration. Charles X.* Paris, 1928.

De La Gorce, P.: *Louis Philippe*. Paris, 1931.
De La Gorce, P.: *Histoire de la Seconde République*, 2 vols. Paris, 1910.
De La Gorce, P.: *Histoire du Second Empire*, 7 vols. Paris, 1905.
Dino, Duchesse de: *Chronique de 1831–1862*, 2 vols. Paris, 1909.
Faguet, E.: *Politiques et Moralistes du XIXe siècle*. Paris, 1891–1929.
Falloux, A. de: *Memoires d'un Royaliste*, 4 vols. Paris, 1888.
Favre, J.: *Gouvernement de la Défense Nationale*, 3 vols. Paris, 1875.
Lavisse, E.: *L'Histoire de la France contemporaine*. Paris, 1875–1914.
Loliée, F.: *Le Duc de Morny et la Société du Second Empire*. Paris, 1909.
Malo, H.: *Memoires de Madame Dosne*, 2 vols. Paris, 1930.
de Mazade, C.: *M. Thiers*. Paris, 1884.
Metternich, Prince de: *Nachgelassene Papieren*, 8 vols. Paris, 1884.
Reinach, J.: *La vie politique de Léon Gambetta*. Paris, 1918.
Renard, G.: *Les étapes de la société française au dixneuvieme siècle*. Paris, 1913.
Senior, N. W.: *Conversations with distinguished persons during the Second Empire*, 2 vols. London, 1880.
Simon, J.: *Le gouvernement de Monsieur Thiers*, 2 vols. Paris, 1878.
Thiers, L. A.: *Discours Parlementaires*, 12 vols. Paris, 1893.
Thiers, L. A.: *Notes et Souvenirs. La Revolution de 1848*. Paris, 1902.
Thiers, L. A.: *Occupation et liberation du territoire*, 2 vols. Paris, 1903.
Thiers, L. A.: *Correspondances, 1854–1865*. Paris, 1904.
Thiers, L. A.: *Notes et Souvenirs*. Paris, 1905.

RECOMMENDED

Barrot, O.: *Memoires*, 4 vols. Paris, 1876.
Berryer, A.: *Discours et correspondances*, 5 vols. Paris, 1874.
Bourgeois, E.: *Modern France*, 2 vols. Cambridge, 1919.
Bourgin, G.: *Histoire de la Commune*. Paris, 1907.
Broglie, Duc de: *Souvenirs*, 4 vols. Paris, 1886.
Chambolle, A.: *Retours sur la vie*. Paris, 1887.
Chateaubriand, R. de: *Memoires d'Outre Tombe*, 6 vols. Paris, 1845.
Claretie, J.: *Histoire de la Révolution de 1871*, 5 vols. Paris, 1876.
Delord, T.: *Histoire du Second Empire*, 6 vols. Paris, 1905.
Dreyfus, R.: *Monsieur Thiers contre L'Empire, La Guerre, La Commune*. Paris, 1928.
Duvergier de Hauranne, P.: *Histoire du gouvernement parlementaire en France*, 10 vols. Paris, 1872.
Faucher, L.: *Biographie et Correspondance*, 2 vols. Paris, 1868.

Guichen, Viscomte de: *La Rèvolution de 1830 et l'Europe,* Paris, 1906.
Guichen, Viscomte de: *La Révolution de 1848 et l'Europe,* Paris, 1927.
Guizot, F. P. G.: *Lettres à sa famille et à ses amis,* Paris, 1884.
Hanotaux, G.: *Contemporary France,* 4 vols. London, 1903.
Lamartine, A. de: *Memoires inédites,* Paris, 1870.
Launay, Viscomte de: *Lettres parisiennes,* 4 vols. Paris, 1862.
Ledru-Rollin, A.: *Discours politiques et écrits divers,* 2 vols. Paris, 1879.
Lenz, M.: *Geschichte Bismarks,* 1911.
Levasseur, C.: *Histoire des classes ouvrières en France depuis 1789,* 2 vols. 1867.
Malo, H.: *Une Muse et Sa Mère,* Paris, 1924.
Malo, H.: *La gloire du Viscomte de Launay,* Paris, 1925.
Matter, P.: *Le prince de Bismark,* 3 vols. Paris, 1908.
de Mazade, C.: *M. Thiers: cinquante années d'histoire contemporaine,* 1884.
Normanby, Marquis: *A Year of Revolution in Paris,* 2 vols. London, 1857.
Palmerston, Lord: *Correspondance Intime,* 2 vols. Paris, 1878.
Pessard, H.: *Mes petits papiers,* Paris, 1898.
Reclus, M.: *Monsieur Thiers,* Paris, 1929.
Simon, J.: *Thiers, Guizot Rémusat,* Paris, 1885.
Simon, J.: *Souvenirs du 4 Septembre,* 2 vols. Paris, 1876.
Simon, P. F.: *A. Thiers chef du pouvoir exécutif et président de la république française,* Paris, 1911.
Thomas, A.: *Le Second Empire.*
Thureau-Daugin, P.: *Histoire de la Monarchie de Juillet,* 4 vols. Paris, 1892.
Tocqueville, A. de: *Correspondance,* 2 vols. 1872.
Tocqueville, A. de: *Souvenirs,* Paris, 1893.
Von Hohenlohe, Prince: *Memoirs,* 2 vols. London, 1906.
Von Hübner, J.: *Neun Jahre der Erinnerungen eines oesterreichischen Botschafters im Paris,* 2 vols. Berlin, 1904.
Washburne, E. B.: *Recollections of a Minister to France 1869–1877,* 2 vols. New York, 1887.
Weill, G.: *Histoire du parti républicain en France,* Paris, 1900.
Weill, G.: *La France sous le Monarchie Constitutionnelle,* Paris, 1902.
Weill, G.: *Histoire du mouvement social,* Paris, 1905.
Zévort, E.: *Histoire de la Troisième République,* 4 vols. Paris, 1895.
Zévort, E.: *Theirs,* Paris, 1892.

INDEX

☆